From the Battlefield
to the Big Screen

From the Battlefield to the Big Screen

Audie Murphy, Laurence Olivier, Vivien Leigh and Dirk Bogarde in WW2

Melody Foreman

FRONTLINE BOOKS

First published in Great Britain in 2022 by
Frontline Books
An imprint of
Pen & Sword Books Ltd
Yorkshire – Philadelphia

ISBN 978 1 52673 771 7

Typeset by Mac Style
Printed in the UK by CPI Group (UK) Ltd, Croydon, CR0 4YY.

Pen & Sword Books Limited incorporates the imprints of Atlas,
Archaeology, Aviation, Discovery, Family History, Fiction, History,
Maritime, Military, Military Classics, Politics, Select, Transport,
True Crime, Air World, Frontline Publishing, Leo Cooper, Remember
When, Seaforth Publishing, The Praetorian Press, Wharncliffe
Local History, Wharncliffe Transport, Wharncliffe True Crime
and White Owl.

For a complete list of Pen & Sword titles please contact

PEN & SWORD BOOKS LIMITED
47 Church Street, Barnsley, South Yorkshire, S70 2AS, England
E-mail: enquiries@pen-and-sword.co.uk
Website: www.pen-and-sword.co.uk

Or

PEN AND SWORD BOOKS
1950 Lawrence Rd, Havertown, PA 19083, USA
E-mail: Uspen-and-sword@casematepublishers.com
Website: www.penandswordbooks.com

Contents

List of Plates   vii
Preface   ix
Introduction   xiii
Acknowledgements   xvi

Part One – Action: Audie Murphy   1

Part Two – Lights: Laurence Olivier   41

Part Three – Camera: Dirk Bogarde   125

Notes   219
Bibliography   225
Index   227

Dedication

This book is dedicated to the memory of my father – David Felix Foreman (1916–76) who served in the Royal Engineers during the Second World War and became misty-eyed at the memory of dancing with the famous actress Dame Anna Neagle during a celebrity armed forces event in 1945. And it was from my mother Winifred 'Nancy' Anne Foreman (née Read) (1924–66), who was in the Women's Auxiliary Air Force (WAAF), that I appear to have inherited a great admiration for the writer, artist and legendary cinema icon, Sir Dirk Bogarde.

List of Plates

Audie Murphy

1. Audie Murphy – the war hero.
2. The Hollywood star Gary Cooper was greatly admired by Audie Murphy.
3. American troops and the tank 'Eternity' on Red Beach 2, Sicily, July 1943.
4. American armour and infantry in Coutances, Normandy, France in July 1944.
5. US infantry fought in freezing conditions in 1944.
6. Audie Murphy's 3rd Infantry Division in Nuremberg, in the spring of 1945.
7. Audie Murphy in 1951 in *The Red Badge of Courage*.
8. The writer and director John Huston
9. A poster of *To Hell and Back* in 1955.
10. Audie Murphy's grave in Arlington National Cemetery.
11. The actor Tony Curtis.

Laurence Olivier

1. Laurence Olivier in 1939. (*Carl Van Vechten*)
2. David Niven .
3. The twin-engined Airspeed Envoy aircraft of the type which appeared in *Q Planes* (1939).
4. 'Churchill's Man in Hollywood', the director and producer Alexander Korda.
5. Olivier as Nelson and Vivien Leigh as Emma Hamilton in *That Hamilton Woman* (1941).
6. The trusty Fairey Albacore in 1943 was an aircraft often flown by Olivier.

7. The Supermarine Walrus seaplane.
8. Olivier on the wing of a Fairey Albacore. (*Courtesy of Royal Navy Fleet Air Arm Museum*)
9. Olivier in 1944 as the fifteenth-century warrior king in *Henry V*. (*Getty Images*)
10. Sir Laurence Olivier as Air Marshal Hugh Dowding in the *Battle of Britain*.
11. Lieutenant Commander Douglas Fairbanks Jr KBE DSC.
12. Foreign newspaper correspondents visiting the set built for *Henry V*.

Dirk Bogarde

1. The young British Army officer Derek 'Pip' van den Bogaerde. (*Photograph and copyright of the Dirk Bogarde Estate*)
2. RAF Medmenham where Lieutenant van den Bogaerde learned aerial photographic interpretation.
3. The cap badge of the Queen's Royal Regiment.
4. Women's Royal Auxiliary Air Force Section Officer Constance 'Babs' Babington Smith.
5. Captain 'Pip' van den Bogaerde somewhere in Europe in 1944 or 1945.
6. Lieutenant van den Bogaerde examining aerial photographs. (*Courtesy of the Medmenham Collection*)
7. Aerial photograph of Peenemünde in Germany.
8. 'Satyrs Wood 1918'. (*Photograph and copyright of the Dirk Bogarde Estate*)
9. Dirk Bogarde and Tom Courtney in *King and Country* (1964). (*Getty Images*)
10. Joseph Losey. (*Getty Images*)
11. Sir Dirk Bogarde being interviewed by the author Melody Foreman in 1991.
12. A painting of Piccadilly Tube Station in 1941 by Derek van den Bogaerde.
13. Dirk Bogarde's 'thank you' letter to the author following the publication of their groundbreaking interview which appeared in *Kent Today* newspaper in 1991. (*Author's collection*)

Preface

As I write this a Lancaster Bomber has just roared overhead, quite suddenly and yet unmistakably loud. Its four Rolls-Royce Merlin engines at full blast and sparking thoughts of days gone by when it was originally flown by a generation who represented the resonance of duty this book commands.

I am lucky to see this iconic aircraft now beautifully cared for by the Battle of Britain Memorial Flight aircrew during this the 75th Jubilee Year of HM The Queen in 2022. Serial number PA474 is one of only two airworthy Avro Lancs flying in the twenty-first century but how gallantly it performs its new role as a reassurance of the past – an unforgettable symbol of liberty adored by millions of people related to long-ago military personnel who gave their all for our today.

And whilst we must salute the storming work carried out by all those enthusiasts and specialists who restore and fly aircraft of the Second World War – the Lancasters, Spitfires, Hurricanes, Mustangs and Harvards – so too must we applaud the film production companies taking care of historic cinema treasures and re-releasing them in full restored glory with additional content to further explain and enrich their history.

I am referring to Studiocanal's latest wartime classic re-awakening of *Appointment in London*. The original film, made in 1953 by Mayflower Films, stars Dirk Bogarde and Diana Sheridan and is hailed as one of the finest ever made about RAF Bomber Command. And, to see the Lancaster in its full, awesome and authentic might in the air there's no better film!

Appointment in London proved to be one of Dirk's favourites as it was the first ever picture which enabled him to plough his real-life wartime experiences as a photo-reconnaissance interpreter into a genuine understanding of a character – in this case RAF Wing Commander Tim Mason who in the film takes part in a risky ninety missions with Bomber Command. During the war Dirk and many other intelligence officers of

RAF Medmenham analysed aerial photographs to enable the squadrons of brave men who flew Lancasters over Germany to drop bombs on designated targets. *Appointment in London* succeeds in its longevity also because of its excellent script and book by former Bomber Command pilot, the composer Wing Commander John De Lacy Wooldrige DSO, DFC*, DFM (1919–58). A friend and contemporary of William Walton (who wrote the film score of the epic film *Battle of Britain*), Wooldridge was killed in a car accident in 1958. But not before he'd seen his memories of Bomber Command turned into a big-screen classic.

His son Hugh Wooldridge appears on the new Studiocanal re-release. He explains:

> When I was younger we used to like playing a game of who we would like to invite for dinner but the person I'd really like to meet was my father, John. My mother was Marguerita Scott, a popular wartime actress on stage and screen and known in the 1970s as Mrs Pomphrey in the UK television hit show, *All Creatures Great and Small*.
>
> During the Second World War 55,000 men of RAF Bomber Command were killed in action and yet even so the British public had a difficult time with the Royal Air Force. There was a lot of jealousy and no one really knew what the RAF did but they wore smart uniforms and were able to live at home or at least in the UK. This was difficult for families of soldiers and sailors forced to live abroad. But, the RAF were taking the war directly to the heartlands of the enemy – a time when the Nazis were bombing our cities night after night. Those who lived near airfields would count the number of aircraft that went out and those that came back. My father John flew Mosquitoes at first (also known as the 'Wooden Wonder') with 105 Squadron. By 1942, aged 23, he was piloting Lancasters and joined Guy Gibson's famous 617 'Dambusters' Squadron.

In *Appointment in London* viewers watch the super-fast twin-engine 'Mossie' drop flares over the targeted sites for the Lancaster aircrews.

In all Wing Commander John Wooldridge flew and survived a massive ninety-seven missions over Germany in a Lancaster. He was asked by Bomber Command chiefs to 'be invalided out' because if anything happened to him it would be bad for the squadron's morale. This is the story which he went on to write as *Appointment in London*. His work as a composer continued to be in demand and he counted among his friends the conductor John Barbirolli.

Hugh added:

My father wrote the film score for *Angels One Five* about RAF Fighter Command but he was keen his story of flying with Bomber Command was told. I am pleased my father chose Philip Leacock to direct *Appointment in London* as he had a very fine reputation as a documentary film maker and what makes this film important is its documentary feeling. It is the real deal showing what it was like living on an RAF squadron during the Second World War.

The film score written by Wooldridge includes a special orchestration denoting a thrum of an engine which is introduced during particularly poignant scenes revealing the character Wing Commander Tim Mason's devotion and sacrifices made out of duty.

Hugh explained:

It was my dad who suggested Dirk play Mason. It would be Dirk's first heroic role. There went on to be many stalwart British actors in this film, including Dirk's long-time friend the actor Bryan Forbes who plays Pilot Officer Peter 'the brat' Greenho. It was Tim Mason who represents all Wing Commanders during wartime including my father who went on to get letters from aircrew from all over the world to say 'thank you' for representing us.

Historian and author of *The Pathfinders* Will Iredale appears as a commentator in the new re-release of *Appointment in London* and confirms its importance as a superb representation of the heroic crews of Bomber Command. And as a vehicle for stars like Dirk this classic war film goes down in history as one of the best. A fact recognised so acutely by Studiocanal which to date has re-released more than 100 classic cinema favourites.

A Studiocanal spokesperson said:

"The black and white film stock of *Appointment in London* looks crisp and clean in Blu-ray, and the high-definition accentuates the emotional reactions of the players, bringing out subtle details in their performances. It's beautifully lit too, with effective use of shadows, half-light and night shoots. The sequences on board the Lancasters are successfully immersive, placing the audience in the thick of the action. Philip Leacock's contribution to cinema with this film was a step along that road. It will especially appeal to aficionados of Second World War films. Dirk's magnetic lead performance – itself a stepping stone to the greatness he would later achieve is sure to appeal to fans of his work".

Melody Foreman
August 2022

Introduction

With the talent to entertain cinema audiences on both sides of the Atlantic, those who had their names up in lights had great power, firstly as role models and secondly as valuable assets to the all-important wartime propaganda films made and screened both in Britain and the USA. Stars of the big screen will always fascinate generations of people. They have the guile to consolidate our dreams of escapism with illuminated performances that resonate resoundingly with our lives loved and lost. Dream-like, potent, distinctive and often profound, who doesn't want to watch and appreciate such genuine wartime-made classics as *Casablanca*, *49th Parallel*, *The Canterbury Tale*, *Mrs Miniver*, *First of the Few*, *Henry V*, *The Great Dictator*, and *In Which We Serve?*

And then later came the arrival of the legendary post-war favourites – *Appointment in London*, *The Dam Busters*, *Dunkirk*, *The Longest Day*, and so many more including the 1998 Oscar-winning epic, *Saving Private Ryan*.

During the war many men and women often admitted they joined the armed services just to help their idols Betty Grable, John Wayne and Leslie Howard fight the enemy.

This book also explores how those actors who joined up to defend our freedoms appeared in films of the war genre. And what's so remarkable about these pictures is their power to report history in an accessible format. The complexities over the moral questions remain but representations of real events have an important role to play in our understanding of military conflict.

Therefore to examine the combined histories of real life battlefields and big screen careers I have divided this book into three sections entitled – Lights, Camera, Action – but not necessarily in that order, as war is war and if we didn't consider military 'action' as the first and foremost story then much of our cultural life would be very different. Each section of this book explores its own very different star and their associates and recounts a raft of extraordinary often unique experiences.

In the section I've entitled 'Lights' we look at the military, theatrical and cinematic life and times of the British actor Laurence Olivier (1907–89). Just how did he manage the serious demands of wartime around such an already famous and culturally multi-dimensional life? Indeed such was the resounding power of Olivier's wartime performance as Shakespeare's *Henry V* his memory lives on today not only on screen but through the work of his son Richard Olivier who wrote a compelling book revealing how the play can be used to motivate and inspire leadership in the modern world. In wartime of course his father drew on real life military experiences to present an authentic performance on screen as the heroic fifteenth-century warrior king.

And it's well worth remembering that Olivier's second wife was the beautiful Oscar-winning actress Vivien Leigh who in wartime showed she was no coward either. Leigh, then the world's most feted female star, swapped her fame for heroism by risking her fragile health to entertain the troops in the hot, tumultuous deserts of war-torn North Africa. Her life was never the same again.

By 1969 the creation of war films was rarely as quick or as easy as it had been when their purpose was primarily urgent propaganda. Instead of a production taking a few weeks to shoot, it could take a few years. A good example is revealed in the 1960s as what became one of the world's most popular war films, *Battle of Britain*, struggled to fly onto the big screen. Its creation required a Promethean effort which began around 1966. Long drawn-out wrangles over the finance, casting, politics and the distribution nearly resulted in the project being axed. When *Battle of Britain* finally premiered in 1969 we see Laurence Olivier in a unique position of starring as his real life war hero – Head of RAF Fighter Command Air Marshal Hugh Dowding GCB, GCVO, CMG.

For part three of this book entitled 'Camera', I've focussed on another great British star, Dirk Bogarde (1921–99) whose wartime work with photographic images was essential to RAF Bomber Command. He served as a British Army intelligence officer and was always tremendously proud of his military career. After the war, Bogarde forged another dynamic relationship with the camera – this time in front of it as the star of many ground-breaking films which included several war-themed epics. One of them in particular was about an operation he'd been part of in his own military life at Arnhem in 1944. Some 30 years later he was among the star-studded cast in the 1977 film *A Bridge Too Far*. I was once lucky enough to meet the enigmatic Bogarde, a complete of hero of mine while working as a newspaper reporter.

And for the first section entitled 'Action' – how could anyone not be engaged primarily by the jaw-dropping military experiences of Audie Murphy who became the USA's most decorated soldier? On top of that he made film history in 1955 when he starred as himself on the big screen in his own life story – *To Hell and Back*. The scene when he jumps up on a burning tank, takes hold of its machine gun and single-handedly wipes out advancing enemy infantrymen who were 'killing his buddies' is unforgettable. Astoundingly, this all happened in his real life. After the war and despite the glamour of Hollywood fame, Murphy became a man deeply haunted by his past.

Today the study of war films often leads to the question; should they all be classed as 'anti-war' films? The genre certainly encapsulates stories about the actions of everyday characters who find themselves in situations forced upon them by an enemy. So without the bad guys to be defeated where is the story? And which films are most accurate?

The original 1930 version of *All Quiet on the Western Front*, directed by the great Lewis Milestone, gets top billing by film historians. Why? Because it was about men as a collective force and was about as authentic as it could get, especially as it was written by Erich Maria Remarque who as a German soldier had fought in the trenches of the First World War.

And while no one can forget the magnificence of Steven Spielberg's Hollywood treatment of *Saving Private Ryan* (1998), its realism is called into question by the American Professor of Philosophy Andrew Fiala who points out the film's focus on the difficult search for one individual didn't reflect the mindset of real-life US commanders like George Patton who regarded battle as strictly a 'team effort'. Patton wasn't one for condoning those who wished to engage in a private war. Interestingly enough, Patton's strident opinions on how wars were won was shared by the young Audie Murphy who during interviews only ever wanted to talk about the bravery of the men he had served alongside.

In 1945 the actor Lionel Barrymore told his friend, the Hollywood star Jimmy Stewart who was by then a decorated USAF bomber pilot hero: 'Jimmy, don't ever forget that when you act you move millions of people, shape their lives, give them a sense of exaltation. No other profession has that power … except maybe politics.'

Melody Foreman
March 2022

Acknowledgements

I'd like to extend my thanks to all those who offered their support during the writing of this book – some of which took place during lockdown as the world battled the Covid pandemic.

My family and of course the ever clever cats did a great job of checking up on all progress! Also Dr Julian Brock's superb organisational skills are always as ever much appreciated.

The expert guidance provided by Dr Barbara Siek (The Dirk Bogarde Estate/Brock van den Bogaerde) Micky Ojeda (Dirk's medals); Ruth Pooley, Curator at the Medmenham Collection; Archivist Barbara Gilbert at the Royal Navy Fleet Air Arm Museum: Larryann Willis, Executive Director at The Audie Murphy Research Foundation, was outstanding and must be heartily applauded for their time and patience during my research. And to the brilliant Professor William Uricchio who inspired and encouraged my passion for film studies during my scholarship year at Utrecht University in The Netherlands, I am deeply grateful.

I also salute the journalist and author Will Iredale for contributing words of support and raise a glass to our mutual friend the late, great Fleet Air Arm pilot hero Flt Lt Keith Quilter DFC who was undoubtedly a much better aviator than Sir Laurence Olivier!

And ever thanks go to the many awesome war veterans I have met over the years including the great Sir Dirk, plus I extend deep gratitude to the autobiographers and biographers especially the great writer John Coldstream for sharing his insights and knowledge of his friend Dirk. Thanks too must go to Sir Laurence Olivier's biographer Terry Coleman and all those historians and film commentators who made my research a deeply rewarding experience.

Ever thanks too to the Editor at *Britain at War Magazine*, John Ash.

On the roll call of excellent people who know a thing or two about history and the arts I must give a shout out to Juliet B. and Paul H,

Bookish Bella, lovely Charn, Jake and Laura, also helpful Lucy O (whose grandfather flew with Bomber Command during WW2), Anne-Marie and artist Paul Finn, poet M J Sully and Waterstones Bookshop colleagues.

Former Bomber Command pilot and friend Gerry Abrahams is a force of nature and in his late 90s is a busy Trustee at the Spitfire and Hurricane Memorial Museum in Kent. Thank you.

Also a mega-cheer goes out to the talented Alex Ford, artist and film director who created not only the storming artwork for this book jacket but has been a real tonic and pal during each stage of my research. And a big thanks to the brilliant author Will Iredale, and the marvellous Maclellans and MacKenzies. Also Bonnie and Ollie, Gillian, Amanda, Kay B, Anthony and Kathleen B, Angela, Chris and Rob, David Sellick, comedy Dee and Alison Hill – your enthusiasm for this book is much appreciated.

Part One – Action

Audie Murphy

'The true heroes, the real heroes, are the boys who fought and died, and never will come home.' – Audie Murphy

Audie Leon Murphy was the twentieth-century American dream of a true hero – the tough guy with the big heart and the cute smile. He was born a poor farm boy in Hunt County, Texas who survived the Great Depression, joined the US army on his 17th birthday and went overseas to fight evil to prove himself as courageous as any warrior from the Greek tragedies.

Put it like this, if you had to take up arms against an aggressor you'd want Murphy sharing your trench. He had dreamed of being a 'sojer' (soldier) since he could walk and talk. A crack shot with any firearm, loyal to all those he respected, generous in the extreme, sincere and modest, his quiet and steady approach to deadly conflict, embracing it even, made him a natural fighter. When the adrenaline was at its peak he could absolutely zone out and instinctively act upon his duty to stop enemy gunfire that ripped and cracked relentlessly towards his men, his buddies.

Murphy mostly led from the front and yet had no qualms about looking out from the back of the line either. At the point of attack he was like a mountain climber near the top of Everest and experienced an out-of-body sensation which scientists have agreed occurs with any human being pushed to the limits in a determination to succeed and in many cases conquer.

And as America's most decorated soldier ever he remains today as legendary as any all-conquering Achilles of the Trojan Wars. The only difference? Well, Murphy was born in the twentieth century and his weapon of choice when facing the enemy was often his trusty Carbine, Caliber .30, M1. Or if there was a smouldering and broken tank nearby with a fully-loaded working machine gun on the turret then single-handedly he knew that would be an even better weapon to fire at any advancing German infantry who threatened his buddies.

How interesting then during and after the war he downplayed his 'hero' status and felt awkward and shy among gushing strangers in the civilian world. When he signed an autograph he often wrote tellingly: 'Audie Murphy – a fugitive from the law of averages.' But everyone who saw his photograph on the front cover of *Life* magazine in July 1945 was entranced by his boyish face, ready smile and smart uniform tunic adorned with its rainbow of medal ribbons, and among them three Purple Hearts, Bronze and Silver Stars and a DSC for valour.

In the eyes of his adoring fans this 20-year-old could do no wrong. It was as if he had somehow made their own wartime struggles all the more worthwhile. They felt he really was away fighting for them. The fact that 'Murph' had killed up to 250 enemy soldiers while serving his country gave him great kudos at home. Everyone in the US knew his name, and even today so many still do as they flock each year to the Audie Murphy/ American Cotton Museum in Greenville, Texas.

People became enchanted too by his quiet humility – an aspect of his personality that shines through in his now-legendary storming memoir *To Hell and Back*, first published to great acclaim in 1949. He dedicated the book to his fallen comrades, especially Private Joe Sieja who was killed in the Anzio beachhead in January 1944, and Private Lattie Tipton, a father figure, who died in action near Ramatuelle, France in August 1944. The tribute to them is followed by the words 'If there be any glory in war, let it rest on men like these.' In 1955 he became the best-known actor ever to recreate his real-life combat service in a film version of his own autobiography.

When Murphy was quizzed about his remarkable jaw-dropping bravery while serving during the Second World War with Company B of the 15th Infantry Regiment of the famous US Army 3rd Division he told reporters in his laconic Texan drawl: 'Like everybody else I just fought to stay alive, I guess.'

What he achieved from 1943–5 on battlefields in Tunisia, Sicily, Naples-Foggia, Anzio, Rome-Arno, Southern France, Ardennes-Alsace, the Rhineland, and Central Europe earned him a breath-taking thirty-three medals and honours in total. He received every American combat award for valour available at the time of his service, including the

US Army Medal of Honor. He was also presented with high recognitions from France and Belgium.

On 30 October 2013, and more than 40 years since his death in an aircraft crash aged just 46, Major Audie Leon Murphy was awarded the Texas Legislative Medal of Honor. It was presented to Murphy's sole surviving sister Nadine Murphy-Lokey in his old home town of Farmersville. She told the crowd, which included Governor Rick Perry: 'Audie remains a fine example to any young person who wants to achieve something with their life. Make your mind up what you want to do and go for it.' Two years later Audie was hailed an Irish-American hero in a speech by President Obama during a St Patrick's Day event at The White House.

* * *

When the Japanese attacked Pearl Harbor on 7 December 1941 Audie Murphy discovered the Marine Corps was on a massive recruitment drive and within 48 hours he was in the queue at an enlisting station in Greenville.

The teenager's head had been full of ambition to serve his country for as long as he could remember. Now here was his chance. He was already a smart little rifleman and knowing just how to struggle and survive against all odds was firmly planted in his DNA. His father Emmett Murphy, a sharecropper, had walked out and disappeared from the family home for good around 1937 when his son was barely 12 years old.

Murphy, of Irish descent, decided then to leave school to help his mother Josie look after his siblings and run the home. His rifle came in handy as he hunted every day for rabbits and other game to help feed the three younger children. An elder sister, Corinne, then left the home to marry and Murphy suddenly felt the responsibility of being head of the family.

What he lacked in formal education was soon replaced by a special wisdom which would serve him well throughout the war. Murphy was born with a particular instinct to seek out ways to survive. It wasn't a curriculum subject he could learn from his teachers at school. Although people who remembered him from those days recall a kind and intelligent boy with a deep sense of loyalty who was often happiest on his own, and yet quick to lose his temper if he felt an injustice had been done against him. When he was just 16 years old his mother Josie died in 1941 after suffering with serious heart problems. His grief stayed with him for the rest of his life.

Murphy was never one for people he perceived as phoney or liars. Every now and then especially after the war those who knew him remembered how his eyes would suddenly glint with an uncanny coldness and they bore into anyone he believed had crossed him or tried to challenge him unfairly. Death had somehow been woven deep into his psyche by its constant presence during the war and somehow at times he behaved as if he was immune to it. His reactions of course would now be diagnosed as a symptoms of 'battle fatigue' (or PTSD) which left him torn to pieces inside and tortured by nightmares. Witnesses say he slept with a loaded pistol under his pillow every night as if he was ready for the enemy to pounce any time. After the war many of his friends decided against sharing a hotel room with him when they were away on a film shoot. One member of the crew recalled Murphy waking up, shouting and banging his hands against the wall until they were bloodied.[1] It was yet another nightmare haunting Murphy who had to take sleeping pills most nights to help him get any rest at all. In the early 1960s he became one of the first war heroes to recognise the full debilitating force of his memories and it seemed he suffered a form of what is now known as survivor guilt.

Quick to anger even as a boy, Murphy was furious for sure when the Marines turned him away on 9 December 1941 because 'he was too small'. In the 1955 film of his life story, also called *To Hell and Back*, Murphy played himself. We see the recruiting sergeant tell a fresh-faced Murphy it was true the Marines made 'boys into men' but they needed something to start with first! Imagine then how a war veteran of the actor's magnitude felt about having to act out this scene and also re-live many real events of a more horrific nature in the film. Such action cannot have helped his psychological distress as he battled subconsciously and unsuccessfully at times to bury the traumas he'd witnessed before the age of 21.

In real life Murphy, standing at 5ft 5.5in tall, had stormed out of the Marines Corps office and then tried to join the Navy, and then the Paratroopers. Each time he was more or less told by a recruitment officer he was too young and didn't weigh enough. It begged the question over whether he had added an extra year onto his age which was in reality 16½ at the end of 1941. The rules stated he needed to be at least 18. He asked his sister Corinne to sign his enlistment papers declaring him old enough as he'd been born in '1924'. On 25 June 1942 he got the birthday gift he always wanted – a life in a military uniform as a real soldier serving his country. Years later he idly confessed he was actually born in 1925.[2]

From the US Army building in Dallas that day the eager young Murphy was driven 50 miles or so by bus to Camp Wolters to learn all he could about combat as an infantryman. He soon made sure he was an outstanding recruit and his skills with the M-1 Garand rifle and other weapons were top dollar. Imagine his delight when his speed at taking apart and re-assembling his rifle was so impressive he was asked to teach other trainee soldiers. Later on in the war the regular task of cleaning his reliable rifle turned into a sort of therapy for him. As a rookie infantryman Murphy was assigned to the fourth platoon of Company D of the 59th Training Division. He had quickly earned his marksmanship badge and received an even greater award for being highly competent during bayonet training.

After three months learning all he could and with his confidence at an all-time high Murphy was given leave and briefly returned home in his uniform. His sister Corinne was delighted to see him looking so well and walking proudly with a spring in his step. It appeared to many who knew Murphy that the boy they'd last seen in the fields shooting rabbits in his patched britches had suddenly become a fine upstanding young man excited about the adventures ahead of him. Murphy had found his metier. He'd waited for this all of his life and ever since the day while working in the cotton fields as an impressionable boy, he'd revealed his ambition to be a soldier to a veteran of the First World War.

In his memoir he described how the man had shared with him a memory of the trenches. Then the work-weary man lit up a cigarette, coughed, spluttered and cursed: 'That damn gas, nearly eighteen years on and it's still hanging around.' When the man had recovered his breath he squinted at the horizon and told Murphy about a particularly early morning when the Germans had given their position away by walking through damp wheat and leaving a dark track where they had been.

'So what did you do?' asked the young Murphy. 'What would you have done? I lined up my sights on the machine gun, and waited,' came the reply.

Murphy wanted to know more and his companion described a machine gun as 'the devil's own weapon' and once he got the enemy in his sights he 'just pulled the trigger and let them have it.' 'That night', said the man, 'the Germans threw the gas over and I didn't get the alarm until I'd taken a lungful.'

All ears by now Murphy praised the man's actions with youthful optimism and said 'but you whipped 'em!' followed with 'Some day I am going to be a sojer [soldier]'. The man snorted and replied with disgust: 'What fer?' to which the boy answered, 'I don't know.'[3]

Five years later and by the autumn of 1942 it was time to step up his training. This time he was posted to Fort Meade, Maryland making a train journey which was to take almost a week. His professionalism with weaponry, skill at obstacle courses and attention to neatness and orderliness continued to impress. However, it came as an annoying surprise to him when an officer offered him the chance to stay out of the conflict in Europe and work in equipment supplies. Murphy really did stick to his guns at this suggestion, politely turned down the offer and continued his training. He wanted to be the best infantryman in the US Army. He was determined to go into combat and that was that. He was the best recruit they'd ever had, wasn't he?

So he was sent on to the city-like Camp Kilmer in New Jersey where there was a cinema in the grounds. It was here and munching popcorn he saw the 1942 war film *Casablanca* starring Humphrey Bogart and Ingrid Bergman. The teenager had no idea he'd soon be arriving, courtesy of a requisitioned old transport ship called *Hawaiian Shipper*, in Morocco, North Africa – the place where the romantic film noir style scenes which flickered before his eyes on the screen were set. Neither was he aware *Casablanca* was produced to help highlight the military success of Operation Torch – the codename for the Allied invasion of French North Africa and Morocco. '*Casablanca* was a cherished studio film which served a patriotic purpose and was approved by the Office of War Information's Bureau of Motion Pictures,' wrote Professor Andrew Fiala in a 2014 book of essays published by the University of Kentucky entitled *The Philosophy of War Films*. In 1943 Murphy was lucky enough to see the film before he left Camp Kilmer as government officials had banned it from being shown in North Africa because its anti-Nazi theme might cause friction with any Vichy partisans still in the area. (In real life the star of the film

Humphrey Bogart was a US Navy veteran of the First World War who aged 18 had served aboard the USS *Leviathan*.)

The North African Campaign of the Second World War began in September 1940 when the Italian army began to advance into Egypt intending to seize the Suez Canal. British troops and tanks fought it out against the Italian army in a series of battles in Egypt and Libya and then faced the German Afrika Korps led by the dedicated 'Desert Fox' – Erwin Rommel. The job of Rommel's troops was to give military support to the Italian army in order to avoid an Axis (German/Italian alliance) defeat. When the Second Battle of El Alamein took place in October 1942 the British forces, fighting in the heat of the desert sands, beat the Afrika Korps back into Tunisia and left them vulnerable to attack from Allied forces advancing from the other side of the country.

It was British prime minister Winston Churchill, working closely with the US Supreme Commander in Europe Dwight D. Eisenhower, who had encouraged the US to join the Allied invasion of North Africa. Both men knew the only way to defeat the German forces would be to drive them from North Africa and then launch a massive amphibious landing on the coast of Sicily.

The US President Franklin Delano Roosevelt had already been working and thinking fast. In the late 1930s in peacetime the amount of American armed forces personnel and equipment had dropped to an all-time low. By May 1940, fully aware of Germany's monstrous attack on Europe, Roosevelt had estimated he needed a budget of $1.2 billion to build 50,000 new aircraft a year and there was also justification for a new US army totalling at least four million soldiers by April 1942.

Roosevelt knew it was vital to keep Russia on side to help save the Middle East, Burma and India, and the only way towards ultimate victory would be not only to attack the Germans from the air but by a massive land assault too. He had offered to help Churchill defeat Hitler's armed forces as soon as he learned the British had been defeated at Tobruk on 21 June 1942. (By the end of the war in 1945 a total of 16,112,566 men and women had served in the US armed forces.)

From 8 November 1942 British and US troops began landing in North Africa in a bid to squeeze the Italians and Germans into a corner. It was no picnic as Vichy French forces put up a massive and impressive fight to maintain control of the area, especially in Oran and Morocco. It took two days for Vichy leaders François Darlan and Alphonse Juin to surrender their armies but there were conditions which meant Darlan had to be allowed to remain in control as part of a Free French administration. When the Allies arrived in Algiers, however, they had met no resistance at all.

US army veteran Ancil Fisher, a farm boy like Murphy, was among the first US platoons to reach North Africa. He recalled: 'I was bored and wanted to do something else apart from farm work so a friend and I joined the Army. I was always the guy that was easy about taking orders from someone else.' In November 1942 Fisher of the 39th Infantry found himself on a ship heading towards North Africa. On his way across the Atlantic he told God 'if you bring me back from this war I'll serve you for the rest of my life'. He explained:

After we'd landed it was rough. I was in five major battles. I mean, bad ones. And they sent aircraft over there and bombers to drop bombs on that place. Machine gun fire like crazy. In the last of our battles in Africa we lost our Lieutenant. He was our platoon leader and from there on I took his place. And I had a good platoon. If our company commanders sent us out on a patrol and chose me to go the whole platoon would volunteer to go with me but all I needed was three or four guys.

When Fisher encountered a German stronghold one day he dropped to the ground as the machine-gun bullets cracked around him. Slowly he crawled towards them and his men followed until they were close enough to open fire and chuck grenades. Through the smoke Fisher saw five dead Germans and ten of them walked towards him in surrender.

Having survived the D-Day landings at Utah Beach in 1944 he was in France when his quick thinking led him to rescue three British prisoners-of-war. That day he had been led towards the enemy by some French women who gave him false information. Suddenly he realised he was trapped as he came across a German leading three PoWs at gunpoint. There was a second or two of tense silence and eye-to-eye contact before Fisher shot their captor and freed the three who turned out to be high-ranking British officers. For his actions that day the British government awarded him the DSC – the Distinguished Service Cross. For the rest of his long life he kept his word to God and lived a good life until he died aged 97 in Canton, Ohio, in 2019.[4]

The teenage Murphy arrived in North Africa three months later. He had recovered from various bouts of seasickness by the time his platoon, consisting of sixty-five soldiers, followed Second Lieutenant W. Heard Reeves down the gangplank to set foot on dry land in Casablanca on 20 February 1943. Murphy had been temporarily promoted to corporal as Reeves had asked him to keep the men in order during the sea voyage which took the large convoy of thousands of US troops almost two weeks.

They were then sent on by train to US Army headquarters in Rabat where Murphy was assigned to Company B, 1st Battalion, 15th Infantry Regiment of the notable 3rd Infantry Division – famously known as the 'Rock of the Marne' for its outstanding First World War action against the enemy at the Marne River. The rest of 3rd Division had been in North Africa since November 1942 and were led by 52-year-old Major General W. Anderson, a man noted for his tact and calmness in battle. It was Anderson who also helped plan the massive amphibious landings which would lead to the Allied victory.

It was General George Patton who ordered, demanded even, the men of the 3rd Division to 'be victorious'. He had made it clear on many occasions he had little tolerance for what he perceived as cowardly behaviour. Patton's strident words of warrior bravado still rang no doubt in the ears of 1,100 unlucky American soldiers of the 3rd Division as they fell to the guns of the enemy. Research reveals almost 19,000 American soldiers were killed or wounded in the North African campaign.[5]

By the time Murphy set foot in Casablanca there is little doubt General Patton in his shiny leather boots, silver-buckled belt and shellacked helmet was stomping about and spitting over the US Army II Corps' defeat at the Battle of Kasserine Pass in Tunisia. Patton was nicknamed by the troops 'Old Blood and Guts' – our blood, his guts! Patton talked a lot about how men should fight as a collective. 'Teamwork' was one of his favourite words. The ill-fated combat at Kasserine took place in February 1943 with more than 3,300 poorly equipped and inexperienced US soldiers killed or wounded as they attempted to take on the might of the highly experienced German forces which held the area. The remaining 27,000 British and US troops were then forced to retreat. Churchill had predicted such a disaster and claimed such a move was too ambitious as raw US troops were not ready to face the combat-hardened Germans under the overall command of the seasoned soldier and veteran of the First World War, Field Marshal 'Smiling' Albert Kesselring.

Eventually, however, the Allied forces, backed up by with reinforcements and extra firepower, pushed through and claimed the vital access needed to gain ground in western Tunisia. Despite this defeat the 58-year-old Kesselring continued in his role and that year oversaw the impressive German defensive campaign in Sicily with Generals Hans-Valentin Hube, Fridolin von Senger und Etterlin and the Italian commander Alfredo Guzzoni.[5]

Meantime Murphy and his platoon had moved on to Port Lyautey in Morocco to take over the positions left by another infantry company. The 3rd Division itself (approximately 10,000 men) was now led by Major General Lucian K. Truscott II, a man who had no qualms about challenging his superiors, including Patton. Just like Murphy, Truscott was a Texan who had a deep respect for discipline and strong determination. A seasoned cavalryman, Truscott strived to keep his men fit and primed for action. During the First World War as a second lieutenant he patrolled the US borders of Mexico which were then under threat. At the time the German Zimmermann Telegram had implied how Texas and other states could come under the control of Mexico if it were to ally with Germany and declare war on the USA.

As a young man Truscott, just like Murphy, had falsified his enlistment papers, only in Truscott's case it was to apply for officer training in 1917. During the Second World War the doughty major general was recognised by his distinctive rasping voice and was described as 'absolutely fearless' by his son, Lucien K. Truscott III, also a US Army officer who saw action in Korea and Vietnam. Truscott III said:

> For his polo sport and exercise my father played mainly to win and told me never to forget that. And I was told to fight wars to win! My father said, that's spelled W-I-N!. And every good player in the game and good commander in a war, and I mean really good player or good commander, every damn one of them, has to have some sonofabitch in him. If he doesn't he isn't a good player or commander. And he never *will* be a good commander. Polo games and wars aren't won by gentlemen. They're won by men who can be

first class sonsofbitches when they have to be. It's as simple as that. No sonofabitch, no commander.

Truscott had his quirks though and was strangely obsessed about his clothes, believing certain garments had special powers. One of his favourite ideas was to wear a white scarf which had a military map of the area drawn on it. Other lucky charms included his old cavalry boots which meant the enemy stopped firing the minute he pulled them on![6]

But while trooper Murphy was always ready to pick up his lucky carbine in the name of courage, his lively mind at the time had only gambling and the job of babysitting PoWs to occupy it. The Axis forces in North Africa had surrendered on 13 May and in total a quarter of a million PoWs were placed in cobbled together make-do camps before being controversially shipped to camps in the US.[7] Many Americans fighting in North Africa and Sicily were angry about Italian and German PoWs being sent to live in the US while they stayed behind and slugged it out in combat, facing death and the prospect of never returning home ever again.

This issue was raised in a 1979 episode of the hit American family television show, *The Waltons*. In the eighth series a wartime story titled 'The Spirit' involved a young German-American PoW named Paul (played by Ned Bellamy) who had escaped from a US Army-run camp in North Carolina. Hungry and cold, he had been living rough until he befriended a child named Jeffrey (played by Keith Coogan) who lived at the Walton family home in rural Virginia. Jeffrey invites Paul to spend Christmas Eve at their house. The unhappy soldier reveals he was born in America and as a boy moved back to Germany with his family. He expresses how much he misses his own kin and little brother back in Germany. The episode reveals he is not the vicious enemy shown in propaganda but a humble, sensitive young man who has been forced to take part in a war. Whilst Paul accepts he must return to the camp he is shown kindness and consideration at the Walton homestead even though the war had seriously affected the family and friends in the neighbourhood.

Back in 1943, and more than three decades before *The Waltons* hit the small screen, Murphy was still desperate to get involved in battle and faced a frustrating wait. This time he felt he was twiddling his thumbs by being the platoon messenger in Arzew in Algeria. 'Instead of combat, we were given another long, monotonous period of training,' he recalled.[8] On 7 May he received his promotion to Private First Class.

His hopes were high, however, when he thought his platoon was going to be sent on to join the action in Tunisia. He even wrote about his excitement to his sister Corinne. But he soon discovered the Promethean efforts of half a million Allied troops with 1,800 tanks, 1,200 field guns, and thousands of aircraft ensured the German and Italian defences finally gave way on 13 May 1943. He wasn't heading for Tunis after all but sure enough his time would come and very soon.

Major General Truscott had received orders to lead the 3rd Division, including 'Murph' and his trusty comrades of Company B, to join the war in Sicily – the invasion was codenamed Operation Husky – on 10 July 1943. The nimble Murphy, then assigned as a 'division runner', was among thousands of US troops who landed on the south coast of Sicily at the port of Licata which sits between Agrigento and Gela. The landing crafts carrying tons of equipment and men had managed to reach the edges of the port with relative ease and little resistance. The new six-wheeled DUKW (Duck boat) amphibious truck created in 1942 was proving a major asset to the US troops and would play its part in the Allied victory in the Mediterranean theatre

At this time a British Royal Navy Reserve Lieutenant by the name of Alec Guinness was preparing to command a landing craft bound for the shores of Sicily. Guinness, aged 29 by then, was already a seasoned actor and his star was in its ascendancy when war broke out. His courage at sea was just as remarkable and as well as taking part in the Sicily campaign in 1943 he also helped supply equipment to Yugoslavian partisans in Italy. His post-war films include the famous *Malta Story* (1953) and *Bridge over the River Kwai* (1957).

But back in 1943 Murphy was complaining that his platoon arrived on the shores of Sicily three hours too late owing to various delays and planning issues during the landings. Strangely enough it was confusion surrounding an amphibious landing that almost led to certain death for Lieutenant Alec Guinness. A muddle over which craft was heading where nearly led to a fatal collision. Guinness' quick thinking and seamanship saved the boat and more importantly the many British Commandos on board. Murphy said when his Company B finally set foot on dry land most of the fighting at Licata was over. Of the thousands of men of the 3rd Division who had arrived earlier, 100 of them had fallen that morning to Italian guns. Murphy recalled: 'If the landings hadn't gone snafu [Situation Normal All F**ked Up] we would have come ashore with the assault waves. That was what I wanted. I had primed myself for the big moment.'[9]

A rare photograph of the landing reveals how the beach was beset with high winds causing the Duck boats to float about offshore like unwieldy 'shoeboxes'. A line of US troops have no option but to form a human chain to unload each heavy vessel now lurching dangerously close to them.[10]

Early in Murphy's memoir *To Hell and Back* as he vividly recalls his war in Sicily, we soon get to know a few of the men he respected enough to describe and write about so vividly. Characters like the brave little Pole 'Mike Novak' who insisted on making the coffee, described all Germans as 'sonsobeeches' and noted Murphy as a 'true friend'. Then there was 'Brandon' who regretted walking out on his marriage and yet treasured the memory of his wife and nine-year-old daughter who wore her hair in plaits and wrote to him, often sharing the news with his buddies keen to hear about her life back home, her school work and games. 'Snuffy' features regularly too, along with a hearty Cherokee native American named 'Swope' – also known as 'Horse-Face'. 'Kerrigan' was among Murphy's potty-mouthed right-hand men at times until in 1944 Kerrigan received 'the million dollar' wound in his arm which put him out of the war forever. In real life 'Novak' was Private Joe Sieja and 'Brandon' was Private Lattie Tipton – both men, to Murphy's distress, were killed in action. 'Snuffy' and 'Swope' also died in battle. Although the commentaries and banter in Murphy's book are laced with dark humour about death and buddies being awarded 'a wooden cross' for gallantry, what shines through is the unbreakable bond between each 'dog-faced' man as they endure the onslaught of combat together. No one dared look too much into the future. To get through another day unscathed was always a miracle.

Murphy was only a mile from the enemy lines in Sicily in 1943 when he recalled:

I am well acquainted with fear. It strikes first in the stomach, coming like the disembowelling hand that is thrust into the carcass of a chicken. I feel now as if icy fingers have reached into my mid-parts and twisted my intestines into knots.

Each of us has his own way of fighting off panic. I recall Novak and try working myself into a rage against the uniformed beings who killed him. But that proves futile. At this distance the enemy is as impersonal as the gun that blew Little Mike's [Novak] pathetic dreams into eternity.[11]

By the time Company B began to climb the dusty terrain on the banks of Agrigento Province around fifteen miles inland, the once-cosy friendship between Hitler and Benito Mussolini was almost at an end.

Among the Allied commanders the story was very different. The British Generals Harold Alexander and Bernard Montgomery, Air Marshal Arthur Tedder and Admiral Andrew Cunningham worked smoothly with their US military counterparts, Generals Dwight 'Ike' Eisenhower and George Patton. Prime Minister Winston Churchill and US President Franklin D. Roosevelt Roosevelt encouraged communication between the commanders although historians have written how Montgomery could be insensitive to the opinions of others and could be a 'thorn in their side' when it came to agreements over battle plans. A compromise, however, was usually reached as each leader knew the lives of so many young men were at risk. They all agreed air and naval power would be key to the success in Sicily where the unprecedented large scale amphibious landings were to prove an important precursor to D-Day at the Normandy beaches the following year.

Hitler and Mussolini (Il Duce) had fallen out after the Allies' hard-won victory in North Africa and Tunisia. The Germans didn't trust the Italians and vice versa. Rommel didn't believe the German army should be in Sicily at all and thought the Italians should defend their own island as his troops, now getting low in numbers, were needed to attack and defend territories further inland. Hitler, however, decided to try and safeguard Italy, a country Churchill claimed was the 'soft underbelly' of Europe, from the Allies in order to concentrate on further power-grabs across Europe and Russia.

By April 1943 and thanks to Allied air and naval power the people living on the island of Malta, just 60 miles from Sicily, were rescued. Any German units who had been posted to Sicily at the start of the war in Europe had been moved out by January 1941 to fight on the Russian Front. Whilst the Luftwaffe continued its bombing campaign on Malta, the RAF and Royal Navy had moved in to defend the little British colony from enemy attacks. Pilots at RAF Ta Kali were able to take off and reach the skies over Sicily. They could shoot down the marauding Luftwaffe which was by now low in numbers and unable to prevent the American bombers from targeting Sicily.

For the Sicilian people life too was grim. Food was scarce and fear lurked in the hearts of everyone on every corner of every rubble-strewn street. Thousands of Italian men and good Sicilians were being slaughtered. It appears too that Italy's own King Victor Emmanuel II was more anxious about the fate of the royal family than that of his own people now facing starvation. He was unable, it appears, to stand up to Mussolini who at the height of his popularity had impressed a tired and defeated population with his passionate political speeches. (Victor Emmanuel, who had reigned for almost 46 years, abdicated in 1946.)[12]

Watch any Pathé newsreel of wartime Sicily and see clusters of tattered troops, their sunburned faces greasy and drawn as they patrol dusty, ruined streets. Their helmets are tilted back on their heads in a jaunty manner and a kind of relief at the opportunity to celebrate a victory of some kind. But by the tense way they are walking it's easy to tell they are not totally relaxed just yet. They know a sniper could be anywhere, or the Luftwaffe might make a sudden last-ditch attempt to strafe them from the air, and maybe the enemy was still lurking behind a heap of rubble that was once a family home.

Meantime, and away from the news cameras, the terrain facing Murphy and the men of his platoon was rough, hilly and proving difficult to capture. Not only were they coping with the usual unbearable summer heat of Sicily, they felt hemmed in between pockets of woodland and small fields. They were under pressure to flush out the enemy with regular attacks made possible by men like 'Murph' who was always ready to make the all-important solo reconnaissance run for information about where to strike. Then the waiting game, watching out for the enemy, the movement of a branch or a bush, then knowing as soon as he'd pulled the trigger and shot one of them hiding out ahead, the rest would know his position. Murphy would run, fast and often bent double to avoid being hit. 'He was the fastest ever to run crouched over like that,' recalled one of his pals. 'And he could cover quite a distance like that too!'

Years later Murphy's agility and nimbleness did not go unnoticed either by his friends in Hollywood. 'When he moved "Murph" was feline … like a cat,' explained actor Michael Dante at a film convention in 2016. Dante had appeared alongside the star in two popular Westerns – *Apache Rifles* (1964) and *Arizona Raiders* (1965). He recalled:

> I used to watch Audie and observe him and one day we were between shots and he took my Colt gun as if he was grabbing a woman's hand. His movements were so quick and I have big thick hands but his hands were so smooth and swift as a lady's hand. He would have shot me four times before I'd got my big finger on the trigger. His hands and the tendons were so loose. They were perfect for a sniper and of course he had all the equipment God could give him.
>
> Put it like this I could understand why he survived the war because he was just like a cat. Sometimes I'd be in a conversation with him and somebody else would come along and I'd look around and Audie had gone. Disappeared. Where did he go? He was so smooth.[13]

For Murphy, now ready for action in Canicatti in 1943, the insane behaviours of the political personalities of the Axis were far from his mind as he went on patrol that day. Suddenly he saw two Italian officers jump on their horses and make off into the distance. He dropped to one knee, took aim and fired. Sure enough both men fell dead instantly.

When he was told by his Lieutenant 'You shouldn't have done that', Murphy replied that it was 'his job, wasn't it?', and claimed the Italian officers would have killed them both if they'd seen them first. The Lieutenant sighed and said Murphy, who that day had made his first kill of the war, had probably done the right thing. Soon afterwards Murphy justified his actions when he remembered a comrade called Griffin who was killed instantly when an enemy shell landed nearby. He wrote in his memoir how the Lieutenant had rightfully understood 'all human life is sacred but had not accepted the fact we have been put into the field to deal out death'.[14]

When on 13 July 1943 the platoon was cornered on a hill Murphy, like a Greek warrior, leapt up and began firing like hell from the hip and running straight at the enemy, yelling loudly for his comrades to follow him. It was this action that earned him a promotion to corporal with the warning from his commander there may come a time soon when 'Murph' would have to take over a squad. What's interesting are the comments Murphy made about his attitude to combat. He said there was a great difference between audacity in battle and actual courage or foolishness. 'Audacity is a tactical weapon and nine times out of ten it will throw the enemy off balance and confuse him. However much one sees of audacious deeds, nobody really expects them. They are not in the rule books. I found that retreating was the most dangerous manoeuvre possible ... if you have no defence, attack.'[15]

On 20 July orders came through from Patton to reach the town of Palermo 300 miles to the north. Corporal Murphy, like thousands of other men, was unable to fight off the debilitating effects of malaria which included vomiting, exhaustion and blackouts, and had no choice but to spend a week recovering in hospital. Soon back on his feet he arrived as Company B were dug in to a hill taking care of a machine-gun emplacement. The rest of the 3rd Division had moved forward to face battle at San Fratello before continuing on to Messina in a bid to drive the enemy away from the port.

Two days later, on 22 July the British Eighth Army was in combat on the north side of Mount Etna with the US Seventh Army driving forward from the east. Murphy and many other men of the 3rd Division discovered the journey towards the Furiano River was tough. The roads were destroyed, the ground desolate, the dust was intense and left clouds of chalk around them waist high. When they were forced to crawl on their stomachs to avoid mines they found bridges had been smashed and devastation all around.

Finally on 3 August Company B with the 1st Battalion, 15th Infantry reached San Fratello – 60 miles away from General Patton at Messina. Their arrival was not a welcome sight for the Germans of the 29th Panzergrenadier Division and at the Furiano River Corporal Murphy discovered the enemy had positioned themselves to shoot down, mortar and obliterate as many men of the US battalion as they possibly could. Within seconds the bombardment and firing started and never seemed to end. Murphy noted one US soldier sobbing hysterically. The man threw his arms around the commander and screamed that he 'couldn't take any more'. The man continued to bawl as he was sent to the rear. 'We watched him go with hatred in our eyes,' wrote Murphy who heard his pal Kerrigan say: 'If I ever throw a wing ding like that, shoot me!' Murphy replied: 'Gladly.' It seems the young corporal shared Patton's disgust at cowardly behaviour and yet soon came to realise 'the fighting would not run out and there was plenty of war for everybody'.[16]

Four days later on Saturday, 7 August, the 3rd Division found itself hemmed in, constantly under attack and unable to move towards Messina. Furious at the delay Patton ordered an amphibious assault from the other side of San Fratello which he believed would help provide cover for the 3rd Division to continue its advance to join the Allies in Messina. To his annoyance only one landing craft could be spared and that was strafed and bombed by the Luftwaffe before it set off. The following day four more DUKWs were piled high with men and equipment and despite being attacked by the Luftwaffe's Ju 88s they made it through to form Patton's back-up advance.

By now Patton was high on a hill watching the battle take place. Through his binoculars he saw his troops being blasted by enemy shellfire. Retaliation came in the form of the mighty offshore guns of the US Navy blasting San Fratello and with the extra US troops surrounding them the Germans retreated early on Monday, 9 August. Corporal Murphy had watched the action from his guard post at a gun encampment. Of his first real experience of battle he declared he had 'acquired a great respect for the Germans as fighters. It has given me an insight into the fury of mass combat.'[17]

At this time, as the earnest young corporal was scrambling his way through the dusty war-torn roads towards Messina, one of Hollywood's biggest stars was a short distance away offshore floating in the deep blue Mediterranean aboard the US Navy's amphibious flagship USS *Monrovia*. New York-born Lieutenant Douglas Elton Fairbanks Jnr was already a legend to cinemagoers who had watched him in awe on the big screen in such swashbuckling hits as *The Prisoner of Zenda* (1937), *Gunga Din* (1939) and *The Corsican Brothers* (1941). He could list among his friends British film stars who would also go on to serve their country during wartime – Laurence Olivier and David Niven. However, Lieutenant Fairbanks would be far away from the studio sets in Los Angeles by 1941 because as a reserve naval officer he was 'more than pleased to take his papers, report for duty and help end the war.'[18] That year he found himself aboard the aircraft carrier USS *Wasp* to assist in the mission to get Spitfires off the deck to reinforce Malta.

As a friend of Lord Louis Mountbatten the actor and naval officer had travelled to England to join a Commando team taking part in special operations which involved the art of military deception. Sure enough his intelligence skills and flare for confusing the enemy did not go unnoticed by Admiral Kent Hewitt, the US commander of the amphibious forces heading for North Africa.

Fairbanks' ideas to outsmart the Germans were to prove highly effective and formed part of the successful 'Beach Jumper' missions which focussed on mock amphibious landings with a couple of hundred brave men who didn't suffer from seasickness and were highly adept at carrying out operations at night by sea. Their job was to fool the enemy into thinking a real beach assault was under way thus directing away the attention from the actual landings taking place further along the coast. Lieutenant Fairbanks' proposals were tried out for the first time in Sicily as part of Operation Husky. They proved to be a success, and each time the 'Beach Jumpers' were deployed throughout the Mediterranean theatre they caused mayhem for the Germans.

This brilliant method of deception was also used when Fairbanks sailed to Southern France in August 1944 where the amphibious landings at Provence included Corporal Murphy. For his honourable service during the Second World War Lieutenant Douglas Fairbanks was awarded a raft of medals including the British Distinguished Service Cross (DSC). After the war Douglas Fairbanks Jnr KBE DSC returned to Hollywood and continued his career as a film star. He remained on call with the US Navy Reserves as a Captain until 1955. His medals included the US Silver Star for conspicuous gallantry, and the notable Legion of Merit.

Just across the water from the USS *Monrovia*, Corporal Murphy and Company B were waiting anxiously to hear when they'd be leaving Sicily. The enemy had retreated and the Americans were keen to advance to Italy. Operation Avalanche began just before dawn broke on 9 September 1943. Over several months of this fierce battle more than 300,000 men from up to fourteen countries joined the Allied effort including those brave fighters of the Italian Resistance movement.

Once again Murphy and Company B waited for almost two weeks before they could follow their comrades of the US Fifth Army led by Lieutenant General Mark W. Clark and attack the beaches of Salerno at Battipaglia. When they arrived on 21 September, up to 1,300 US soldiers had been killed and many more wounded. The Germans were not going to give in easily.[19]

What followed was almost a year of intense combat for Corporal Murphy and B Company as they were confronted with the enemy around every corner, along every road, field and copse. He was moving slowly along the Volturno River with two other soldiers when they faced a surprise attack. One man was shot dead and Murphy and his remaining pal rapidly retaliated by throwing hand grenades and letting rip with a machine gun. Five Germans were killed. By October the weather had turned cooler and the trees began to shed their leaves. It was about the time Murphy and a few pals of Company B found themselves taking cover in a dark, damp, flea-ridden cave. They did their best to hole up and keep watch on the area around them. The banter between each soldier is recorded in Murphy's memoir and the dialogue is a lively exchange of views littered with bawdy observations and grand gestures. They hear about each other's plans and even dare discuss the future. Every man has heard the stories and anecdotes many times before. Father of one Brandon, it seems, wants to make it up with his wife, see his little daughter grow up, study and become an engineer.

Little Mike Novak from Poland has his heart set on a farm in America 'where nobody can take it away from you.' Snuffy gets drunk and irritates Kerrigan and an Italian-American soldier called Antonio asks him to shut up. 'Horse-Face' the Cherokee (Private Abraham Homer Johnson) reckons he can hear enemy artillery fire about 200 yards in the distance. They all climb out of the darkness of the cave and see the rain coming down in steel rods.

By the third day water is becoming scarce and they decided not to eat the meagre, dry army rations of biscuits and salty meat as it would make them thirsty. Antonio told Murphy he was going out for some air. Nobody spotted he was carrying an empty canteen to fetch water. Suddenly the sound of a German machine gun cracked the air and they saw Antonio tumble and Murphy noted how a bone is sticking out from the rest of Antonio's broken leg. Then more bullets tear at Antonio's body until he lays dead with a face frozen into an expression of terror. It was not long before the sound of battle echoed around them and the enemy was wiped out. Relief arrives from across the river and they can leave the cave and top up their supplies. Their next destination is Mignano. Their pal Antonio was now at peace in the land of his forefathers.

Soon enough the 3rd Division had orders to cross the river and meet the Germans head on in a full-scale attack. In doing so and in a violent bid to secure the area the 3rd Division suffered the loss of 300 men. Further on and the Americans found themselves trapped in mud, deep in a valley. The Germans had buried themselves out of sight in the two mountains either side. Murphy's courage never failed him and on Mignano Monte Lungo Hill 193 Company B fought off a terrifying attack. In the process they killed three German soldiers and four were taken prisoner. For the enemy the bitter frost they felt in the air had met with the chill of death. By December that year Murphy had been promoted to sergeant of Company B's third platoon and yet reckoned he was only given three stripes just because he was lucky to still be alive. Now sitting with his pals huddled in a freezing quarry they listened to the crash of artillery fire around them. They drank their grouty coffee and considered their next move.

In late January 1944 the Allied forces attacked Anzio Beach (Operation Shingle). Murphy was ready to join the first assault but was struck down again with malaria and taken to a hospital in Naples. Seven days later he was back with Company B again and caught up in the vicious battle at nearby Cisterna where at first the Germans proved impenetrable. By now, his memoir records that Little Mike Novak (Joe Sieja) and the pal they call 'Swope' were dead. The brutality at Cisterna should never be forgotten. By 30 January the US 1st and 3rd Ranger Battalions had already made good headway from the beach. The canny Germans though allowed them to gather at the tip of an area shaped like a horseshoe and began to attack from the sides with full force. It was Murphy's job leading the men of Company B to go in and help rescue their comrades now trapped and unable to escape. In his memoir Murphy dramatically compared the enemy assault to 'a fiery blanket woven by their guns which never lifts. We may as well be hurtling naked bodies against a wall of spears.'[20]

The Battle of Cisterna cost each side dearly. While the Allies, including the 504th Parachute Infantry Regiment, managed to gain some of the area the Germans and their massive tanks were victorious and continued to successfully defend Cisterna until May 1944. In total 803 Allied troops, many of them inexperienced in battle, did not make it home. Four hundred US Rangers were taken prisoner. It was at Cisterna that Murphy told new recruits not to feel ashamed as there was nothing wrong if they felt scared or wanted to cry.[21]

What was left of the 3rd Division including Murphy and Company B returned to Anzio to await further orders, this time from Major General John P. Lucas who had taken over from Major General Truscott. Another medal, this time a Bronze Star with 'V' device, was earned by Staff Sergeant Murphy who along with his men on 2 March decided to attack a German tank which had passed by their hiding place. The crew were killed and the tank completely wrecked by the force dished out by grenades. Days later he discovered his valiant actions had earned him a Bronze Oak Leaf Cluster to attach to his Bronze Star. It could now accompany the Combat Infantryman Badge he'd won alongside other heroes of Company B.

When Staff Sergeant Murphy collapsed one day he once again woke up and found himself in hospital. This time a bad dose of the flu had floored him, which was hardly surprising when we think about the freezing damp and nerve-wracking experiences inflicted upon his immune system. The flu, it could be argued, was another symptom of chronic battle fatigue which US Army medical reports of the time admitted was seriously damaging the physical and mental health of many men. Murphy, who as a young soldier brushed off the idea he was suffering from shell shock or battle fatigue, was lucky to receive help in hospital from a kindly blonde nurse he calls 'Helen' in his memoir. She became one of his best friends in real life and although she turned down his offers of marriage he always felt ready to share his thoughts with her – a rare honour from a man who fiercely guarded and controlled his emotions, often, it would turn out later, to the cost of his mental wellbeing.

But despite the men's exhaustion there was great faith placed in the troops led by British Generals Harold Alexander and Oliver Leese, and US General Mark Clark from the start of the Mediterranean campaign. All three men had steered their armies towards Rome in a bid to finish the war as soon as possible. On 17 January 1944 the bloodshed began at Monte Cassino (the Battle of Rome) and before they could freely march into the ancient city there was four months of intense fighting ahead for dog-tired troops despairing at the all-too-familiar sight of casualties, many of them friends, who were being placed on stretchers dead or alive, each day. The Allied victory at Monte Cassino came at a cost. The Allied forces made up of men from Britain, the US, India, France, Poland, Canada, New Zealand, South Africa and Italy totalled 240,000. By the end of the battle in late May the casualty figure was around 55,000. The Germans' total strength was 140,000. Their losses numbered 20,000.

By 4 June 1944 the streets of Rome, by now turned into rubble by US Air Force bombing raids, had been cleared of enemy forces. The Italian people were ecstatic to feel free again, and felt nothing but hatred for the fascist regime which had ruined their lives, killed their men and turned their city into a place of fear and dread. When Murphy and Company B, now sadly depleted of many soldiers it had begun the war with, got to Rome there was no fanfare, no cheering crowds to greet them as the great saviours. Instead he recalled they were 'like ghosts prowling around with nothing to see or do'.[22]

They were in a restaurant when the characters 'Kerrigan' and 'Brandon' got drunk and join in a fight against Air Force men who had several Italian women around them. This boisterous skirmish involving chairs being thrown is re-enacted in Murphy's 1955 film of *To Hell and Back*. When the Military Police arrive at the behest of the agitated restaurant owner the men calm down and claim it was all a bit of 'friendly banter between them after one man tripped and fell into the Air Corps guys by mistake!'

On 15 August 1944 military records reveal Murphy and the rest of the 3rd Division took part in the fourth beach assault in Southern France. As they headed towards the coast they heard the rattle and boom of German artillery fire. It was daylight as they'd poured out of the landing craft just south of St Tropez. The intelligence was good and when Murphy headed up 'Yellow Beach' he knew the job of the 3rd Division would be to attack up to 30,000 German troops who after a short while were forced to retreat further inland. From here the advance of the 3rd Division would prove a tough mission. Up to 200,000 enemy soldiers were waiting for them and Sergeant Murphy and Company B sprang into action, flushing them out of their hiding places.

Accompanied by two members of his platoon he attempted the ascent of a hill which had been part of the French Maginot Line. Suddenly he heard a crack of a gunshot and watched the GI in front of him crumple dead to the ground. The remaining GI was shot dead within the next few seconds. Now alone and fully aware the enemy knew his position Murphy dropped low like a cat and swiftly made his way into a small ravine for cover. From here he continued his advance until he almost collided with two German soldiers. In the seconds it took for them to realise he was there Murphy lifted his rifle, pulled the trigger and killed them outright. In a split second he experienced a great wave of detachment from the action he'd just taken. In his memoir he describes the sensation as 'things slowing down and becoming clarified'. His mind was now set on a plan. Now that he'd seen where the Germans had dug their foxholes and were manning machine-gun posts aimed directly at the American soldiers at the bottom of the hill his adrenaline was on a high as he swiftly made his way back to an area where he could grab a loaded heavy machine gun from his comrades.

Alone he carried the gun to a place of cover where he use his sniper's eye to pinpoint the enemy and let rip. He shot at the range of foxholes in his sights and when he ran out of ammunition he ran back for more to continue his solo assault. His pal Lattie Tipton (known as 'Brandon' in *To Hell and Back*) accompanied him now. They went forward firing their weapons and chucking grenades. When Tipton spots a German soldier waving a small white flag as if to surrender Murphy instructs him to stay down. Tipton ignores him and remarks how his sergeant is turning into a cynic. Tipton stands up, believing the idea of a truce is genuine, and the enemy shoot him dead. Murphy cries for a 'medic' and cannot stop the tears from falling down his face. Too late. His friend who had been with him through so much is dead. From that day on Murphy wanted to downplay any sort of 'hero' status. Tribute is paid to Lattie Tipton on the opening page of his book *To Hell and Back*.

For a while the Americans met only weak resistance from the Germans until they faced more deadly combat as they attempted to head for Marseille and Toulon where both ports were now being attacked by the Allies. By the middle of September 1944 the 3rd Division was on its way to Montélimar. Once again Sergeant Murphy was called upon to do his duty and protect his men. He had remarkable luck on one occasion in discovering the enemy by chance and surprising them with an attack. At one time a group of German soldiers guarding artillery were having breakfast when Company B struck them with a burst of bullets. One enemy soldier stood up and aimed straight at Murphy who also fired. When Murphy opened his eyes the man was dead. Once again his rapid reaction had guaranteed he lived another day. Knowing there were more Germans in the area he grabbed a bazooka and blasted away ahead of him and left the enemy with no choice but to surrender.

Another mission included a search for snipers lurking in the houses of Montélimar. He records in his notebook the terrible sight and smell of so many dead men and horses lying along the broken roads. The battle intensifies as the 3rd Division slowly advance. Fuel is running low until more was found at the liberated city of Besançon in eastern France on 8 September 1944.[23]

The plan was to meet with Patton's Third Army at the Rhine but along with so many GIs Sergeant Murphy was beginning to feel 'burned out'. The feeling was intensified just after he realised he had narrowly escaped death yet again when a mortar shell exploded next to him. In the blast all he lost was the heel of his boot and skin from his foot. He also had one hell of a headache as he was taken to hospital, only to return soon afterwards ready and outwardly steady to go forward into battle again.

His sense of detachment had begun to kick in as he battled to survive. He had no real friends left in Company B, many of them having been killed or wounded so badly it had bought them a ticket home to the US. It was during a conversation with Kerrigan a few days earlier when the comment about being in a war was like 'going to hell and back' is first recorded in Murphy's famous memoir.

One day, as Company B made its way to Le Tholy in the Vosges department of north-eastern France, Sergeant Murphy decided to follow behind a patrol group mostly because he was tired of the tedium he felt at that particular moment and his mind was racing back to and fro over various memories which made him sad. His professional mind was his safest bet at all times now and he was proven right as the patrol was attacked. Murphy worked fast, fired his carbine then threw grenades, killing four German soldiers and wounding another four. The US group he'd tailed were lucky to be alive as Murphy escorted them back to camp. Another medal was pinned to his chest – this time he had earned a Silver Star.

Murphy's bravery continued to astound his commanding officers. One time he felt like a boy again and took his rifle out hunting where he took out a German sniper lurking in the woods. On 3 October 1944 and after a fierce battle involving US Sherman tanks the enemy retreated and ensured a slightly safer passage for Company B until they encountered another potential ambush. In a place called L'Omet and in weather which chilled the bone he slid on his stomach across the deep frost to various places of cover from where he could take aim like the skilled sniper he was and prevent another enemy soldier from killing any more men of his platoon. Before long he was promoted to Second Lieutenant. The boy from Hunt County, known for his rifle skills, was proving one of the US Army's biggest assets even though he believed his lack of education would hamper his promotion through the ranks. But as the future reveals it wasn't the case as his actions in several more harrowing battles in France earned him more promotion.

On 26 October that year he was shot in the hip at Brouvelieures. The German sniper who wounded him swiftly received a deadly bullet between the eyes from Murphy's rifle. Murphy's injury kept him in hospital at Aix-en-Provence until January. A Bronze Oak Leaf Cluster was awarded to him and was attached to his Purple Heart. He found solace during his long conversations with a nurse named Carolyn Price who heard all about his life back home and the younger siblings he was desperate to help when the war was over. It's extraordinary to think of what he had achieved in his life up to that point. When he first began to communicate from the heart with Carolyn he was just 19 years old.

By the end of the month and still recovering from the disabling effects of his hip wound, he was promoted to commander of Company B. By now his men were fighting off enemy attacks in the Colmar Pocket in the mountainous region of central Alsace. Sergeant Murphy's next death-defying action was to prove, 10 years later, a brilliant and dynamically compelling scene in his famous 1955 film of *To Hell and Back*. It shows how single-handedly Second Lieutenant Murphy grabbed a field radio, jumped on top of a burning tank and fired its machine gun at rows of German infantry heading towards him and his platoon. He kept his finger on the trigger of the gun for up to an hour and shot at least fifty enemy soldiers in between talking on the radio to his unit about the situation. By now he was wounded in the leg and had run out of ammunition. Also the tank, full of fuel, could blow any minute. The only option now was to get back to his men who he had earlier ordered to stay back. He refused an order to do the same.

The scene re-enacted so astutely by Murphy for the film reveals the tension of a breath-taking situation which inspired him to write about the action: 'For the time being my imagination is gone; and my numbed brain is intent only on destroying. I am conscious only that the smoke and the turret afford a good screen, and that, for the first time in three days, my feet are warm.' Once the firing has stopped and he watches what's left of the enemy run back towards Holtzwihr, he recalled: 'As if under the influence of some drug, I slide off the tank destroyer and, without once looking back, walk down the road through the forest. If the Germans want to shoot me, let them. I am too weak from fear and exhaustion to care.' The reason he gave for his deadly solo attack on the German infantry that day was that he had to do it because they 'were killing his friends'.[24] When Company B advanced again to attack any remaining Germans Murphy stayed with them. His actions, no doubt carried out in his complete blind faith in his purpose in life, earned him the Medal of Honor. The 3rd Infantry Division received the Presidential Unit Citation. Murphy was promoted to First Lieutenant.

After almost two months of fighting the 3rd Division, with a casualty list totalling 4,500, left the war-torn Colmar Pocket. It was time for some rest and recreation (R and R) and Murphy visited Paris. His battle honours now included a Legion of Merit and he soon discovered, as was the traditional procedure, he was to be taken off the front line to work as a liaison officer. He wasn't happy and wanted to march forward with his men to Germany. It seems his nickname of 'Young Blood and Guts' among some of his platoon was ringing true. On one occasion he couldn't resist going to the aid of Company B when it was stuck behind the Siegfried Line. Always the warrior out to protect his fellow soldiers, he grabbed his rifle, found the desperate GIs and helped plan their next move forward thus putting them back in touch with their unit. He recorded how no one had noted his absence from headquarters that day.[25]

When Murphy was offered the opportunity to train as an officer at West Point he decided the rigorous pre-entry academic exams would not suit him and he declined. He had left school aged 12 remember, and although he was told by senior officers that accommodations could be made for his lack of formal education, he probably realised the absurdity of it all, especially as he'd won every single medal the US Army could bestow upon him. It would be bizarre surely to become a student again at the mercy of officer/teachers very much less experienced than himself?

Murphy was very much an individual character, he was his own man by now even though his baby face at just 20 years old, belied the wisdom of a battle-hardened soldier.

Towards the end of the war in Europe the 3rd Division continued its advance to Germany where between 17–20 April 1945 they faced yet more combat in Nuremburg against an enemy prepared to fight to the bitter end. The 3rd Division then went on to plant the Stars and Stripes flag in the town of Salzburg, and finally the men of the 7th Infantry took control of Hitler's precious hideaway and Nazi command post on a mountainside near Berchtesgaden.

Lieutenant Murphy stood nervously on an airfield near Salzburg on 2 June as he waited to be presented with his blue-ribboned Congressional Medal of Honor by General Alexander Patch. Soon afterwards the French and Belgian governments awarded him yet again their greatest military respects in the form of the Croix de Guerre with palm. Back home in Texas he was officially honoured by the state and the newspapers hailed his homecoming as a time of great glory. He was their boy and he was their hero. When the US Army aircraft landed at San Antonio airport he was met by excited reporters and photographers and a crowd of well-wishers all anxious to shake his hand.

Back in his home state of Texas he was free to relax a little, and realised there was no need to keep looking over his shoulder. The streets and fields weren't ruined with rubble and decay either. He was finally able to breathe again. But always, always as the sun shone down he remembered the friends who didn't make it. Murphy recognised too it was the dead who deserved the honours, not him. When he was discharged on 21 September, having expressed a preference to return home in 1945, he was signed off with a 50 per cent disability classification as a member of the Officer Reserve Corps.

On the day he returned to his home town of Farmersville thousands of people lined the streets to see him and his sister Corinne welcomed him home. In August of that year he had bought a property in Farmersville for Corinne and her husband Poland Burns on the condition they shared it with the siblings Beatrice, Nadine and Joseph Murphy who had been left in a church children's home while he was away at war.

By now his life was about to change again. Murphy, now a national hero and feted wherever he went, wore a uniform as a Major in the Texas

Army National Guard. Most of his role was in a training and promotional capacity focussing on the military development of new recruits. But behind the poster-boy looks there remained a young man struggling to overcome the debilitating effects of memories detailing horrific conflicts. His traumas were so bad and so many they proved more than enough to share between a hundred lifetimes, let alone Murphy's mere two decades on this planet. When he recognised he was suffering with battle fatigue he found some solace in writing poetry to honour his fallen comrades.

In 1950, now aged 25, he was not sent to fight in the Korean War although there's little doubt his survival training, rich with professional experience, had come in useful to those young soldiers he'd assisted during his time back at camp. By 1957 Murphy had stepped back from all active service with the Texas National Guard and by 1969 his status with the US Army Reserve was that of 'Retired'.

The Film Star

Today as we watch re-runs on the television of any Western there's a good chance the name 'Audie Murphy' will loom large at the top of the credits. There'll be a lot of shooting of course, as Murphy's expertise with any gun is usually utilised to the full by an astute director mindful of the star's extensive military background. Playing either a hero or a villain, Murphy had legions of fans who adored his earnest youthful looks and watched on the big screen how he fought every battle with style often embellished with an unerring natural justice. When he was victorious in any way his character would tip his hat with the end of his Colt 45 pistol and shrug off any congratulations. Maybe the actor behind the slight smile didn't have to act much after all?

But how did Murphy become a star of the big screen? While he had adored watching Gary Cooper films as a child, he never considered fate would take him, the poor boy from Farmersville, to Hollywood. But in 1945 that 12-year-old who was once so desperate to become a 'sojer', found himself in Los Angeles sitting wide-eyed in a luxurious mansion belonging to the legendary James Cagney. And it was the redoubtable Cagney, star of so many classic films, who had spotted Murphy's face glowing with victory on the front cover of *Life* magazine. Cagney ran a production company with his brother William. They thought Murphy would be ideal for cinema. They knew audiences wanted a new face to idolise, and what with Murphy's status as a war hero how could Cagney Productions fail to give America a new star?

After a conversation with his new protégé Cagney organised acting lessons for Murphy and offered him a contract. And yet while the war hero persevered at his new profession he soon tired of the extreme left-wing political behaviour of his classmates, and the relentless speech and diction exercises which aimed to quash or at least tone down his strong Texan accent. There were also academic film history classes to attend. It wasn't long before he'd had enough of the Actors Lab and decided to give up his tortuous schooling there. However, while he wasn't a red-flag waver like many of his former classmates Murphy did sign a petition against the unfair actions of the House Committee on Un-American Activities (HCUA) which was paranoid about Communism infiltrating Hollywood. The HCUA blacklisted anyone it believed was guilty. Actors, screenwriters, directors, musicians, studio crews and bosses were all targeted if their sympathies were deemed politically dubious.

Murphy's venture into politics was brief and even then he was motivated only by his sense of fairness. He did make a speech in front of other celebrity war veterans in Hollywood including Douglas Fairbanks Jnr about the problems facing less fortunate US servicemen and women who returned from the war with no home, no job and few prospects. Murphy's support for a Democrat politician who disagreed with the HUAC was noted by the FBI. But, in essence he was a soldier-poet who had no ambitions to use his status as America's most decorated war hero to promote a political career for himself, even though prevailing parties of the time urged him to strongly think about it.[26]

His association with James Cagney came to an end in 1947. He never made a single film with the Cagney Brothers production company but despite this they agreed to loan out the student actor to Paramount. Soon enough Murphy landed his first ever appearance on the big screen in the suitably-themed *Beyond Glory* which was set in the Second World War. Ironically the character he played was that of a cadet named Thomas and the scenes would show him at West Point. The star of *Beyond Glory* was the diminutive Alan Ladd who plays 'Rocky Gilman' – a bright young soldier who believes he is to blame for the death of his commanding officer (Daniels) during service in Tunisia. 'Rocky' falls in love with the officer's wife Ann (played by Donna Reed) and at a hearing questions arise about the truth of Daniels' death. Gilman, it turns out, did not kill his CO who witnesses said had died in battle earlier on in the day in question. Murphy might have had only eight words to say in the film but they got him noticed.

For appearing in *Beyond Glory* he was paid $3,000 by Paramount Pictures. More luck was on its way when he met US Signal Corps veteran and screenwriter David 'Spec' McClure who became a close friend. In 1947 both men began work on Murphy's autobiography, *To Hell and Back*. McClure's contacts in Hollywood extended far and wide. He had worked closely as a writer for Walt Disney and he was also a friend of Hollywood's famous gossip columnist, the fiercely Republican Hedda Hopper. From there on, in his pal McClure, Murphy realised he had found himself a great chief of public relations.[27] Despite this, however, Cagney had relinquished all claims on Murphy, admitting there was no ill feelings it's just that the war hero 'couldn't act' and therefore there was nothing he could do for the company.

Cagney's criticism is perhaps a little harsh especially as Murphy had since found a more suitable acting coach who was working as Head of Talent for Universal Studios. Her name was Estelle Harman. She taught her students the Konstantin Stanislavski method which encouraged the actor to be independent and use instinct when creating character. Her war hero of a student obviously felt happier under Harman's guidance as personally he was unquestionably about as individual as you could get. Murphy was who he was. Fact. Among those who took part in Harman's popular classes were other Second World War veterans destined for stardom. They included former US Navy servicemen Tony Curtis and Rock Hudson.

Murphy's first leading role was in a 1949 film produced by Allied Artists called *Bad Boy*. Suddenly the money began to roll in after he signed a seven-year contract with Universal Studios. In today's money he was earning more than $12,000 per week. Over the years of course this figure would increase dramatically and later fall equally as fast when his obsession with gambling and horse racing got out of control.

From 1948 and during the next 21 years the clean-living Murphy, who never drank or smoked, appeared in more than forty films. Some good, some not so good as many Westerns were classed as a 'B' movies and produced double-quick to make a fast buck for the film company. Never once would Murphy agree to appear in a commercial advertising alcohol or cigarettes. He always said booze made his stomach flip, and smoking was a killer. His attitude proved to be one of the more progressive of the time.

Two notable A-star classics for which he earned praise from the critics included a film about the American Civil War called *The Red Badge of Courage* (1951) which was inspired by an important 1895 novel by Stephen Crane. Murphy's fellow war veteran James Whitmore, who served with the US Marine Corps, narrates the film. *The Unforgiven* (1960) was the second A-lister. Both films were directed by the great John Huston – an alpha-male type character of 'Hemingway-style' who took no prisoners. Among his legendary films are *The Maltese Falcon* (1941), *The African Queen* (1951) and *The Man Who Would be King* (1975). He was known for shooting films which involved people fighting together for a common goal and how their motivations could become corrupted and defiant. He was always interested in conflict, truth and freedom. Murphy loved working with Huston who was able to coax out of him the best performance with gentle but firm encouragement. On set, though, Murphy often looked sad and withdrawn. And if he wasn't needed to film on any particular day Murphy would try and clear his mind by riding his horse around Huston's awesome Californian ranch.[28]

Why did he get on with Huston? There's every chance he admired the Nevada-born director's professional detachment and single-minded focus on the job in hand. Like Murphy, the great director was a no-nonsense kind of guy. Some called Huston the 'Renaissance man' of the US film industry. And like Murphy, he had served with great courage during the Second World War and had been awarded the Legion of Merit and promoted to Major. In 1942 as Captain Huston of the Signals Corps he had been tasked to make three films about the conflict, *Report from the Aleutians* (1943), *The Battle of San Pietro* (1945) and *Let There Be Light* (1946). The last one was banned until 1981 because it revealed veterans suffering the effects of psychological damage. When Huston worked with Murphy six years later on *The Red Badge of Courage* there's little doubt he could see into the heart of the young man's own battle with war-induced trauma. This sensitivity and understanding towards Murphy and his struggles was no doubt played out by Huston in his honest, thoughtful and straightforward approach towards him.

By now, however, Murphy had soon discovered he intensely disliked the Hollywood social scene. He thought it was full of so many facile, insincere characters and found it difficult to believe in anyone he thought was a phoney. He was never keen on parties where deals were made and careers were sprinkled with more glitter and gossip. To him none of it was real. Murphy's first wife was the actress Wanda Hendrix who was very much into the show business hubbub. When she discovered her husband had no interest in trying to be someone he was not the marriage went downhill and they were divorced in 1951. The marriage had lasted just two years. It didn't take long at all for Murphy to marry again. This time a former airline stewardess called Pamela Archer agreed to be his wife and from the union came two sons – Terry Michael in 1952, and James Shannon in 1954.[29]

Life was beginning to improve for the actor around this time even though he still awoke at nights grieving for his dead pals of Company B having re-lived his most intense war experiences in his nightmares. *To Hell and Back* had proved a big seller when it hit the bookshops in 1949. The book had been created over 18 months from detailed notes Murphy had made on scraps of paper during his wartime service. His screenwriter pal David 'Spec' McClure spent weeks at the actor's home in Hollywood ensuring the memoir was written in Murphy's own voice.

When the war hero was invited to France to receive the Légion d'honneur and Croix de Guerre he took McClure with him. Both men were able to spend time enriching the memoir by walking through hundreds of miles of battlefields where the action had taken place. To Murphy's amazement, and hidden beneath the undergrowth in woodland near Holtzwihr in the Alsace region of France sat the twisted and burned-out remains of the tank he'd stood upon during his famous heroic solo attack on the enemy. (Today, there is a memorial at the site.) During Murphy and McClure's research trip they rediscovered the places which had left a lasting and often bitter memory. Even though four years had passed since Murphy had stood on the spot where his pal 'Brandon' was shot dead, and other tragic events had occurred, to US Major Murphy the fledgling actor, it all felt like only yesterday. His memories, sharp and raw, no doubt provoked a range of emotions during the visit with many as vivid as they were traumatic.

In February 1949 The Henry Holt Company went down in cultural history as the publisher of the first edition of *To Hell and Back*. In December 2020 a signed copy of this famous book, without the dust jacket, fetched $2,000 on an online auction site. The large sum paid indicates how the legend of Audie Murphy will never die. The book, a bestseller, did even more to endear him to the hearts and minds of the American people.

Later on, when Murphy made the Westerns *Sierra* (1950), *Kansas Raiders* (1950) and *The Cimarron Kid* (1952), he had the chance to work alongside fellow former Actors Workshop student Tony Curtis again. According to Curtis' memoir, however, the ugly side of Murphy's fiery temperament had begun to alarm many people who worked with him in Hollywood. The signs of his PTSD showed themselves in their full frightening glory to Curtis one day.

Curtis, a handsome US Navy veteran who in 1951 was popular with boys and girls because of his awesome DA (Duck's Ass) hairstyle' recalled:

> In *Kansas Raiders* I remember we shot most of our scenes on a back lot. I had very few lines, but I did a lot of horseback riding. I played a member of the Dalton gang, and Audie played Jesse James. Everybody, including me, was afraid of Audie. I didn't feel that way about many people, but Audie was different. At the time he was dating an actress named Peggy Castle, a girl I didn't particularly like.
>
> I was walking down the corridor at Universal Studios, and Audie grabbed me by the lapel and pulled my face down to his. He snarled 'Did you say anything bad about Peggy Castle? She told me you were talking bad about her'.
>
> 'No,' I said. 'Believe me, Audie, I don't know what you're talking about.' I didn't like the way he was yanking me around but I couldn't help but think of all those Germans he had killed. Thankfully, he accepted my answer and walked away.

It was a brave Curtis who dated Murphy's ex-wife, the glamorous Wanda Hendrix. According to Curtis she experienced the full horror of Murphy's PTSD. He once was in such a jealous rage he held Wanda captive with a gun. 'It later came out that he was suffering from post-traumatic-stress-disorder as a result of everything he'd been through in the war, but we didn't have a term for it then. All Wanda knew was that she wanted out,' recalled Curtis who at the start of his brief romance with Wanda admitted how he tried not to worry about Murphy coming after him.

One day when both actors had to rehearse with pistols for a quick-draw scene Murphy predictably was always fastest. When Murphy won time and time again he put his pistol in Curtis' stomach and pulled the trigger. 'I heard a muffled explosion. I looked down at myself and saw smoke and smelled it. I couldn't believe it and thought Murphy had found out about my date with Wanda. I fainted at the thought of dying,' recalled Curtis. When he came round again he was surrounded by faces looking down at him. Audie apologised and said he'd played a trick by using one hand to fire a cap gun he'd hidden behind his back as he used his other hand to point his six-gun pistol in Curtis' stomach. 'From then on, Audie was really nice to me, and we even became friends. But I never went out with Wanda Hendrix again,' he explained. (Murphy, however, allegedly said he disliked Curtis.)[30]

Now a reliable mainstay of the Western genre Murphy was always happiest when socialising with the crew who enjoyed listening to his jokes and banter. By mixing with carpenters, scene designers, the props department staff, lighting and cameramen he was reminded of his army days as he relaxed into discussions about the practicalities of a film. He also liked to gamble and often unlucky many remember him losing a lot of money. If he counted you as a friend he'd take you to the racetrack in southern California. When a business venture he'd invested in was a success he enjoyed the income but when it failed and he lost out he would shrug it off. He was a risk taker and cheated on his wife Pamela. He laid the blame for his excesses on his war service and came to realise he was also tremendously bored much of the time. Nothing, it seemed to him, could match the thrill and ultimate adrenaline rush of deadly combat. In 1962 he told the *Dallas Morning News* how war had 'robbed' him 'both mentally and physically'. He explained: 'It drains you. Things don't thrill you any more. It's a struggle every day to find something interesting to do.'[31]

Twelve years previously the film rights to his autobiography had been snapped up by Universal-International. By 1954 studio bosses made the decision to get *To Hell and Back* on to the big screen. At the time Murphy wasn't overly interested in playing himself, especially as he had lived the real thing. He expressed his desire the film should not be all about him and his medals but a tribute, as the book is, to his fellow soldiers. If the film was to be made, he conceded, Tony Curtis should play him because 'he'd be a good fit'.[32]

However, after many clever and persuasive conversations with Murphy conducted by producer Aaron Rosenberg and director Jesse Hibbs who had already worked with Murphy, an agreement was reached. Murphy was 30 years old in 1955 but his baby face as a 17-year-old soldier had remained more or less intact. He felt his role was to oversee the authenticity of the film. Especially as studio bosses decided the book was too bleak, gritty and sad. They wanted a film which contained uplifting scenes, humour even, which would attract big audiences and make the box office rocket sky high. Murphy, a keen advocate of the truth, had a tough job on his hands! And he was determined to be involved in every way he could during each shoot. The Universal Studio bosses gave him 60 per cent of the $25,000 paid for the rights, as well as $100,000 and 10 per cent of the net profits for starring and acting as a technical advisor.[33]

After various meetings a location was chosen which worked well for everyone on board. Shooting *To Hell and Back* was to begin in September 1954 at Fort Lewis in and around the rugged terrain of Yakima Training Center near Washington. The US Army, in full appreciation of the film's promotional value, happily provided authentic equipment and trucks when required. To add authenticity and gravitas to Murphy's steadfast belief the film, like the memoir, should be a tribute to the action and courage of the armed forces as a collective. General Walter 'Beetle' Beddell Smith was chosen to be its narrator. Beddell Smith had served as Eisenhower's Chief of Staff throughout most of the Second World War.

It was Murphy too who cast the tall, serene actor Charles Drake to play the solid father figure of GI Lattie Tipton. They had worked together on *Gunsmoke* and Murphy knew Drake was as reliable an actor as they come, just like Tipton in real life. He then cast his own 4-year-old son Terry Michael Murphy to play his younger brother Joseph as we are shown the 1930s family scenes at the beginning of the film. Child actor Gordon Gebert appeared as the 12-year-old Murphy.

The total cast listed in the credits numbered more than sixty. In the military ceremony shots of top brass presenting Murphy with a medal, hundreds of real troops from Fort Lewis were filmed marching past in his honour. The technical aspects of *To Hell and Back* were vigorously overseen by Murphy who had appointed Colonel Michael Paulick as his own key advisor on the set. Paulick was a former comrade he had once rescued during the war from enemy attack in the Vosges Mountains. Murphy also trained the film crew how to create the environments surrounding soldiers on the front line. He was happy to grab a shovel and dig foxholes. He wanted it to look as authentic as possible. However, some parts of the film did get the glossy showbusiness treatment as desired by producers seeking to lift the story out of its gloom. In the book Murphy describes in detail the misery of snow, mud, filth and bitingly cold temperatures his men experienced during certain battles. Certainly his real-life action atop the burning tank destroyer took place in snowy conditions. But when the film got behind schedule there was no option but to continue shooting it in the dry bright area which doubled up as Sicily, Italy and Southern France.

As an actor Murphy was always professional, he showed up on time, he knew his lines and took on board everything director Jesse Hibbs (a former US professional football player) told him. However, he had confessed how re-enacting the battle had made him feel guilt for the men who never made it back. He admitted too how hard he struggled to push his memories of war to one side only to have them 'explode' in his dreams at night.[34]

It was Murphy's performance, many critics said later, which gave the film an edge and took it beyond the many run-of-the-mill productions in which the actors performed too mechanically. Murphy, they rightfully noted, was convincing in the role as his real soldier self. *The New York Times* reviewer wrote: 'Murphy lends stature, credibility and dignity to an autobiography that would be routine and hackneyed without him.' The actor was at his happiest too as if performing each scene was just a natural event for him.

Actors including Marshall Thompson as Private/Corporal Johnson and Jack Kelly as Private/Staff Sergeant Kerrigan were praised for their performance too. 'The soldiers were played with a human quality that makes them very real. Fighting or funny, they are believable. The war action shown is packed with thrills and suspense,' said the reviewer in a July edition of *Variety* in 1955.

A few weeks before the publication of such noteworthy comments, the pre-publicity for the film about the United States' most decorated soldier was effusive. Murphy embarked on a tour to help promote the film, meeting several key politicians in Washington keen to enlist his help in a national campaign to crack down on juvenile delinquency and narcotics.

To Hell and Back was premiered at the Majestic Theatre, San Antonio in Murphy's home state of Texas on 15 August 1955. When a man named Chin Lun who knew Murphy during the war spotted him at the Boston premiere of *To Hell and Back* in 1955, he introduced himself. Murphy then told Chin: 'There's an awful lot of phonies in this business, you know.' Chin then replied with: 'A lot of people think I'm a phony when I say I know Audie Murphy. They look at me like, why would a guy like Audie know a guy like you? Well I did.' Chin Lun had served with 'Baker Company' (506th Infantry Regiment) from 15 March 1945 until the end of the war. He went on to describe the wartime Murphy as a skinny, very friendly, fragile looking little guy weighing between 105–110lbs.[35]

By April 1956 the profits had reached a whopping $6 million. It was the most money Murphy would ever make from a film role and he used some of it to buy a ranch in California. The idea of a sequel, *The Way Back*, was floated by David McClure but it didn't go any further than the discussion stage. Studio executives felt unable to put up the finance as they were concerned it would have to be all too real about Murphy's post-war life and audiences would not be interested in a story of battle fatigue and unhappy soldiers. Although Murphy secured the rights to any follow-up film of his life to guarantee ultimate control, nothing ever made it onto the screen. *To Hell and Back* was not only unique in the genre of war films because of its unprecedented autobiographical weight, but it had further established Murphy as the US's number one war hero. Its recipe for success was perfect.

It was in a February edition of *TV This Week* magazine in 1958 that Audie Murphy's article 'War and Westerns' was published. He had just finished filming a television drama about the Civil War called *Incident*. He wrote:

After I finished *To Hell and Back* I promised myself I'd never do another war story. But I came to realize this is as foolish as saying I'd never do another western – just because I had already done one. I feel there are an unlimited number of good stories that can be portrayed against the background of war, whereas under any other circumstances they would not be believable. I do admit, however, no one wants war stories for a steady diet. It's something we all want to forget but people can be shocked into stark, quick reality when brought face to face with men in battle.

War stories can also be much more honest than the average western. If a western hero ever showed signs of fright he would be laughed off the screen, even though he comes up against a life and death matter. He can be tense but not scared. However, put the same leading man in a uniform, transfer him from a western street to the Western Front, give him a rifle instead of a six-shooter and if he shows fear the audience understands him; they sympathize and he can do everything up to running away without losing a fan. Maybe this comes about because war, at one time or another, has been so close to most of our population today. There are few men who face battle who won't admit they have experienced fear, and they know, in true life, the line between being a hero or a coward is a fine one.[36]

Audie Murphy died in an aircraft crash in May 1971. He is buried at Arlington National Cemetery.

Part Two – Lights

Laurence Olivier

Skin of Our Teeth

The Thornton Wilder play *The Skin of Our Teeth* gets its title from the King James Bible, Job 19:20: 'My bone cleaveth to my skin and to my flesh, and I am escaped with the skin of my teeth'

With his dark, brooding good looks, a wealth of experience in British classical theatre and his leading man status in Hollywood, Laurence Olivier was already a major star when the Second World War broke out. In 1939 he delivered a storming performance as Heathcliff in *Wuthering Heights* which earned him an Oscar nomination for Best Actor. In March the same year he starred in a British comedy spy film *Q Planes* (in the US it was called *Clouds over Europe*) which the US *Vanity Fair* magazine praised as 'an excellent summer diversion' with its 'anti-German propaganda neatly tucked away'. In contrast the British version of the film opened with scenes showing storm clouds over the Houses of Parliament to introduce the seriousness of impending war.

On 3 September 1939, after Prime Minister Neville Chamberlain announced over the BBC airwaves 'this country is now at war with Germany', Olivier and many British actors in Hollywood decided to take action. So they contacted the British consul in Los Angeles to find out if they could return home and join up. Many of them, including Ronald Colman, Herbert Marshall, Cedric Hardwicke, Nigel Bruce and Basil Rathbone, MC, had served gallantly in the First World War.

At this point they were all officially told: 'Do nothing for the moment but stay put and await further instructions.' The advice certainly applied to any actor over 31 years old which included Olivier. But some British stars felt uneasy with the message. Most of them felt it was their duty to share the burden of war and help their fellow countrymen and women across the Atlantic on the Home Front. The British ambassador in

Washington, Lord Lothian, stood firm and told them: 'You are here in America on legitimate business. Yet what would Germany give to have such a corner as you actors have in the making of American pictures for the world market? And if Englishmen are to be portrayed in those pictures, how much better that real Englishmen act the parts rather than actors with monocles and spats.'[1] The situation was complicated though. Many Brits in the US, including specialist film crews, had signed long contracts with the studios. The Hollywood producer David Selznick was anxious because if his stars were called back to join the armed forces then his investments would come crashing down. Selznick is reputed to have said the studios 'would be in a pickle' if these actors all left for England but 'not so much as a pickle as that of Poland, I grant you!'[2] In the 12 months before the outbreak of the Second World War, a total of 264 feature films had been screened in British cinemas. Out of these just 50 were made in Britain. As Hollywood had provided 172 of the total number it more than proved it was the film capital of the world.

The day Britain declared war on Germany the 32-year-old Laurence Olivier was on board a yacht in Catalina Harbour in California with his friends. They'd spent the weekend trying to forget the grim prospect of a war in Europe. Now they had to accept it was official. The actor Douglas Fairbanks Jr and his wife Mary Lee had organised the party on the yacht in an attempt to cheer up their British pals. Fairbanks had known Olivier since 1931. That day, sipping champagne and trying to enjoy herself too, was Vivien Leigh who had just recently finished filming *Gone with the Wind*. Leigh rocketed to fame as Scarlett O'Hara in the full-colour American Civil War epic which hit the big screen in December 1939. On the day of the party, and already married to a British barrister named Herbert Leigh Holman, she was chaperoned by her mother Gertrude in order to help keep her affair with the married Olivier a secret. Among them was the aristocrat and First World War hero Nigel 'Willie' Bruce (Honourable Artillery Company) known for playing Dr Watson in the early Sherlock Holmes films. All in all they made for a friendly bunch until the mood took its dive in to sombreness, tension, and Olivier's outbursts of anger.

After hearing the news war had broken out in Europe Olivier recalled the reaction of all on aboard: 'Many of us burst into tears at once. Along with most other inhabitants of the earth, we felt blighted right through: careers, lives, hopes. Shortly reaction set in. Doug [Fairbanks] knew what drink existed for and a consequent hysteria began; my own manifestation of this was a show of frank vulgarity.'[3]

Fairbanks summed up the feeling and explained:

The world seemed in dread anticipation. Hitler had disavowed an older non-aggressor pact, this time with Poland. Suddenly, he blasted his way through that country's western front, while his new strange bedfellow, Stalin, by pre-arrangement rolled over Poland's eastern front. Great Britain and France warned them both that they would honour their guarantees to Poland unless the invaders withdrew immediately. An answer was expected by the morning of September 3. On that day our little yachting party had slowly been gathering on deck in silence, grouped around the radio, spirits cringing.

The radio suddenly broadcast Big Ben's deep chimes. Then a solemn BBC voice announced, 'The Prime Minister, the Right Honourable Neville Chamberlain'. Chamberlain calmly and briefly reported the situation and said that by the deadline a reply from Herr Hitler had not been received.

No one spoke. No one could. However apocalyptic our thoughts might have been, we could not have envisaged that the next five years would record the most awesome, horrible, and obscene indulgence in human fratricide since mammals first evolved from the primeval sludge. Over forty million human beings would lose their lives as a result of the next five years of the Second World War.[4]

Aboard the yacht in Catalina Harbour that day everyone was mostly drunk. Olivier even more so, possibly as he struggled to take on board the idea his homeland was in crisis. He was fired up enough to lower a boat into the sea and begin rowing manically around various other yachts declaring they were 'all done for'. He yelled 'this is the end' so loudly at various astonished onlookers they felt compelled to complain to the authorities about a mad Englishman and his verbal abuse. They believed the culprit to be the actor Ronald Colman who, whilst he was in the area, was in truth innocent of all charges. It seems the identity confusion may have had something to do with the fact both Olivier and Colman sported pencil-thin moustaches which were de rigueur for male Hollywood stars of the day.[5]

Ironically Olivier's likeness to Colman had frequently been a bugbear to him. (Both men shared the same birthplace of the comfortable suburbs of Surrey, England.) Olivier had experienced the humiliation of being second choice to Colman for roles more than once. Most notably in 1938 the director William Wyler had wanted the versatile Colman to star as Heathcliff in *Wuthering Heights*. When Wyler discovered Colman was unavailable to walk the Yorkshire moors with the mythical wild, wilful Cathy, his second choice was Olivier who went on to make it his own even though producer Sam Goldwyn complained about him being 'the ugliest actor ever known'. It appears Goldwyn was always a charmer!

On the day war was declared the British star David Niven was with his friend the actor Bob Coote (noted for his characterisations of military types including RAF Flying Officer 'Bob Trubshawe' in the awesome Powell and Pressburger 1946 film *A Matter of Life and Death*). Both men had drunk too much at another party and had fallen asleep on a dinghy on its way to take them to Fairbanks' party in Catalina. Niven wrote in his memoir: 'When we arrived and joined the others we found a sombre group. No one knew quite what to do; like millions all over the world it was beginning to dawn on us that we were pawns in a game that got out of control.'

The star was right. Everything had changed for so many people. Just a few weeks beforehand Niven had been a young actor building a successful screen career and had portrayed the character of Edgar Linton alongside Olivier's Heathcliff in *Wuthering Heights*. By 3 September he knew he'd have to join the real theatre of war. Niven's own family had strong military connections. His father William had died fighting in the Gallipoli campaign in 1915, and his maternal grandfather William Degacher had served as a Captain in the South Wales Borderers. The actor's great-grandfather had been killed in the Anglo-Zulu War of 1879. Unsurprisingly, the patriotic Niven, who had himself already served as an officer in the Highland Light Infantry from 1930–3, felt compelled to return home and re-join his unit. He was among the first to leave Hollywood and get back into uniform and do his duty.

On 30 September 1938 when the Munich Agreement was signed by Adolf Hitler and the British Prime Minister Chamberlain, Olivier appeared in his first war film. Did he suspect the espionage theme of

Q Planes (backed by the great British film impresario Alexander Korda who was also secretly working for British Intelligence) was something of a prophecy of what was about to hit the world for the next six years? There's little doubt Korda had inside knowledge of the fragile political situation in Germany that year. The Hungarian-born Korda was a friend of Winston Churchill. They had been introduced by Lieutenant Colonel Claude Dansey, a mutual acquaintance who had served with Churchill in the Boer War. Dansey was the head of British Intelligence in Rome who enjoyed Korda's taste for intrigue and his sharp intelligent mind. When Churchill's political career hit the rocks in the 1930s, Korda had offered his dejected friend lucrative work as an editor and script advisor. Churchill was a fan of Korda's films about war heroes, and had enjoyed *The Four Feathers* (1939) because the story was similar to the politician's own youthful military experiences.[6]

Olivier began work on *Q Planes* (*Clouds Over Europe*) with Ralph Richardson in September 1938. Both actors had been friends for some years and had appeared on stage together in Shakespeare's *Othello* (Richardson as the Moor of Venice and Olivier as Iago). *Q Planes* was shot at Denham Studios, and at Brooklands Racetrack where in the background to some scenes we can see fine examples of the Airspeed Envoy, the de Havilland Dragon Rapide and the de Havilland Tiger Moth.

At first the film had the working title of *Foreign Sabotage* and was loosely inspired by a true story involving the disappearance of a prototype of a highly effective new bomber made by Vickers Wellesley. This aircraft was built with a specially designed geodesic fuselage which was the brainchild of Sir Barnes Wallis who was later famous for his 'bouncing bomb' and the Dambuster raids. In the late 1930s new aircraft were being reported as 'missing in strange circumstances' over the Channel. A search was instigated at the orders of the Air Ministry which put Sir Robert Vansittart who was Chief of the British Secret Service, in charge of the investigation. Vansittart who was always highly suspicious of the Germans, believed something dodgy was a foot and it wasn't twelve inches! He was also a good friend of film mogul Alexander Korda who was one of his approved British agents. When part of the real aircraft was allegedly found in a garage in Kiel in Germany there was suspicion it had been shot down by a Nazi submarine. Convinced of this, the Secret Service under Vansittart's instruction funded *Q Planes* in order to let

Hitler and the Luftwaffe know they had worked out ways to defeat any enemy attempt at aircraft sabotage.

In the film a bowler-hatted Ralph Richardson stars as Major Hammond who as the secret service boss was the early inspiration for the character of John Steed played by Patrick McNee in *The Avengers* hit television series of the 1960s. Olivier assertively plays the character of test pilot Tony McVane who is employed by the Barrett & Ward Aircraft Company which is developing a range of new military fighters and bombers.

When two aircraft suddenly go missing over the Channel McVane is keen to help solve the case. Having made friends with Major Hammond and then becoming romantically involved with Hammond's sister Kay (played by Valerie Hobson) who is a newspaper reporter posing as a waitress in the works' canteen, McVane goes all out to find out the truth. When he takes to the skies to look for the aircraft he is brought down by a mysterious ray of magnetic light which is beamed out by an innocent-looking German salvage ship the SS *Viking*. As the aircraft hits the top of the water a large crane from the ship lowers a harness and brings it aboard. The crew and passengers are taken prisoner and McVane is re-united with those men already captured from previous 'missing aircraft'. *Q Planes* ends well when McVane and the other captured air crew break out of a locked room aboard the SS *Viking* which is manned by a German crew thus confirming the link to villainy and pro-Nazi activity. Major Hammond soon discovers what is unfolding aboard the ship and sends the trusty Royal Navy in HMS *Echo* to rescue McVane and those who had been captured. A bloody battle on board to seize control of the ship saw most of the German crew wiped out. It was the ending Vansittart and Korda loved – the British were victorious over enemy skulduggery.

Film historians argue *Q Planes* is a 'neutral spy comedy' – a genre which followed Alfred Hitchcock's hits including *The 39 Steps* (1935) and *The Lady Vanishes* (1938). In America in June 1939 the film received positive reviews, although in Britain the famous critic Dilys Powell described Olivier as 'dashing but undistinguished'. There was also criticism because the opening had been changed for US audiences.

By the time the picture, distributed by Paramount, hit the big screen on 2 March 1939, both Olivier and Richardson had learned to fly aircraft in real life so the controls in a cockpit were not alien to them. Richardson had introduced his friend to flying in the mid-1930s when he took him for a flight over the London Aero Club at Hatfield (which during wartime became home to the women's section of the Air Transport Auxiliary). Olivier never forgot the thrill of flying and became determined to forge himself another occupation as a pilot. Sure enough he found a gruff and bullying instructor who would eventually turn him into a pilot even though there is evidence to prove he wasn't 'a natural'. The trainee aviator's lessons took place firstly at Hatfield in England. Then when he was in the US he flew around Clover Fields in Santa Monica, California, and the Metropolitan Airfield in Hampden County, Massachusetts, and he even flew over the Hudson River. Vivien Leigh and Korda often waited on the ground and watched the actor's airborne demonstrations with fear and trepidation. During the course of a few weeks he had smashed up three aircraft, much to everyone's dismay. But perseverance and fighting for what he wanted was one of the actor's key attributes. Finally after completing his 200 flying hours Olivier was granted his pilot's licence. His enthusiasm for aviation was to prove useful as within 18 months it influenced his decision about his military career.[7]

But while he was roaring about the skies in an attempt to ignore the inner knowledge he would never be completely at ease as an aviator, he found himself among the British colony of actors who had begun to suffer a torrent of criticism for 'moving to the US to avoid the war in Europe'. Many stars were named and shamed in a 'Gone with the Wind Up!' smear campaign, including British singing star Gracie Fields. By 1940 Fields had moved to the US to be with her Italian husband Mario Bianchi who had lived there since he was 10 years old. Although Fields took part in fundraising concerts to help the British war effort it was many months before she could move on from the bad publicity which had almost ruined her reputation as Yorkshire's favourite big-hearted lass with the voice to match. In 1940 there was no one to wish her luck or even wave her goodbye. The notable film producer Michael Balcon joined in the attack and wrote an article for *The Sunday Dispatch* which questioned the morality of British 'deserters', these 'isolationists who are being allowed to accumulate fortunes without sharing in any way the hardships their fellow Britons endure gladly for our cause'.[8] The cheeky chappy with the ukulele George Formby agreed with Balcon and so did Sir Seymour Hicks, Controller of the Entertainments National Service Association (ENSA), who was at Drury Lane preparing productions for the troops.

He said the older actors like Hardwicke and Bruce who had fought in the First World War were obviously exonerated from negative judgement, but he said he'd like to include the young 'shirkers' in Hollywood on a 'Roll of Dishonour'.

To make matters worse the German consul in Los Angeles was revelling in the situation because it helped prevent pro-British films from being made and distributed. Then after the author J.B. Priestley made a broadcast to support the smear campaign, the British consul decided to act and put the British public in the picture. The relevant War Office committee was contacted and a statement from the consul was published in *The Sunday Dispatch* on 25 August 1940 to explain there had been a recent update to the rules which recommended actors under the age of 31 should return home, and any older film stars should 'stay put and carry on working' and await further instructions. The statement read:

> I understand this ruling has been, to all intents and purposes obeyed. It is therefore quite unfair to condemn older actors, who are simply obeying this ruling, as 'deserters'. Moreover, the maintenance of a powerful nucleus of older British actors is of great importance to our own interests, partly because they are continually championing the British cause in a very volatile community which would otherwise be left to the mercies of German propaganda, and because the production of films with a strong British tone is one of the best and subtlest forms of British propaganda. The only effect of undesirable broadcasts like this [Priestley's] is to discredit British patriotism and British-produced films; neither do Americans like having British dirty linen washed for their benefit in public.

Shortly after the consul's message had hit the newsstands a meeting was called with British actors in Los Angeles to make it clear all negative publicity must be stamped out. He also told them there was no point in 'an immediate stampede home', and the greatest immediate need back home was for 'equipment not manpower'.

The assembled party, who had taken time out from shooting their latest films, were advised to offer their services and be ready to be called upon if needed. Each man was advised to do his best to raise funds for war charities and events which included a personal appearance. A meeting was then arranged with Lord Lothian – the British Ambassador in Washington.

Cedric Hardwicke and Cary Grant were chosen to represent the British colony of actors. The ambassador informed Lord Halifax back home of the action now being taken and it was also agreed a special committee of actors representing the British colony should work closely with the consul and a retired British Army colonel. Those actors put forward for the task were: Basil Rathbone, Ronald Colman, Cedric Hardwicke, Herbert Marshall and Brian Aherne.

In his memoir Aherne recalled how everyone behaved 'extremely well' and justified 'Lord Halifax's faith in them'. The honest Aherne praised Rathbone's sterling efforts as President of the British War Relief Association. 'He travelled endlessly and worked tirelessly over the West and deserved a large share of the credit for the enormous sums of money and gifts of comforts and supplies that were collected by this Division. Had he been in England, he would surely have received a knighthood.'[9]

* * *

In 1939, and despite critic Dilys Powell's recent frowning description of his performance in the quick turnaround film *Q Planes*, 'Larry' Olivier with the extraordinary voice and an all-consuming desire to 'become the greatest actor in the world' had already achieved many professional victories. Indeed he was described by the great director Franco Zeffirelli as 'the most disciplined man he had ever known'.

Olivier was already famous for storming the London stage in a variety of leading dramatic roles. By the end of the year he had become a cinematic heart-throb following his Oscar-nominated performance as Heathcliff in Sam Goldwyn's production of Emily Brontë's novel *Wuthering Heights*.

But beneath the glitter of fame his personal life was in conflict with his professional glory. Firstly there was tension between him and his co-star Merle Oberon during the making of *Wuthering Heights*. Olivier was desperately keen for his new love Vivien Leigh to play the tormented Cathy but Oberon, who was married to Korda, was chosen instead. Leigh had been offered the role of Isabella but turned it down. Olivier disliked Oberon who had already established herself as a leading Hollywood name. She too had left the set in an outrage when by accident he drooled on her and then refused for a while to apologise. Tensions were high between them. Psychologically Olivier felt he must wear two masks – one to successfully play stormy Heathcliff and another to reassign and hide his objections to working with Oberon.[10]

The production company was keen to retain a moral code among its casts, and executives were waiting for Olivier's divorce to come through from his first wife of 10 years Jill Esmond (the mother of his eldest son Tarquin). Leigh was waiting too for her official separation from her then husband Herbert Leigh Holman with whom she had a daughter, Suzanne.

Whilst life on the set of *Wuthering Heights* had been as dramatic and tempestuous as Emily Brontë's story itself, Olivier became a firm admirer of the demanding director William Wyler. In a television interview with Michael Parkinson in 1970 the actor said it was Wyler who persuaded him one could do anything with the medium of film. 'Why you could even put Shakespeare on film!' And of course Olivier went on to do just that but not before he'd offered Wyler the job first. He recalled: 'During the war when I made *Henry V* I found out William was a Major in the American Army and he was staying at that time at Claridge's Hotel. So I went to him and asked him if he would direct *Henry V*. He said "no thanks I can't you'd better do it yourself". If it hadn't been for Wyler I would never have thought of making a movie.'[11]

Wuthering Heights was also the picture that heralded the creative camerawork of Gregg Toland who devised the new deep-loaded shots which could include two characters at once. It was a new way of filming and Olivier noted Toland always worked with Wyler. When the actor played Hamlet in the 1948 film version it's worth noting Toland's dynamic cinematography using dark shadows creates great dramatic effect. The film was, as Olivier admitted, reminiscent of Orson Welles' 1942 legendary epic *Citizen Kane*, which had Toland's style written all over it.

In 1939 Olivier was in Hollywood with the beautiful yet troubled Leigh when he was cast to play the dashing and sinister character of Max de Winter in Daphne Du Maurier's *Rebecca*. The film was produced by mogul David O. Selznick. Once again its star was desperately disappointed his beloved Leigh had not been cast to play opposite him as the second Mrs de Winter. The director Alfred Hitchcock was adamant the role went to Joan Fontaine. Of course Olivier's dispute was pointless as by this time his lover was already contracted to play Scarlett O'Hara in the legendary full-colour epic *Gone with the Wind*.

The actor had a lot on his mind at the time. He knew full well the war in Europe was going badly at home in Britain and can be forgiven for believing everything he knew and loved, his very roots were now under great threat. Important childhood memories, his young adulthood and his doting family and myriad of friends needed his protection or wanted him to join them in the call to arms. The call of duty was powerful. This was as great a role demanded of him as from any of Shakespeare's great history plays in which he was star so very many times.

In his memoir Olivier vividly recalled 1939. He wrote:

> There was a general directive to all our countryman abroad who did not already have a commission or were not within the required age group to stay put; did we not appreciate that if every Englishman living abroad were to come gallantly dashing home, the public services would have to face an additional population of anything up to half a million extra mouths to feed and extra hands to find employment for? It was a painful situation, and wretchedly embarrassing with the Americans who for once were our not very enthusiastic hosts. Many of them seemed far from certain whose side they were on. There was an enthusiastically pro-German feeling in those areas of the United States containing extensive proportions of German immigrants. Milwaukee, for instances, was largely German speaking. Whether it would be useful or not, I soon began to feel it would be better for us to go home and take whatever came. And so the 1930s went limping out, on a note as baleful and grim as a fog-horn on a dark night.[12]

By the beginning of 1940 Leigh had agreed to start work on MGM's tear-jerking production of *Waterloo Bridge*. She plays ballet dancer Myra Lester whose lover is killed in the First World War and having abandoned all faith in humanity she becomes a prostitute. The American actor Robert Taylor stars as British Army Captain Roy Cronin who meets Lester by chance as he crosses Waterloo Bridge during the Second World War. They begin a relationship which is soon thwarted by the tyrannical woman who runs the ballet company. And, when Cronin is captured at the Front, he becomes a prisoner of war and is absent from Lester's life. Leigh always claimed the character of Myra Lester was one of her all-time favourite roles, especially as she had the opportunity to reveal her own natural gracefulness as a dancer. She also felt the film helped acknowledge the struggles on the Home Front in real-life wartime Britain.

By this time she was a major star and had the power to call the shots. After just one film (*Gone with the Wind*) she had risen above the greatest names like Joan Crawford and Irene Dunne who had strived for years to reach the giddy heights of the Hollywood system. Scarlett O'Hara, whose personality was not unlike that of the actress who created her, ruled supreme. Imagine the furore then which erupted when a New York advertising agency put Robert Taylor's name at the top of the billing for *Waterloo Bridge*. The action resulted in a breach of contract which left Selznick at MGM furious especially as negotiations over fees and casting had proved a long and complicated process. It was another disappointment for Leigh on top of the fact she had desperately wanted Olivier to play Cronin.

What the film did prove, however, was that Leigh was a superb actress. In the *New York Times* Bosley Crowther wrote: 'Miss Leigh shapes the role of the girl with superb comprehension, progresses from the innocent, frail dancer to the bedizened streetwalker with such surety of characterization and creates such an appealing naturalism that the picture gains considerable substance. Leigh is as fine an actress as we have on the screen today. Maybe even the finest.'[13] The film opens with a scene from the Second World War which helped Leigh feel she was using her talents to illuminate the struggles experienced by so many on the Home Front in Britain. *Waterloo Bridge*, directed by Mervyn LeRoy, also marked a time when the 'Phoney War' and all its frustrations among the people of Britain was at its peak. It hit the big screen in May 1940 and was an instant success at the box office.

In that same month the great producer Alexander Korda was called to a special meeting with Britain's Minister of Information, Duff Cooper. Both men had been instructed by Churchill to communicate. During their top-secret conversation Korda was encouraged to produce films which would help influence American opinion about the war in Europe. It was agreed Korda's company London Film Productions would also provide cover for secret agents working across Europe. Korda's decision to leave Britain and travel to America in the early summer of 1940 to plan his new covert role in Hollywood brought him a torrent of criticism from many in the industry who believed he was 'deserting' the country in its hour of need. Patriotism was high as the aircrews of the Battle of Britain were now fighting it out with the Luftwaffe in the skies of southern England. What critics didn't know was the truth behind Korda's mission. He took many risky flights in military aircraft to and from Britain to the US to fulfil his promise to Churchill.

Korda met with Olivier in New York to discreetly inform the actor he would like to work with him on propaganda films. At the time in 1940 Olivier wasn't overly keen to remain in America as he wanted to return to Britain with Leigh and get involved in the war effort by using his piloting skills. But the charismatic Korda persisted and called them to say he had the perfect film for them both and it would be one that Churchill himself would adore. They agreed and signed a contract to make *That Hamilton Woman* – the story of naval hero Admiral Horatio Nelson. Churchill was thrilled.

* * *

The patriotic Laurence Kerr Olivier was born on 22 May 1907 in Dorking, Surrey. He was the son of local Anglican clergyman Gerard Olivier who married the kindly Agnes Crookenden around 1900. Their eldest child Sybille was born in 1901. It was Agnes who insisted her youngest child Laurence join his brother 'Dickie' at All Saints' Margaret Street Choir School in London to obtain a healthy and spiritual education. Astute as ever, Agnes was well aware her husband felt the noisy Laurence (also known as 'Paddy' for his fiery temper) had been an unwanted late addition to the family, and until her early death in 1920 (Olivier was 13 at the time) she did her utmost to ensure the welfare of her youngest son was equal to that of her other children.

At school he met a boy named Douglas Bader who would grow up to be known as one of the RAF's most famous pilots. It was a cheeky young Bader who once held Olivier underwater in the school swimming pool and irritated him with 'saucy language'. But it was Olivier who later in his life confessed to feeling guilty for administering two whacks of a cane to Bader as punishment that day! Bader soon got his own back by bowling his adversary out at cricket![14]

Three decades later Bader, who had both legs amputated after a flying accident in 1931, went on to became a notable RAF fighter ace in 1940 during the Battle of France, Dunkirk and the Battle of Britain. He fought on against the Luftwaffe for some months after until he was forced to bale out over France and become a PoW on 9 August 1941.

In 1969 (as we shall examine more fully later in this book) his old school sparring partner Olivier appeared as his former boss – Air Chief Marshal Hugh Dowding in the legendary 1969 film *Battle of Britain*. Bader had been signed up by production executives in 1968 to serve as an important technical advisor on this legendary picture directed by Guy Hamilton. Bader, two years younger than Olivier, had obviously forgiven him for the schoolboy caning, for when he bumped into him one day and learned the actor had joined the Fleet Air Arm he said: 'I want to congratulate you. I think it's a thoroughly good show your coming back to join up like this. I want to say "Bravo!"' At this Olivier, by now staring at the glittering array of medals including the DFC* (Distinguished Flying Cross and Bar), and DSO (Distinguished Service Order) adorning his former schoolmate's RAF tunic, replied: 'I want to say more than Bravo!' Sir Douglas Bader CBE, DSO & Bar, DFC & Bar, DL, FRAeS died in 1982.

Not long after his mother's death the schoolboy Olivier had already begun to show great promise in drama productions but at the time he believed he was destined to follow his 'Father Olivier' and become a clergyman. His powerful voice would project well in the pulpit. There was no doubt about his natural talent for theatre as school reports show how the only subject he deemed worthy of any effort was drama.

The Very Reverend Gerard Kerr Olivier, however, had no wish to force his son's interest in a clergyman's life and heartily recommended the theatre to him as a future career. When Olivier reached the age of 17 his father insisted his son become a student at the Central School of Speech and Drama. It was here, under the tutelage of the great voice coach Elsie Fogerty, that Oliver's sister Sybille had excelled. Once the young actor with the large eyebrows and great sense of fun had similarly impressed Miss Fogerty he was offered a bursary and trained with notable theatrical names such as Dame Peggy Ashcroft.

In 1926, having learned the essentials of stagecraft and a gift for characterisation, he was spotted by Sybil Thorndike and her husband, the actor Lewis Casson, and soon found work with the Birmingham Repertory Company. The variety of character roles helped expand his performance skills and he met another young actor who would prove a lifelong pal – Ralph Richardson. Fifteen years later, in his uniform of a Royal Naval sub-lieutenant pilot, it was Richardson who recommended to Olivier that he join the Fleet Air Arm and help the war effort.

Back in 1928, however, Olivier was about to appear at the Apollo Theatre in the West End as Captain Stanhope at the premiere of a notable and still much revived play set in the trenches of the First World War – *Journey's End* by R.C. Sherriff. It was a production which offered him an opportunity to understand the lives of men forced to live in squalor and survive the horrors of a seemingly endless conflict. The playwright and author Sherriff had in real life served in the trenches with the East Surrey Regiment and was badly wounded at Passchendaele in 1917. His drama takes place near Saint-Quentin, Aisne, France in 1918. The characters are officers of a British Army infantry company who await orders to drive back an overwhelming German military offensive designed to break through Allied lines. The play which is fuelled by suspense and varying levels of tension among the officers was called *Journey's End* because that phrase was in the last line of a book Sherriff had been reading at the time.

Olivier revealed: 'This play was a masterpiece. Although I could recognise the possibilities of the role of Captain Stanhope I told James Whale, the director, "there's nothing but meals in the play" but he replied that was all they had to think about in the mud of the trenches during the war.'[15] The actor, who was just 21 at the time and full of ambition, admitted he used *Journey's End* as an 'audition' in the hope he would get spotted and offered the leading role in Basil Dean's stage production of P.C. Wren's book *Beau Geste*. (The silent Hollywood film version starring Ronald Colman was made in 1926.)

At the time as a young actor he didn't realise *Journey's End* would become a theatrical legend and be hailed as one of the most powerful and evocative theatre and film productions ever to represent the plight of those serving in the 1914–18 conflict. The character of Captain Stanhope was in fact ideal for him as it provided some intimate knowledge of military conflict, camaraderie and class hypocrisy. He'd find that useful when he joined the armed services himself in the Second World War. *Journey's End* had taught him how men used their intellect and their emotions during times of war. In his own real life situation it soon became all about motivating the Allied troops with his storming performances in various important propaganda films and plays.

Beau Geste by P.C. Wren captured his imagination in 1928. It tells the story of three English brothers who join the French Foreign Legion following their discovery that a valuable and precious diamond has been stolen from the home of a wealthy relative a year or so just before the outbreak of the First World War. It is a powerful and compelling adventure tale and it is easy to understand why Olivier sought an outlet for his passion to play a swashbuckling kind of hero with a whole myriad of darkness clouding a troubled soul. However, the play ran for only two months in the West End whilst *Journey's End* with Colin Clive in Olivier's former role of Captain Stanhope ran for several years (and still does) and toured triumphantly in the late 1920s in New York and Chicago to rave reviews. Ten years later in 1939 the now theatrically seasoned Olivier could shake off any regrets about his short run as John Geste in the West End as he went on to successfully star in the Campbell Theatre's radio production alongside Orson Welles.

The 1930s would prove tremendously busy for the handsome young Olivier who was fast realising his ambition to be the 'greatest actor that ever lived'. The new decade would also prove culturally significant in the United States and Europe as political turmoil and economic challenges gripped global populations. Firstly the Wall Street Crash of 1929 in the US had sent its brutal consequences across the world provoking insecurity and fear. In the United States in 1933 nearly 14 million people were unemployed. After President Franklin D. Roosevelt swept into power in December 1932 a National Recovery Administration was set up which led to new support for unions. Economic growth began to flourish and roads, buildings and the arts received generous subsidies. Hollywood was to benefit with the new Works Progress Administration (WPA) seeing 8.5 million people back into work. Industries were becoming stronger and prosperity began to creep back into communities still ever watchful about where they spent any spare dimes rattling around in the safe. Roosevelt's biographer Jean Edward Smith noted: 'He lifted himself from a wheelchair to lift the nation from its knees.'

In Britain and Europe the devastation caused by the First World War had left communities broken and despairing. The pressure on film and theatre artistes to provide maximum escapism was never so fierce as it was then. In Hollywood the Studio System was created and the conglomerate of small companies which ran the industry during the silent era had little choice but to accept changes when the 'talkies' arrived. Sound was here to stay and with it came the opportunity to attract audiences and box-office cash into cinemas. Along came the 'Big Five' companies – RKO (Radio-Keith-Orpheum), 20th Century Fox, Warner Brothers, Paramount (formerly Famous Players–Lasky whose big-name director was Cecil B. De Mille) and Metro-Goldwyn-Mayor (Loew's/MGM). These were the majors who owned cinemas with a linked-in distribution set-up. Then came the minors otherwise known as the 'Little Three' – Universal, United Artists and Columbia, all of which produced a raft of high-quality films on a par with those made by the Big Five.

The 1930s became known as the 'golden age of Hollywood' even though the subject matter of most films was monitored closely by the 'Hays Code' (named after its creator Will H. Hays) which set out strict morality rules for each production. At the time the conservatism of the decade led to a strong belief that the so-called debauchery and loose behaviour of the 1920s Jazz Age had caused a far too Bohemian attitude towards the fundamental purpose of culture.

However, the Officials of the Motion Picture Producers and Distributors Association which accommodated the Hays Code were battling a raft of complications owing to the public scandals in the film industry of the 1920s and should not be condemned as the old miseries of the industry. They also served to encourage good public relations and their aim was to keep government censorship and meddling out of the industry. However it was the Code which demanded films containing content like 'sexual perversion' (homosexuality), crime, violence and bad language should be forbidden.[16] Rhett Butler's famous last line 'Frankly, my dear, I don't give a damn' (delivered superbly by actor and Second World War hero Clarke Gable) in Gone With The Wind had the MPPDA in a sweat for weeks. Finally permission was given to keep the line in the film. It's unimaginable to think how else they could have concluded this legendary epic! Somehow Rhett whispering meekly: 'I'm not returning here again,' just doesn't have the same impact! The MPPDA trod a fine line and whilst it permitted over-saucy lines and innuendo it did save the production companies money by ensuring expensive and explicit scenes were not included. If any director tried to slide such things into his film they would always be spotted and snipped out during the final edit. All these censorship rules in Hollywood were of course well in place by the late 1930s and being ever so slightly massaged by one or two brave directors. The dramatic innuendo of film noir would soon be arriving on the big screen as the 1940s beckoned, with sultry women characters and the man in the shadows offered to cinema audiences.

Meantime in Britain the ambitious Olivier continued to extend his theatrical range and appeared to much acclaim as Hamlet in 1937 at the Old Vic. He revealed a talent for presenting a tale of conflict which stemmed from both inside and outside the character. His new love Vivien Leigh was cast as Ophelia. That year they both appeared on screen too in *Fire Over England* which was set during the time of England's Elizabethan victory over the Spanish Armada. Olivier played the young hero Michael Ingolby and Leigh stood out as the love interest, a character named Cynthia. It was her performance in this film which went on to convince the producers of *Gone with the Wind* that she would be perfect to play the legendary Scarlett O'Hara.

By 1940 and with Europe already in the grip of the Second World War, Olivier and Leigh starred on the Broadway stage in Shakespeare's *Romeo and Juliet*. The play was not a success but since they had both been granted divorces from their previous spouses they were able to marry in August of that year at the San Ysidro Ranch in Santa Barbara.

It was at this time Olivier had almost managed to free himself of his obligations to Hollywood and return to Britain to help the war effort. He contacted Churchill's Minister of Information Duff Cooper to declare his intent but was advised to stay in Hollywood. When the anxious actor asked why he couldn't go home and do his duty he was told to go to New York and visit the film director Alexander Korda who Churchill had put in Hollywood to assist British Intelligence.

It has been rumoured there was a hidden agenda to the situation and a theory was put forward by some historians that Olivier had been recruited by the Special Operations Executive (SOE) to work for a propaganda organisation as he was prone to be a target for Nazi agents. Whilst the actor never disputed such thinking there is little proof it was fact, but as it all added some mystery to his work in the United States then he went along with it all. Although such recruitment to the SOE is unlikely,

Olivier fanned the flames though by the coy response 'My ego is too great to reveal my secrets. It serves my ego to keep things to myself.' He knew then that anything he could do by appearing on the screen to encourage the US to join the war effort would be a significant result.

When Korda encouraged Olivier to star in *That Hamilton Woman* he told him: 'Propaganda can be a bitter medicine. It needs sugar coating, and Lady Hamilton is a very thick coating indeed.' The indefatigable Prime Minister had been discussing the production for weeks and telegrams between himself and Korda went to and from the US. The discussion over the film's title proved to be a lively debate. In 1940 both men were aware of the fragile political situation which existed between the US government and Britain. Extra attention was needed to not infuriate the American government as the US was not at that time at war with Germany. Anyone in Hollywood who had expressed sympathy with Britain was treated and exploited with great tact.

Great diplomacy had been at the forefront when it came to the choice of who should create a screenplay which would have a subtle but strong propaganda subtext. Eventually, an Austrian writer and director called Walter Reisch, and Britain's R.C. Sherriff of *Journey's End* fame, took up the challenge of creating plot and dialogue for *That Hamilton Woman*. In a letter to film historian Karol Kulik in 1973, R.C. Sherriff wrote:

> There was always a very strong pro-British feeling in Hollywood with producers and directors. I was on a committee organised by the British Consul which was intended to watch over films that might have embarrassed the American government as being too much against Germany before the War was declared. Among these pictures were *Mrs Miniver*, and, of course, *Lady Hamilton*. I was never at anytime conscious that our activities as British citizens in writing these pictures were under any Government suspicion, although clearly it would obviously have been wrong to emphasize their British bias.[17]

The beautiful Leigh agreed to star as Emma Hamilton (1765–1815) who in real life had embarked on a torrid romance with the great Royal Navy hero Lord Nelson (1758–1805). Work began on the film in September 1940.

Alex Korda's creative younger brother Vincent Korda and Julia Heron designed the glorious sets and were nominated for an Oscar in 1941.

Jack Whitley won the Academy Award for Best Sound. *That Hamilton Woman*, despite all diplomatic efforts exercised by the writers, was pure propaganda for the British war effort. The audience was seduced into associating the dictatorial, tyrannical traits of the aggressive French military and political leader Napoleon with the behaviour exhibited by Adolf Hitler. The idea it was about one of history's greatest love affairs was Korda's convenient coating of sugary glitz to hide the film's true motive to persuade Americans to take Britain's side in the war effort. And some might agree one of Nelson's speeches in a particular scene had Churchill's hand to it. It certainly did nothing to convince the US Senate that Korda was politically neutral.

In a brilliant and compelling performance Olivier as Nelson addresses the British Admiralty:

Lord Spencer, gentlemen, you're celebrating a peace with Napoleon Bonaparte. Peace is a very beautiful word as long as the impulse of peace is behind it. But, gentlemen, you will never make peace with Napoleon. He doesn't mean peace today. He just wants to gain a little time to re-arm himself at sea and to make new alliances with Italy and Spain, all to one purpose. To destroy our Empire! Years ago I said the same thing at Naples. I begged them, I entreated them not to give way but they wouldn't listen to me, and they paid the price. But that was a little Kingdom miles away in the Mediterranean. But this is England our own land. Napoleon can never be master of the world until he has smashed up us – and believe me, gentlemen, he means to be master of the world. You cannot make peace with dictators. You have to destroy them. Wipe them out! Gentlemen, I implore you, speak to the Prime Minister before it is too late. Do not ratify this peace!'

At first the US censor tried to ban the film because it 'glorified adultery'. In real life Admiral Nelson was already married during his affair with his mistress. Lady Hamilton gave birth to his illegitimate daughter, Horatia Nelson Thompson, in 1801. Whilst nudity was never revealed in *That Hamilton Woman*, the telling glances of lust between the characters was enough to make the Motion Picture Production Code committee jump with unease.

Korda was told by the censor he should have checked out the morality of the screenplay before work went ahead. Rapidly, Walter Reisch and R.C. Sherriff were called in to write a scene to save the picture from the axe. This master stroke showed Nelson's father strongly berating him for neglecting Frances for the adulterous attentions of Lady Hamilton. Finally, the new scene meant the censor could give *That Hamilton Woman* the all-clear. It was a near thing as Korda was already under suspicion for his heavy-handed pro-British sympathies, and he had been summoned to answer a raft of awkward political questions in the US Senate.

When *That Hamilton Woman* hit the big screen its box office receipts totalled more than $1 million. Not bad for a film which took just five weeks to shoot. Churchill loved its clever subtext and hailed it as his favourite film of all time. His friend Korda paid for the latest cinema equipment to be installed at Churchill's beloved home Chartwell at Westerham in Kent. Guests who included a raft of stars including Vivien Leigh were often treated by the avuncular Churchill to a showing of *That Hamilton Woman* and other pictures about heroism and adventure including later the first James Bond film, *Dr No*.[18]

Olivier didn't regard the film as an important piece of cinema history. He had lost money on his stage production of *Romeo and Juliet* in 1941 just before he agreed to play the great Nelson.

He wrote:

The inclination to get the hell home was irresistible. I was fortunate enough to have Duff Cooper for a friend; married to Lady Diana Manners, he was at this time Minister of Information. Telephoning obviously presented some difficulties, especially long distance, but calls to government high-ups went through like silk. I decided 'This deed I'll do before this purpose cool' and to get him when he was sure to be in his London office. This turned out to be during our [*Romeo and Juliet*] matinée about 4pm. The call went straight through from the stage door, of all places. I asked him if there might be a job for me even though I was beyond enlistment age, or any way in which I might be useful in his department. Within a few days came the following cable: 'Think better where you are Korda going to be there.'[19]

It was followed by a call from Korda about *That Hamilton Woman* and suddenly the 'money situation' became less 'poignant'. The money enabled Olivier to ensure his son Tarquin and first wife Jill Esmond could stay safely in Hollywood and Vivien's daughter Suzanne could be cared for by her grandmother Gertrude in Vancouver, Canada.

It was during the autumn of 1940 as Olivier persisted with his flying practice that he received a visit from British director Michael Powell who wanted him to appear in *49th Parallel*. The title came from the line of latitude which is the border between the Canadian provinces of British Columbia, Alberta, Saskatchewan and Manitoba (to the north), and the US states of Washington, Idaho, Montana, North Dakota and Minnesota (to the south).

Meantime Olivier, already known to Powell from his early days at Denham Studios, was offered the role of 'Johnnie', a French-Canadian trapper who stands up to the malicious crew of a sunken German U-boat who descend on the neutral Hudson Bay during the early days of the Second World War. Olivier listened intently to Powell and agreed to appear providing contracts were amicable. He also informed Powell he planned to return to England at the beginning of 1941 to join the Fleet Air Arm. The actor agreeably joined the rest of the principal stars of *49th Parallel* who, to assist the war effort, had agreed to a special fee of £2,000 for two weeks work, tax-free.

Powell recalled:

I went to the studio on Santa Monica Boulevard where Alex Korda had completed *The Thief of Baghdad* and was now producing the film about Nelson. I didn't want to see Korda or old friends as I wanted to get back to my unit in the Canadian Rockies. Larry [Olivier] came out to see me in his Nelson suit, black patch over his eye, empty sleeve, cocked hat, the lot. He repeated his promise we had made during an earlier telephone call about playing Johnnie the trapper if the Fleet Air Arm agreed. I could have kissed him; maybe I did![20]

Some time, however, before the dynamic Powell approached Olivier about the role of 'Johnnie' the beginnings of one of the most successful wartime propaganda films had begun to take shape. Whether or not the ultimate significance and power of *49th Parallel* was ever acknowledged by Olivier is not known. Maybe he didn't feel it was important to mention it in his autobiography as his appearance lasted all of 10 minutes. This 'bit part' however earned him rave reviews and he was praised highly by notable publications like *Variety*. The actor obviously took note as he is recorded as asking himself: 'Had I learned something about the economy and directness of film acting from my days in Hollywood?'

It is tremendously important to salute Powell for his resolution then to tell the story of Canada and its role during the Second World War. First instigated by the Ministry of Information with a film section led by Kenneth Clark, it was Powell who had been impressed by an article written by Beverly Baxter about Canada's involvement in the conflict – a prophetic piece of writing which almost predicted the United States was soon to join the Allied cause against Hitler's tyranny.

An original idea by the Ministry to make a film about minesweeping had now been replaced by Powell's enthusiasm for the Canadian project. He was given a £5,000 advance to visit the country and research his ideas. The timing of his artistic concept couldn't have been better as, by the middle of 1940 with the aggressive Luftwaffe exercising its might over the south-east corner of Britain and the trauma of the Dunkirk evacuation still hurting the population, he knew just how important it would be to muster support from the US for all the Commonwealth countries including Canada now fighting the threat of a Nazi invasion. Within days of the film unit's arrival in the Canadian Rockies the visionary screenwriter Emeric Pressburger came up with a script about a handful of German submariners who become stranded in the wilds of Canada after their U-boat is sunk. Their plan is to find their way to the then neutral United States and escape back to Germany. The film (also known as *The Invaders* in the US) was the third film made by the remarkable Powell and Pressburger duo whose chemistry in the industry had begun to explode into a powerful force on the big screen and for millions of cinema-goers.

Spurred on by the thought of casting Olivier and other stars, Powell, Pressburger and the technical crew behind *49th Parallel* headed off to the Canadian Rockies to shoot the outdoor scenes. They did this before meeting again with Olivier in January 1941. It was decided the interiors would be filmed at Denham Studios back in Britain.

By this time Olivier was ready to play his role as Johnnie the Trapper. It gave him a chance to reveal his acting range to rare effect, starting at a loud and busy pace as the hearty French-Canadian who sings in the bath, and then after a fight with the Germans dies from a gunshot wound. In real life a genuine trapper by the name of Tony Onraet was stationed in England at the time with Canadian troops. It was Onraet who coached Olivier and helped him capture the accent and rumbustious personality of a French-Canadian Frontiersman. It was the adoring Leigh who described her husband's performance as 'the best thing he's done in films ... '.

The finances of *49th Parallel* were organised by the British producer John Sutro. This enabled Powell to freely exert his creativity and shoot the sequences he wanted in the illuminating landscapes of far-flung Canada. Indeed from Powell's memoirs we learn there was so much footage there was an immediate hunt for a good editor. When the young David Lean, fresh from the set of George Bernard Shaw's *Major Barbara*, was found to take on the task Powell was overjoyed. Decades later at a film conference Lean would pay tribute to *49th Parallel* and yet joke how when he started work on the film there was so much footage it would have lasted for eight hours if shown in full! Despite initial expenditure going way over its original £68,000 budget *49th Parallel* was a commercial success and raked in $5 million US/Canadian dollars. In Britain £250,000 was accrued at box offices all over the country.

But as the film was in progress in the autumn of 1940 Olivier was very keen to return home. He also felt there was great uneasiness in Hollywood and complained its pro-Nazi sympathisers were 'lurking around every palm tree'. By then many of his friends too had joined the armed forces including New York City-born Douglas Fairbanks Jr who was commissioned as a reserve officer in the United States Navy, and David Niven had re-joined his British Army unit back home. Olivier was furious with any British actors who tried to work out publicity-driven and legitimate ways to remain in Hollywood. He scoffed at their attempts to play cricket matches to fundraise and hold parties for the 'boys at war back home'. Olivier believed they should all return to Britain if they really wanted to make a difference.

The British actress Lynn Fontaine (wife of American stage director Alfred Lunt) told Noel Coward. 'Larry is learning to fly every day, so that means he will be good. He says he is going to be an ace!' Hollywood star Olivia de Havilland also spread the information about the actor's adventures in the air and said despite several dangerous incidents in which he'd written off three aircraft 'Larry was fearless, undaunted and oblivious.'

But aged 33 in 1940 meant there was no way the RAF would accept him as a fighter pilot. It was then he accepted his fate and took his friend Ralph Richardson's advice to join him in the Fleet Air Arm. If Richardson could do it at 37, then Olivier was in with a good chance too.

In his autobiography Olivier wrote:

Vivien and I married in Santa Barbara on August 21, 1940. We were now free to go just as soon as we had discharged our obligation to this, the last professional commitment we would engage ourselves to for... how long? But we were off and away.

We were two of twenty-three passengers on the American ship *Excambion* – not what you would describe as a queen among ocean liners. We endured the most apprehensive voyage I have ever known. The captain, for a start, was a German. Of course, we had no right to assume that he was not loyal to his American citizenship, but we could not rid ourselves of the fear that all was not well.

Our fears were confirmed as the voyage, which was not to England but to Lisbon, Portugal, proceeded. New Year's Eve, which usually provokes extra jollity on a sea voyage was quite nightmarish on this occasion. The toasts on this last evening of 1940 were boisterously made by the captain himself with the declamation 'Deutschland über Alles' followed by a 'Heil Hitler'.

We felt far too greatly outnumbered. I'm afraid, to rise bravely to our feet and declaim 'God Save the King' or even 'There'll Always be an England'. There was a US naval lieutenant at our table, sporting pilot's wings over his handkerchief pocket, to whom I, perhaps foolishly, raised my glass and offered a toast 'To the American and the British Naval Air Services'. To my horror he turned my toast aside and said 'I prefer ... to all pilots trying to get home.'

Olivier pointed out his description of that journey home may sound 'over-dramatic' but there was a constant nightmare of being forced to walk a rope-ladder to a waiting U-boat and taken to a prisoner-of-war camp, and Lisbon in Portugal, allegedly a neutral country, was as packed with spies 'as a pomegranate is with pips'. The flight home in a Dakota to Bristol wasn't uneventful. A fire in the cockpit put everyone's nerves on edge and the sight of the captain rushing about with a fire extinguisher left passengers feeling they were about to meet their maker.[21]

When the Oliviers touched down in relief at Bristol Airport on 10 January 1941 they ran to the passengers' lounge as an air-raid was on and ack-ack guns boomed around them. There were no red carpets, no palm trees or sunny skies to greet them when they reached their hotel either. They found a semi-demolished building which had been hit by a bomb courtesy of the Luftwaffe. The outside wall of the hotel was now a giant tarpaulin which failed miserably to shelter the guests from the chill. It was a bleak welcome home for two of the world's greatest film stars who spent the night trying to keep warm in their coats.

The following day they made their way back to Durham Cottage, their home in London, and were greeted by friends including Ralph Richardson wearing the uniform of the Fleet Air Arm, and the theatrical set designer and painter Roger Furse who was in the Royal Navy. In 1943 Furse was to design the costumes for Olivier's classic film of Shakespeare's *Henry V.* Also at the welcome party was the actor John Mills who was by then serving in the Royal Engineers, Richard 'Dickie' Olivier who was a Royal Navy Volunteer Reserve when he greeted his starry brother (Dickie survived the war only to die aged 54 in 1959 of leukaemia), and the actor Jack Hawkins who had joined the Royal Welsh Fusiliers.

After the joys of a happy homecoming Olivier applied to the Admiralty to join the Fleet Air Arm. At his first medical examination a nerve defect was revealed in one of the actor's ears – a problem caused during his flying training when he went through a rough storm. But with support from an independent doctor who said the defect was so slight it would not make a difference to a pilot's ability to control an aircraft, Olivier was given the go-ahead for non-operational flying. But before he could spend much time in uniform there was the actor's earlier promise made to director Michael Powell to fulfil and so after a few days grace to work on his French-Canadian accent he made his way to Denham Studios to shoot his scenes in *49th Parallel.*

By now this film and its extraordinary story had gathered a long list of big names on its cast list – Leslie Howard, Eric Portman, Raymond Massey, Anton Walbrook, Raymond Lovell and Glynis Johns who replaced the actress Elizabeth Bergner originally cast in the role. Bergner was an ex-German national who feared the Nazis would kill her if they were to take over Europe. She had also refused to work with the Hutterites after a woman from the strict community slapped Bergner for smoking and painting her nails.

Audiences follow the lives of a party of six Kriegsmarine sailors who go ashore from their U-boat in the Hudson Bay to look for supplies. When their submarine is destroyed by the Royal Canadian Air Force they must find their way to freedom and during their journey each one is either killed or captured. When Lieutenant Hirth (Eric Portman) and his crew chance upon the home of a French-Canadian trapper 'Johnnie' (Laurence Olivier) and his friends at a Hudson Bay Trading Post they murder an Eskimo and after several aggressive, bullying conversations the innocent freedom-arguing 'Johnnie' is killed too.

The Germans then shoot dead the pilot of a floatplane along with some of the local Inuit, steal the aircraft and attempt to fly south. When one of the sailors is ordered to throw items overboard because the plane is too heavy he is killed by a bullet fired by an Inuit. The aircraft soon runs out of fuel and crashes into a lake in Manitoba. Another Nazi is killed and the survivors decide to walk on.

A friendly farming community living by the simple disciplined order of the Hutterites take them in and the sailors try and fit in, believing this rural way of life is Germanic. A speech made by Lieutenant Hirth (Portman) glorifying Hitler is angrily rejected by the community's leader Peter (Anton Walbrook) and Lieutenant Hirth decides to take leave of the camp but not before killing his comrade who has decided to remain with the Hutterites as a baker and give up Fascism and all it stands for. The story then sees the remaining Nazis turn up in Winnipeg where they discover the police are on their tail and watching the border. The death toll is mounting as they murder their way towards Vancouver where they plan to catch a steamship heading for Japan.

One man is arrested and the two left attempt to cross the Rockies on foot. It is at this point they meet a writer, Philip Armstrong Scott, played by Leslie Howard, who thinks at first they are tourists who have lost their way. When the Nazis tie up the writer and destroy the contents of his large tent including valuable artworks, books and his unpublished manuscript they make their escape. But the injured Scott manages to break free and along with his men chase the German sailors. Finally they catch one and Scott beats him up before calling the police. Only Hirth is left and just when he thinks he is safe on a train towards the American border he encounters another stowaway – a US soldier (Andy Brock played by Raymond Massey) who after a fight with the Nazi finally persuades border guards to send Hirth back to Canada.

It is a gripping story which reveals Powell's genius as a director and Pressburger's remarkable screen-writing at its best. Shadows, landscapes and subtle performances emanating from the souls of the wicked and the good, the pure and the innocent, come together to authentically expose the horrors of a tyranny imposed by fascism driven by the delusions of Adolf Hitler. Powell's determination to create a film with an edge as sharp as his talent was proven in the scene which involved the actor Eric Portman as Hirth making his Hitleresque speech to the crowded Hutterite dining hall. Once again we can turn to his passion for authenticity as in real life the Hutterites had allowed him to film at their farm in Winnipeg.

Powell recalled:

There were a hundred men, women and children seated on long wooden benches at the long, wooden tables, and we had picked every face. More than half of them were Germans and German Jews, refugees from Hitler. We ran a rehearsal several times with Eric mouthing his part, but occasionally his voice rang out as he reached a climax. You could feel the temperature in the room rising as these true victims of Hitler's oppression realised what we were attempting to do and say, with the added knowledge that Hitler's soldiers and airmen were amassing for the invasion of England.

Every word of the long speech that Eric and Emeric had worked out together rang true, the minted gold of liberty. I don't know how these things happen, but before we had run the rehearsal twice people were filtering in from the other stages and surrounding the big set to listen to the performance. As usual, when I have a big emotional scene to direct, and particularly in this performance of Eric's, which was sheer witchcraft, I planned to shoot it in one continuous take and let the pauses come naturally with the emotion.

By the time Eric finished the speech after about four and a half minutes we saw so many onlookers and extras sharing in the emotion and identifying with the reaction to it. When Eric's voice rang out with 'Brothers! Germans!!' with that peculiar brazen insolence that was a speciality of the Nazi orators, and of their leader, our flesh tingled and the palms of our hands grew moist, and when at the climax Eric yelled: 'Heil Hitler!' and his four companions leapt to their feet with the Nazi salute, I could feel all those hundreds of people take the insult like a blow. I yelled 'Cut!' and started clapping, and everyone on that huge set and around it joined in a roar of applause. After that, the film's reputation was made.[22]

In the film the gentle reply from the character of Peter, the wise and solemn leader of the community was, 'No, we are not your brothers'. It was the perfect and ultimate putdown to the fury of Nazi lunacy.

The awards for the film with its dramatic musical score by Ralph Vaughan Williams are notable. Screenwriter Eric Pressburger scooped an Academy Award for Best Story, and there were also nominations for the Best Picture and Best Screenplay awards. (It was rightful compensation for Pressburger, a Hungarian by birth, who had initially been treated with hostility by the suspicious British and at one time he had been arrested for being 'a foreign alien'.) *49th Parallel* was seen by 9.3 million people on its release on 8 October 1941.

Sadly, a young member of the cast was killed just before the film hit the big screen. Teenager William Leslie Falardeau, who appeared in the rescue floatplane scene just before the Nazis seize it, was killed in an air accident in Britain during his service with the Royal Canadian Air Force. On 1 June 1943 British star Leslie Howard also died in tragic circumstances. The Luftwaffe shot down the aircraft he was flying in from Lisbon to Bristol in 1943. (It was the flight route operated by the same company used by Olivier and Leigh in January that year. The same flight had been on the Nazi radar as convenient transport for spies.) Howard, a cinematic giant known for his role as Supermarine Spitfire designer R.J. Mitchell in the wartime propaganda films *First of the Few*, and as the archaeologist-come-spy Professor Horatio Smith in *Pimpernel Smith*, was among the seventeen passengers who died that day. Although the aircraft BOAC Flight 777 was supposedly in a 'non-war' zone (the Bay of Biscay) there is a suggestion that the Germans believed Churchill was on board or that they targeted it especially to murder Howard who they hated for his effective anti-German propaganda films.

The actor was already a hero of the First World War having served with the Northamptonshire Yeomanry until he suffered severe shell-shock and relinquished his commission in 1916. Twenty-three years later of course he famously appeared as Ashley Wilkes with Leigh in *Gone with the Wind*. Howard was aged just 50 at the time of his death.

In February 1941 Olivier's decision to join the Fleet Air Arm came good and he stepped into the cockpit of a Miles Magister for a flight test. The tough little Magister was a single-engined aeroplane often used as a trainer. Following a successful flight in front of a commanding officer named Goodyear, a temporary commission was provided and a posting to the Royal Navy Air Station HMS *Daedalus* at Lee-on-Solent, Hampshire followed in mid-April 1941.

By then the proud actor-pilot had received an envelope in the mail containing a tiny sprig of white heather and two four-leafed clovers glued to a piece of paper. The envelope came from his old drama teacher Miss Elsie Fogerty who had been able to find out the exact day he was leaving to start his service in the Fleet Air Arm. It was her way of wishing him good luck and it was the day both the actor and his wife closed up Durham Cottage and drove to Lee-on-Solent where Acting Sub-Lieutenant (A) Olivier RNVR began his training.[23]

In the spring of the previous year Kent-born Lieutenant Commander John Casson of 803 Squadron (FAA) – whose parents were the theatre legends Lewis Casson and Dame Sybil Thorndike – had been keen to welcome Olivier when he discovered the actor was interested in military flying. He was happy to take Larry 'under his wing'. Casson had a strong link to Olivier as his parents were great friends with the actor's former drama coach Miss Fogerty who had once hailed Casson's actor father Lewis for 'having the purest of stage voices'.

Born in 1909, Casson grew up to carry the fine looks of his noble mother Sybil and yet answered the call of the sea and the air as a young adult. When he agreed to help Olivier further his flying ambitions he already had served with the Fleet Air Arm since the late 1920s and was a very experienced pilot. But on 13 June 1940 and some months before the Oliviers arrived at Lee-on-Solent, the brave Lieutenant Commander Casson was in a two-man Blackburn Skua with gunner

Lieutenant Peter Fanshawe. The Skua had just enough fuel to stage attacks over Norway from the Orkney Islands. That day after taking off from HMS *Ark Royal* they led a dive-bombing attack on the damaged German battleship *Scharnhorst* which was berthed in Trondheim Harbour. While carrying out a manoeuvre during a dogfight the Skua suffered engine failure and it was shot down. The aircraft crash-landed in a Norwegian fjord and Casson and Fanshawe were captured and taken to Germany as prisoners-of-war. The raid that day, made by just a handful of Skuas and Swordfish aircraft, was a disaster and the tiny FAA aircraft proved to be no match for the Luftwaffe's Me 109s. The operation became known in the history of naval battles as 'Black Thursday'. Eight of the fifteen Skuas from 800 and 803 Squadrons were shot down during their attack on the Scharnhorst. One Skua pilot who managed to return to the *Ark Royal* was 24-year-old Donald Gibson, much later to become Vice-Admiral Sir Donald Gibson. In his memoirs Gibson compared the attack on the *Scharnhorst* to the Charge of the Light Brigade and said: 'In future all admirals should ideally be shot at in an aeroplane while they are still young.'

After Casson and Fanshawe were rescued from the icy waters Casson was first taken to Dulag Luft (Frankfurt), then transported to Stalag Luft III in Poland. He acted as a code-master for MI9, the branch of British Intelligence tasked with helping PoWs to escape and downed airmen to evade capture, and assisted Fanshawe in his role as a member of the Stalag Luft III 'Great Escape' Executive Committee. Casson used his storming theatrical pedigree to be the leading actor in the camp with fellow actor and FAA observer Rupert Davies of 812 (Swordfish) Squadron. Peter 'Hornblower' Fanshawe was also a member of the 'Great Escape' Executive Committee in Stalag Luft III. Fanshawe was the real sand dispersal specialist at the camp and his expertise was exactly reproduced in the 1963 film *The Great Escape*. In real life Fanshawe was transferred to Belaria camp shortly before the escape took place. (In 2007 the actual Skua flown by Casson and Fanshawe was raised from the fjord from a depth of 242m. The aircraft is now displayed after full restoration in the National Norwegian Aviation Museum in Bodoe. An incomplete Skua raised from a Norwegian lake in 1974 is on display at the Fleet Air Arm Museum near Yeovil in Somerset.)

Whilst Olivier's own service with the Fleet Air Arm was not to be as dramatic as that of Casson and his comrades at sea, he remained determined to serve his country. This the actor made clear to anyone who knew him. Olivier recalled:

> I had to take a conversion course to service types of aircraft, and proceed from there as appointed. My great dread was I might be sent to the RNAS in Trinidad, a situation of despairing loneliness, utter boredom, and inevitable separation from Vivien; the dread was exacerbated by the knowledge that all naval appointments were for two years duration. Vivien was about to star in *The Doctor's Dilemma* at the Haymarket.[24]

Research into the Fleet Air Arm reveals that new recruits like Olivier flew seven types of aircraft including the Miles Magister, Hawker Osprey, Westland Lysander, De Havilland Tiger Moth and Puss Moth, Hawker Hart, Fairey Swordfish, Percival Proctor and Blackburn Shark. The Tiger Moth was a biplane and the Hart which was made of wood and canvas was a reliable fighter aircraft which had already seen active service in the later 1920s against the Afghans on the North West Frontier.

Being a determined man keen to succeed at everything he did Olivier made morale-boosting little notes in his course book about flying, the rules of the cockpit and inspirational thoughts. He wrote: 'Never give up'. And 'The strength of gentleness (women driving) … It takes a good head to navigate a craft to its destination but a better one to lead it to its destination after losing the way. Only by continuous self-badgering can one achieve proper attitude of alertness for flying'. Then under a heading 'Reverence for the Machine' he'd scribbled 'Gentle handling, train to be cautious – aim for the expert touch'. Funnily enough his commitment waned somewhat when under a heading of 'Elementary Flying Drill' he had written 'Phone Ritz … '

For the first three weeks of basic training Acting Sub-Lieutenant Olivier was stationed with his friend Richardson at Worthy Down, near Winchester. Here, serving with 755 Squadron at HMS *Kestrel*, he was lucky to find another actor and pilot Lieutenant R. Douglas-Finlayson was on hand to help put him through his paces. Of their days in the Fleet Air Arm, Douglas recalled: 'It was my job to help Larry become accustomed to the "routine". He seemed so desperately keen to "go into battle" instead of doing the dreary job we were stuck with, namely training observers, gunners, etc, in antiquated old Swordfish or whatever else could stagger into the sky. But he had barely got started when he was involved in a hideous incident.'

This happened on Olivier's first day at Worthy Down while Douglas was away for a few hours. When he returned he asked the commanding officer if the new theatrical recruit had settled in well? Apparently not, as: 'the C.O said nothing. He just glared and then pointed out of the window at a wrecked aircraft and two others that had been damaged when Olivier was taxiing on to the runway for the first time. "Good Heavens Sir!" exclaimed Douglas. "Not three!".'.[25] The newly commissioned Sub-Lieutenant Olivier need not have worried about being banished to anywhere as far-flung as Trinidad as finally he learned how to become an accomplished pilot of seven types of aircraft.

HMS *Kestrel* certainly wasn't Jamaica! Instead it was a former airfield which had been discarded by the RAF in 1921. It had been recommissioned by the Royal Navy in 1939 for use by the Fleet Air Arm. The station hit the headlines when the notorious British traitor 'Lord Haw Haw' (William Joyce) maliciously and falsely broadcast that HMS *Kestrel* had been sunk by Hitler's Kriegsmarine!

Initially Olivier was pleased he was serving his country at last and described in April 1941 that his new station was a real challenge as there was a tall hill which offered great difficulties to anyone trying to negotiate a three-point landing. He wrote: 'Only a skilled pilot could make a decent three point landing by putting the aircraft into a double stall at the last moment before actual touchdown.'

But many who knew Olivier said he liked nothing more than to spin a yarn about his own activities including his flying career. Some reported he told them he had written off three aircraft during his training. His close friend the actor and wartime Royal Engineer John Mills reckoned it was often difficult to know exactly what was true and what was fantasy with the Fleet Air Arm's garrulous new pilot. Indeed one of Olivier's biographers, Terry Coleman, claims there is little record of the actor causing such costly aviation accidents. The Commanding Officer at HMS *Kestrel* graded the actor as 'an average pilot'. And it was certainly unlikely he performed any 'glorious aerobatics!' in spite of the 250 hours on his licence. Decades later Olivier went on to admit his role in the Fleet Air Arm was 'unheroic'. He said: 'I never fired a shot in anger and I just taxied air gunners about the sky. That's all I did. Then when I did volunteer for operations I was taken aside by the Ministry of Information to make the pro-Russian film – *The Demi-Paradise*.'[26]

The role of his squadron at Worthy Down was indeed to assist and train air gunners. Lieutenant Olivier ferried crew around the skies so they could take aim and fire at towed targets. Olivier's brief time with the Fleet Air Arm wasn't exactly front line. He recalled: 'A pre-dominant memory was of sitting in the ante-room trying to refuse another gin or kicking my heels in the pilots' room gazing impotently at other aircraft taking off or at the surrounding ceiling zero.' He wrote in his memoir:

Frankly the Navy was using pilots at Worthy Down as taxi-drivers for trainee air-gunners, flying them about the sky while they attempted to keep in wireless contact with base. The pilot's role in the exercise was to inform the gunner of his position through the speaking-tube from time to time.

The one freedom allowed to the pilot was in his choice of route, supposedly one hour out and one back. This virtually confined one to four hours' flying a day, except for the long light days of summer when one could get permission for aerobatic practice.

Another practice that was encouraged was to jump into the cockpits of all varieties of aircraft new to one and practise 'circuits and bumps'. This increased one's usefulness in being able to transport any type of aircraft to other air-stations all over the country.

I got to know the map of England like the back of my hand. From Winchester one could reach Canterbury to the east, Exeter to the west and Coventry to the north. At no time, of course, was it permitted to fly over the Channel – our aircraft were unarmed and the poor gunner would have been a helpless clay pigeon.[27]

But while he grew disillusioned with his time in the Fleet Air Arm he did learn to fly a good variety of aircraft including the Fairey Albacore, de Havilland Leopard Moth, Fairey Fulmar, de Havilland Hornet and Fairey Swordfish. Each one was added proudly to his logbook. The fastest aeroplane he flew was a modern fighter, a Fairey Fulmar. When he wasn't flying he wrote in his diary that his day became a 'complete bore'. He took lessons in parachute packing and then organised demonstration flights for air cadets and teenagers keen to join the RAF.

From the outset of his days in military uniform he found his acting reputation something of a handicap as he strived to gain status as a serious pilot. When he joined some forty long-serving Fleet Air Arm officers at the table in the wardroom on his first day with Douglas at his side for tea he overheard two veteran officers discussing him as 'another actor fellah' who 'didn't look a damn bit like Nelson'. All Olivier could do was smile but this sort of gentle tolerance couldn't last for too long as he soon discovered he was faced with an invisible wall which appeared to deny him acceptance as 'just one of the lads'. He wanted desperately to be seen as a Fleet Air Arm officer who also happened to be an actor and not that 'actor fellow' who pretended to be a pilot.

On 7 December 1941 the war took a dramatic turn. The Japanese attacked Pearl Harbor and all at once the US became allied with Britain. In the meantime Vivien Leigh was finding life back in England a struggle. She realised her life as a doting pilot's wife was not a role she wanted to play forever. Her daily routine of waving her handsome husband and his motorbike goodbye each morning, shopping, gardening and reading had begun to bore her. She began to crave the prospect of returning to her own work on the stage and screen even though throughout her life her mental and physical health had been an issue. Possibly since her childhood growing up in India, she had been living with random and debilitating attacks of tuberculosis.

But with her lively mind and passionate nature she yearned to get back to what she knew. It's hardly surprising. No one could describe Leigh as a wholesome Mrs Miniver type of character at all. As one of the world's most beautiful women and feted Hollywood star she was never really going to settle down in a bungalow three miles from her husband's aerodrome. She was far too adventurous for that. And while she was delighted to have won an Oscar as Best Actress for starring as Scarlett O'Hara in *Gone with the Wind*, she always saw herself as a theatre actress. (She won her second Oscar 10 years later starring as Blanche DuBois in Tennessee Williams' controversial drama *A Streetcar Named Desire*. There was no question Leigh possessed great talent).

When discussing her looks the star once told reporters: 'People think that if you look fairly reasonable, you can't possibly act, and as I only care about acting, I think beauty can be a great handicap, if you really want to look like the part you're playing, which isn't necessarily like you.' The director George Cukor described Leigh as the consummate actress hampered by beauty.

Olivier was not immune to the tedium of his military life and described the war as a loud 'drill' that continues to turn whatever battles have been won. He believed at the time no military or political achievement could stop its relentless drone. He began to admit he too found it difficult being with 'real people' (officers and men of the FAA), those he described as 'rather ordinary'. Olivier felt little sense of community with the Fleet Air Arm, coupled with the fact his life at home was haunted by his wife's evident longing to fly away back to the stage. The actor admitted he found the 'palpable safety' of his service life made him feel like a 'shirker' and while his initial reactions to those film colleagues who had remained in front of the cameras had been derisory he had privately began to wonder if they had been doing a 'more sensible' duty doing the jobs they knew.[28]

Olivier's conscience caused him to question whether he had put on a uniform for appearances sake and then admitting to his selfishness he decided it would be easier for him to serve his country as an artiste. The Fleet Air Arm could move him to operations but as he was 34 years old it meant he could only fly the elephantine amphibious seaplane – the Walrus. Olivier thought about this idea and confessed he liked this aircraft which had been designed by the Spitfire genius, R.J. Mitchell. The actor described it: 'the Walrus was a strange-looking aircraft – a high-wing float biplane with the engine in the top plane, its prop facing after, the fish-tale bow swooped up from the water so that, when skimming along the top of it before take-off or after landing, she looked as though she was travelling backwards. To embark she was hoist from her special top deck of the ship and craned down the water. I loved the whole idea.' Understandably enough some wartime pilots, including Air Transport Auxiliary First Officer Mary Wilkins Ellis, loathed the Walrus and recalled how it was like 'flying an elephant with a mind of its own'. She also remembered the time an ATA colleague and friend almost died when trying to take off in the cumbersome amphibian.[29]

Olivier's logbook revealed he flew a Walrus from Poole in Dorset, west to Teignmouth in Devon, and St Ives in Cornwall. His final flight as a FAA pilot was over Hastings in East Sussex which he described as a coast with 'no defence at all and very, very little blockade to stop the Germans from walking straight in'. He made this remark, however, when the Allies were progressing well in their advance and pushing the Germany military machine away from the French coast. Years later Olivier said: 'I always thought that my performance as a naval officer was the best bit of character work I've ever done.'

His friend Ralph Richardson too noted Olivier was always the actor in the FAA as his shoes were just a tad too shiny, his manner was too debonair and he wore a uniform that was a little too clean-cut. Tarquin Olivier writing in his memoir *My Father Laurence Olivier* said his father definitely felt out of place in his unit near Winchester. He was a film star and could never convince the men in the squadron otherwise. He could never be one of the boys with his brother officers, even if he had wanted to. 'He role-played to keep something between himself and the meanness of spirit he perceived.'

Tarquin pointed out his father's 'loathing' of a particular officer who would make snide remarks like 'How's our film star today?' Lieutenant Olivier then wondered if he ought to infuriate his enemy by charming the beautiful wife of the man he hated. He stopped short when he realised he was turning into Shakespeare's Iago.[30]

But Olivier's issue with rank stayed with him throughout his life. As a Lieutenant he had two gold bars on his sleeve whereas Richardson, a longer-serving officer, had been promoted to Lieutenant Commander and had an extra half stripe – something which bugged Olivier who on the stage had indeed played Iago to Richardson's Othello. If he wasn't too careful life would indeed imitate art! There was something of the 'pompous' about Olivier at this time, reported Richardson, who said how even after the war his friend was obsessed by the idea of class and hierarchy and how it affected people's behaviour.

On 14 May 1942 a somewhat dejected Olivier told his first wife Jill Esmond how he 'admired' the lads of the Fleet Air Arm for their diligence to duty but the officers 'were not up to much'. But there was some relief from the social unease in the officers' mess as when he was not at Worthy Down the actor was performing morale-boosting speeches during 'Warship Weeks'. One day Churchill was in the audience with 10,000 people at the Royal Albert Hall watching Olivier who was on stage 'crystallizing the fighting spirit of the Empire'.

In between his fractured military and professional theatrical lives, the actor knew his wife needed attention and stayed home with her as much as he could. In the spring of 1942 the Oliviers were riding high on a wave of popularity thanks to the box office success of *That Hamilton Woman* – although not every reviewer was kind. C.A. Lejeune in *The Observer* asked why history should be told 'through the eyes of a trollop!' and many critics were biased and believed Korda was a coward for leaving Britain during wartime to make films in Hollywood. Of course in reality Korda was Churchill's man in Hollywood and remained on board as a major producer of British propaganda films, and more often than not the dutiful Korda had to find the finance for each one himself. In 1943 Korda was given a knighthood.

*   *   *

On 12 February 1942 while the actor was carrying out his real life military role in uniform at Worthy Down, the Fleet Air Arm, the RAF and the Royal Navy suffered a catastrophic defeat.

Hitler's navy had been ordered to sail two battleships, the *Scharnhorst* and *Gneisenau*, and the heavy cruiser *Prinz Eugen* out of the harbour at Brest in France. Both vessels had been docked there for some weeks as they underwent repairs and had been repeatedly attacked by British forces. Now Hitler wanted them back home in Germany. So under the codename Operation Cerberus, the ships set sail with the Luftwaffe as escorts. In a serious of extraordinary manoeuvres they sailed right through the Royal Navy's defences and up the Channel until they reached Heligoland in the North Sea.

The British were aware the Germans might take the risk to sail the ships home and the Royal Navy had set up Operation Fuller to be on 'red alert', and the men of RAF Coastal Command were at the ready with air patrols over Brest and the English Channel day and night. They firmly believed the enemy battleships would leave Brest by day and complete the most dangerous part of their journey, the narrow waters of the Dover Straits, by night. This sadly was the first error that led to disastrous consequences.

It turned out the Germans had sixty-six ships in its group accompanying the two mighty battleships with continuous air cover provided by 250 fighter aircraft. They sailed from Brest at night on 11 February 1942 and reached the Dover Straits, more or less unseen, at about 11.00am on 12 February. The Fleet Air Arm's 825 Squadron, led by Lieutenant Commander Eugene Esmonde and comprising six Swordfish aircraft flew out of RAF Manston where they had been preparing for a night attack on the German ships.

The RAF promised Lieutenant Commander Esmonde fighter cover of five squadrons of Spitfires (approximately 60–70 aircraft). Esmonde agreed to lead his squadron in a daylight attack. Just one RAF squadron – No. 72 Squadron led by Squadron Leader Brian Kingcombe – met Esmonde's aircraft for the mission. Fighter cover was provided by only ten Spitfires when Esmonde's courageous 825 Squadron attacked the mighty German convoy. But, against the guns of the big ships coupled with the speed and power of the Luftwaffe, the weary, outdated Swordfish of the FAA stood little chance. Every Swordfish was shot down that day and only five of the eighteen aircrew who set out survived. Esmonde was shot down and killed during the raid. His body, still in his life jacket, was washed ashore in the Thames Estuary seven weeks later.

Despite more than thirty torpedo attacks launched against the German squadron not a single hit was achieved. As a last resort, in the largest Bomber Command daylight operation of the war so far, 242 British aircraft were sent out against the German vessels but all to no avail. Any damage inflicted was caused by mines encountered by *Scharnhorst* and *Gneisenau.*

All members of the FAA's 825 Squadron were honoured. Esmonde was posthumously awarded the Victoria Cross. Gallantry medals were presented to those who survived and a Mention in Despatches was given to those who died during the operation which became known as the 'Channel Dash'. Despite such gallantry the British defeat was a humiliation and morale was damaged on the Home Front. It even sparked fears of a Nazi invasion on the south coast. The Fleet Air Arm had played a major role in a battle but they remained the defeated team.

On the same day as the Channel Dash Lieutenant Olivier was in a confusing and embarrassing situation. He had some days previously agreed he would organise a concert party on behalf of the Fleet Air Arm and his participation involved him performing a sea shanty and excepts from Shakespeare's *Henry V.* The show was badly timed and when the curtain went up at the Garrison Theatre in Aldershot the audience in their khaki uniforms were not impressed by anyone wearing blue. The concert was described as a 'complete fiasco' and each act was booed and hissed – Olivier's performance more than any other. Indeed when he stepped out in his shining armour as Henry V to deliver the famous St Crispin's Day Speech he was shouted down by the angry audience. Despite this he continued and when he fell to his knees to deliver Henry's prayer the mood quietened and the jeering crowd let him finish in silence.

> Oh God of battles! Steel my soldiers' hearts;
> Possess them not with fear; take from them now
> The sense of reckoning.

It was then and only then the audience tuned in to the power of the words which rang out to them during a time of military grief. And as the curtain came down there was applause – but hardly enough to console all those who had taken part in the concert. All of them, including Olivier, knew in their hearts it had been a disaster. The timing really couldn't have been worse.[31]

Some weeks later though, when his rousing proclamations during a morale-raising concert at the Royal Albert Hall were more of a success something brought his growing discontent with the Fleet Air Arm to a head. His speech which used phrases like 'We will attack! We will conquer!' were a provocative indicator of his power as a supremely effective orator. His thoughts turned to returning to Hollywood to be part of the big propaganda machine and assist in the defence of Britain in the best way he knew how. The actor recalled that only 18 months previously Hollywood studio bosses had offered to fund a Spitfire and a bomber if only he would stay and make more films.

Then just as he began to make enquiries about returning to the professional stage and screen full time to assist the war effort he was summoned to the Ministry of Information to see Jack Beddington who was a government advisor on showbusiness propaganda. Olivier was delighted to be asked to appear in two films to promote Britain's fight against the Nazis. Either fate had stepped in to guide his talents to be a more effective weapon against Hitler's tyranny, or his influential contacts realising his discontent with life in uniform, had stepped in on his behalf. The first production was called *The Demi-Paradise*. When he was told the second film would be Shakespeare's *Henry V* he quickly learned he would not only star as the great fifteenth-century warrior king but make his directorial debut too.

Meantime he was told *The Demi-Paradise* was to be directed by Anthony 'Puffin' Asquith, son of the former Prime Minister Herbert Asquith. It was a comedy to be produced by Two Cities Films. Olivier was cast as a Soviet Russian scientist and inventor Ivan Dimitrevitch Kouznetsoff who arrives in England where he can build a pioneering propelling device. The Ministry of Information decided the picture should promote Britain's good relations with the Russians – an idea Olivier recalled was not overly necessary as the Russians had already joined the Allies by 1943 when work began on the production.

But *The Demi-Paradise* (also called *Adventure for Two*) was sound enough and had an entertaining screenplay written by its producer Anatole de Grunwald. The cinematography was under the auspices of Bernard Knowles then known for his work with Alfred Hitchcock. In the film Knowles illuminates, ever so gently, a satirical look on the traditional values so dear to the British. Penelope Dudley-Ward plays socialite Anne Tisdall who is the love interest of Olivier's crop-haired character of Ivan.

The plot includes an examination of capitalist principles, and a frustrated Ivan decides to head back to communist Russia when his invention fails to function effectively. He then returns to England keen not to be seen as a disgrace to Mother Russia and just when the audience think Ivan is about to fail again his great love Anne persuades the local shipbuilders to labour all hours to make the propeller a success – so much so that it is soon installed in any new ship. The happy Russian returns to his home country realising that love really can and does save the day.

Olivier recalled:

Demi-Paradise was amusing to do, Russian accent and all. I had at first a Russian lady to teach me this until I began to find my consonants becoming alarmingly, not to say suspiciously effeminate; I turned to a male Russian who immediately told me everything the woman had told me 'was all wrong'. I did learn to pronounce 'Soviet' correctly as 'Suvyett'.[32]

The actor enjoyed the work and the crew around him got along well. He liked working with 'Del', the director Filippo Del Giudice, who went on to highly recommend Olivier to influential contacts when it came to the production of *Henry V*. Olivier kept the *The Demi-Paradise* crew on board for his legendary Shakespearean wartime epic. Although some critics later described *The Demi-Paradise* as all 'rather silly' it did mean Olivier could well and truly get back to the professional work which suited his talent. The film turned out to be superb propaganda for the Allies and successfully put forward the idea that the Russians (once labelled 'the Red Menace') really weren't such bad folk to have on one's side in a war after all.

'Puffin' Asquith believed Olivier had produced a 'truly creative performance' in this Anglo-Russian film and the character of Ivan was 'so thoroughly imagined and so consummately realised that he contrives to exist quite apart from the film'. Even *The Sunday Times'* legendary sharp-minded film reviewer and journalist Dilys Powell believed the actor deserved a place high up in the ranking of British stars. It seems he had been promoted after all, even though the extra gold stripe he so derided in the military was afforded within the realm of silver screen eminence.

It was while making *The Demi-Paradise* that the Oliviers leased a house (once the home of Noel Coward) in Fulmer, Buckinghamshire as it was close to Denham Film Studios (founded by Alexander Korda in 1936), and London was a short trip away. The new house was conveniently located for Leigh who was by now starring in a successful run of *The Doctor's Dilemma* at The Haymarket Theatre.

While living at Fulmer the couple were surrounded by great showbusiness friends who had also served in the armed forces – John Mills (Royal Engineers but invalided out as a Second Lieutenant after suffering from a stomach ulcer) and his new wife the dramatist Mary Bell. There was Rex Harrison and his then wife Lilli Palmer living nearby. And, just along the road in the beautiful village of Dorney when he was not away at war, lived British Army Major David Niven and his wife Primula.

No amount of food rationing could stop this famous theatrical set from enjoying a party or two. As Olivier was the son of a thrifty vicar he was always given the job of carving the chicken. These festivities became legendary. At one such event the Minister of Information Brendan Bracken was greeted at the door by Olivier wearing only a rug and badly singing Handel's *Messiah*. His wife Miss Leigh was clothed in nothing but a sheet!

At this time there was a suggestion Olivier might appear in Powell and Pressburger's *The Life and Death of Colonel Blimp*. His role would be to play a ludicrous military character created by the awesome cartoonist of the day David Low. However, this proposal was quickly stamped on by the Secretary of State for War – the ever so slightly er … buffoonish Sir James Grigg. There wasn't any way, he blurted, Olivier would be released from the Fleet Air Arm to send up the military command – however clever the satire! (In the end the actor Roger Livesey appeared with aplomb in 1943 as the blustering General Candy aka Blimp.)[33]

Soon enough for Olivier the world of the Fleet Air Arm seemed far away and 'the ordinariness of sitting in the Mess' was over. He had also been disappointed the Air Ministry had decided to take his beloved Walrus flying boat out of service. This, he believed, marked the end of his military career and his belief he might one day go into airborne combat was now just a faraway dream. No more could he get by on the idea he would be a pilot first, actor second.

His disappointment in his military life was soon replaced by a sense of fulfilment though. He was about to attain a full artistic licence to focus on arguably the biggest and most important challenge of his life – *Henry V* – which as Shakespeare had intended was a representation of rightful might against an enemy with plans to invade and conquer 'our sceptred isle'. A military triumph, albeit on film, was just what the country needed as Hitler's bombs rained down on a beleaguered Britain. It would prove another bonus for Churchill and his vigorous propaganda agenda.

Olivier's brother 'Dickie' in the meantime had seen active service in the Channel and the North Sea as a lieutenant aboard Royal Navy ships laying mines near the coast of France. He was awarded the DSO (Distinguished Service Medal) in 1943 for coaxing his crippled ship back home after it had been damaged by German destroyers. His brother 'Larry', however, was already out of his FAA uniform, covered in greasepaint and back in front of the cameras to assist the war effort with a rousing performance about leadership and honour in the guise of *Henry V.*

The film version of *Henry V* had been proposed by a BBC producer named Dallas Bower. At first a short radio programme was made and Olivier in the role of Henry V gave the speech at the Siege of Harfleur which had taken place in 1415. Shortly after the broadcast the Italian producer/director Filipp del Giudice who had worked alongside Noel Coward in the patriotic classic 1942 film *In Which We Serve* joined the *Henry V* production team and assigned Olivier to the role.

In a letter to his son Tarquin, the actor acknowledged his gratitude to the *Demi-Paradise* crew who were to assist him with his greatest-ever project. He wrote:

> *Henry V* I am to produce myself. It's all a great change. Very welcome indeed is the feeling I am doing something I feel I know something about, and over which I have some control. The job I had was beginning to get me down slightly owing to all sorts of circumstances, and I shall feel better when I get back that I shall have had a whack at serving in every way, and that I shall not have wasted the talents I have got.[34]

Olivier was always grateful to the director William Wyler who he'd worked with on *Wuthering Heights*. While the actor admitted Wyler was a tough taskmaster he had taught Olivier to respect the camera and medium of film. 'It was Wyler who gave me the simple thought – if you do it right, you can do anything. And if he hadn't had said that, I think I wouldn't have done *Henry V* five years later,' he recalled.

* * *

While Olivier was giddy with excitement about his new all-encompassing Shakespearean project, Vivien Leigh decided it was time she got back on stage in a bid to rally the troops. So in 1943 and having completed her successful run in London's West End she left home and joined a merry cast whose aim was bring entertainment to British armed service personnel in North Africa. The visit to the hot, dusty sands of Egypt and beyond had been organised by seasoned theatre producer Hugh 'Binkie' Beaumont. Originally Leigh had told Beaumont she wanted to help the war effort as a fire warden in her spare time, or even become a volunteer ambulance driver? The diligent Beaumont advised her instead to use her acting talent and proceeded to invite her to join the 'Old Vic Spring Party' – a collective of performers organised by ENSA.

Fellow theatricals in North Africa included Leigh's friends like the music-hall artistes Dorothy Dickson, Leslie Henson, Nicholas Phipps, Kay Young and the mercurial comedienne Bea Lillie. At first she wondered exactly what she could present to audiences of men beleaguered by the horrors of gunfire and shell shock. Firstly she suggested the Potion Scene from Shakespeare's *Romeo and Juliet* but after a derisory comment from John Gielgud she settled on two dramatic recitations – Newbolt's *Drake's Drum* and Lewis Carroll's *You Are Old, Father William*. She dressed as her famous character of Scarlett O'Hara and after some coaching from Bea Lillie proved a sensation.

Although Rommel's Afrika Korps had been beaten back by the Allies when the Spring Party turned up in North Africa that year, the entertainers experienced exhaustion and episodes often fraught with danger. The tour lasted for three months with the concert party stopping off at venues between Gibraltar and Cairo. Leigh wrote to her husband of her adventures and once she informed him the stage manager had to stay behind in Algeria as there was some suggestion he was a Nazi spy. In a letter from Tunis she wrote: 'Nothing seems to matter though because we are now really playing to the boys who deserve it and haven't seen anything except fighting for months.'[35]

The heat in Cairo reached temperatures of 48 degrees at times. The entertainments were staged in hospital tents and audiences of more than 8,000 men arrived to watch the cast on stages built among sand dunes. One real venue in the raft of makeshift arenas, however, included the awesome Roman amphitheatre at Leptis Magna, near Tripoli. The drama critic and historian Felix Barker was serving as a Desert Rat (Sapper) and witnessed a particular performance at Leptis Magna. He recalled a stunning moment when Leigh, all alone, appeared on stage and was illuminated in the darkness by a single spotlight. He recalled: 'Hardened soldiers who had fought through a gruelling campaign sat spellbound as she recited *You Are Old, Father William*.'

Big names to applaud the players included senior commanders – Generals Bernard Montgomery, Jimmy Doolittle and Dwight Eisenhower. A Royal Command Performance was staged by the Spring Party on the terrace of a villa at Tunis. HRH King George VI recommended Leigh recite his favourite poem by Alice Durer Miller – *The White Cliffs of Dover*. And, after graciously obliging His Majesty's request, Leigh informed him how his choice was 'most inspiring'.

As word got around about the Spring Party many of their friends in uniform came tapping at the tent flaps to congratulate their theatrical pals. Naval commanders and actors Alec Guinness and Peter Bull had left their ships anchored off the Algerian coast and had a signal to 'catch the afternoon show' at a garrison theatre a few miles inland. Guinness recalled bumping in to 'Binkie' Beaumont who was on the phone 'doing business as if he was in the West End of London'. As the time wore on Guinness and Bull became anxious about getting back to their ships which were due to set sail that evening. Leigh, in full charm mode, managed to persuade an admiral to drive them to the coast so they might get back on board without too much stress. In return for his kindness the high-ranking naval chief was promised a kiss and a big drink from the alluring Miss Leigh.

Obviously feeling she was something of a success as a morale-raiser for the troops Leigh decided to remain in North Africa for three weeks in order that she could entertain the sick and wounded in various far-flung heat-soaked hospitals and field units. But in early September 1943, suffering from severe exhaustion, she returned to England. Her husband meantime was in the throes of editing *Henry V*.[36]

Life changed again for Leigh as she decided to rest, recuperate and concentrate on her English garden, much-loved cat and various dinner parties. Her experiences as a wartime entertainer had not quelled her appetite for socialising and by Hallowe'en of that year the Oliviers were hosting parties for David and Primula Niven, John and Mary Mills and Brendan Bracken who was a close friend of Churchill and Korda. But in 1944 and suffering from a cough and high fever Leigh was admitted to hospital and found to be in the throes of tuberculosis. After several weeks bed-rest she was given the all clear and went to work again.

Her role was to be the 16-year-old Egyptian queen in a film of George Bernard Shaw's *Caesar and Cleopatra* and it was to be shot at Denham Studios, produced by the director Gabriel Pascal's own company and financed by Rank. It was noted at the time how Leigh's performance was lacking in enthusiasm, and the famous spark which often lit up her performances had disappeared. It was as if the length of her wartime tour of the desert had sapped her energy and the tuberculosis had affected her vocal chords. The production cost £1.3 million and was not a commercial success. (This was a massive difference when compared to Olivier's propaganda epic *Henry V* with its budget of £475,000. It made more than £1 million at the box office.) The excessive expenditure on the glossy full-colour *Caesar and Cleopatra* was largely down to the director Pascal's fussing and obsession with detail, and whilst initially Leigh got on well with the ageing Shaw he soon turned against her and accused her of 'babbling' his lines. A notorious lecher in his time and known for trying to make free with female actors there's every likelihood his criticism of her was fuelled when she rejected his advances and misguided attempts to pinch her bottom.[37]

When the film was being made Vivien was also pregnant and was thrilled at the thought there would be a new addition to the Olivier family. But after a fall on set she suffered a miscarriage – a tragedy not unassisted by long, intensive and exhausting days standing about in chiffon clothing in cold weather as Pascal urged his cast to present a performance indicative of the heat of Egypt. According to film historians Pascal even insisted real oceans of sand from Egypt were shipped in in order to ensure the colour of the desert was correct for every shoot! Vivien's co-stars included Claude Rains as Caesar, Stewart Granger as Apollodorus and Flora Robson as Ftatateeta.

After the miscarriage Vivien suffered weeks of depression and filming was delayed. There were also further hold ups owing to developments in the war. When *Caesar and Cleopatra* was released in December 1945 it was hailed as 'one of the most popular British films released in the US'. Other less charitable reviews labelled it a 'box office stinker'. It took Leigh six years before she felt able to sit and watch it – and she only did so with Olivier holding her hand, as she had agreed in 1951 to resurrect the Egyptian queen on stage with her husband at her side starring as Caesar.

For Olivier in 1943 *Henry V* was consuming much of his energy and time and yet his commitment to the film was 100 per cent. Not only was his Italian friend and director 'Del' working hard on Rank executives to come forth with the finance he was also aware of propaganda ace Dallas Bower's great efforts to persuade Churchill to cut through red tape to film in certain locations. Churchill was a great believer in *Henry V* as a morale raiser for the troops and agreed that in order to set the fifteenth-century scene a neutral country should be chosen to shoot the film. That location with its harmonious and peaceful natural environment was Ireland. On the train journey to the Emerald Isle the excited Olivier travelled with the poet John Betjeman who was employed as press attaché to the British Embassy. They amused each other by creating lyrics such as 'If I should die think only this of me, I could not live without my Vivien Leigh … '[38] Ireland was a perfect choice as there was no sight or sound of aircraft in the sky and there would be plenty of men in the area who could take part in the essential crowd scenes, especially during the Battle of Agincourt. For its star who was a true Shakespearean through and through, *Henry V* had to 'be beautiful' and he made sure his talented, loud, pot-bellied, cigar-smoking friend 'Del' and the Ministry's propaganda officials were aware of his exceptionally powerful vision of the production.

At first, the actor was asked by the Ministry of Information which had just given him a down-payment of £20,000, to appear at all times in battledress. But this suggestion was soon pushed aside as Olivier worked his magic on the character of *Henry V* and the 'beauty' of the production as depicted in the Limbourg Brothers' book *Les Très Riches Heures du Duc de Berry*.

Henry V was no easy ride. At the outset there were changes of scriptwriter and various ideas about who should direct it were on the table. The look of the film was too seemingly open to all sorts of opinion with the Ministry of Information recommending it should be shot in modern battledress. But Olivier stuck to his own brief that the film would be of 'spectacular beauty'. It was to be dedicated to 'The Commandos and Airborne Troops of Great Britain the spirit of whose ancestors it has been humbly attempted to recapture'.

Briefly, Olivier's preferred choice of director was Terence Young who declined the invitation on the grounds he wasn't experienced enough for such a debut. Olivier was reportedly relieved and was optimistic about 'doing it all' himself. He said: 'The tortuous business of balancing one second-rate director against another and trying to decide which would be worse was really too much. It really feels better for me to be riding a terrible great horse myself than pretending to trust somebody else whose riding I suspect. I'd rather land my own arse in my own ditch than have some hack land it on his!'[39]

The actor also approached the great William Wyler to take up the challenge. (During the war Wyler directed *The Memphis Belle: A Story of a Flying Fortress* (1944) and took great risks flying over enemy territory to get the shots he wanted. His cinematographer First Lieutenant Harold J. Tannenbaum was shot down and killed during the filming.) When Olivier went to see Wyler who was then serving as a Major in the American army, to ask if he would direct Henry V. Wyler told him bluntly: 'Direct it yourself!'

It was clear from then on Olivier was the man to lead the production. By 1944 Britain and its Allies were fighting not only the Nazis, but an enemy in the Far East too.

Henry V was shot in Enniskerry, 30 miles south of Dublin, which then was the estate of Lord Powerscourt. Most of the soldiers were played by extras and more often than not Olivier was the only professional actor on the set. He also stepped into minor roles, disguised, if required. Among the esteemed professionals in the cast of fifteenth-century soldiers was Robert Newton who played 'Ancient Pistol'. Like Olivier, Newton was fresh out of uniform and had served as an able seaman aboard HMS *Britomart* which had been an escort ship for the Russian convoys. Newton had been medically discharged after two years in the Royal Navy. Before joining the cast of Henry V the notable actor with the gruff manner and raffish grin had already appeared in a raft of films and theatre productions before the war and made his mark as the playboy pilot Jim Mollison in the 1942 film *They Flew Alone* about the aviatrix Amy Johnson (played by Anna Neagle) who died flying for the Air Transport Auxiliary in 1941.

As well as Newton on the *Henry V* set was the awesome First World War hero John Laurie (Dad's Army) who appeared in three films with Olivier – *The Demi-Paradise*, *Hamlet* and *Henry V*. In the film we also see the actor Jimmy Hanley who had in real life served as an officer with the King's Own Yorkshire Light Infantry, and then took part in a Commando raid in Norway until a serious leg wound saw him invalided out of the army. Hanley appears as a soldier called 'William' in Henry's noble army. The well-known Irish actor Niall MacGinnis who appears as the character 'MacMorris' saw active service as a surgeon in the Royal Navy during the Second World War. And the stand-out performer Esmond Penington Knight had served on board HMS *Prince of Wales*. During the battle with the German battleship *Bismarck* in the Denmark

Strait he was injured and lost his eyesight for two years. When he took up the role of Fluellen, a Welsh captain in Henry's English army, Penington Knight had recovered some sight in his right eye.

One of the major anxieties haunting the production team was the shortage of film. Olivier realised he could make just two takes of his famous 'Once More Unto the Breach Dear Friends … ' speech. There were also the varying expressions on the faces of the performers which proved an editing challenge for the actor/director when he looked through the footage at the end of the day. This wasn't a film about blood, mud and battle-weary men. Those faces were to play their role in creating a glossy tribute to 'our 'Sceptred Isle' and the divinity of the human spirit. Of course in 1943 Olivier was lucky to find enough men to film the battle sequences at Agincourt. He wanted 650 young men who could appear as archers and cavalrymen. Also there was a hunt for 150 horses, let alone the shoe nails. In southern Ireland the extras agreed to work for £3.10 shillings a week and those who had their own horses received an extra £2.[40]

Olivier wrote and told Leigh how the extras were encouraged to grow beards and their chain-mail was made from old twine woven together and sprayed with aluminium paint. Olivier too adopted a grey horse and like the real Henry V he named the mount 'Blaunche Kynge' (White King). Always keen to motivate, impress, and show his cast he was happy to do his own stunts, one day he decided in one scene he needed to jump from a tree and wrestle with a French cavalryman. The action led to a fractured ankle and a back sprain.[41]

He was aware he had to lead from the front in order for his cast to have confidence in their own performances. It was a time his experience in the real-life military could be put to good use. But it was the first time he had to inspire almost 700 men into action. For some scenes he stood on a beer crate to talk to the crowd of extras. This action also helped him beat back his own nerves. He told them: 'I may sometimes be asking some things of you which might be difficult, perhaps even dangerous, but I want you to know that I shall not be asking anything of you that I shall not be willing at least to try to do myself.' Another time he received a facial injury when an extra on horseback furiously collided with the camera and the viewfinder smashed through into Olivier's face and tore open his gum leaving him with a scar for the rest of his life.[42] Years later Olivier described his upper lip scar as useful for playing harder types of

Nazi like the character of Szell in the 1976 American suspense thriller *Marathon Man*. More often than not he concealed its creases by growing a moustache.

The making of *Henry V* also left its mark on a horse – one which lost an eye. This accident was a mystery to all as every sharp arrow or spear point had been blunted and kept clear of heads belonging to men or their mounts. When the horse went back to its normal job pulling a cab in Dublin its owner was fined for a minor traffic offence. Olivier often told the story of how when the Irishman went to court he asked if the magistrate might be taking it out on a 'poor old war-horse that lost an eye fighting for the Irish at the battle of Agincourt?' The man was then fined for contempt of court![43]

Olivier had high praise for his camera crew whose mastery had successfully manipulated away gloomy skies, and excellent cinematography transformed just 160 men and horses into a total of 1,000! The actor described his connection with the cast as a special natural kinship, 'almost angelic' owing to their childlike ability to have no qualms about showing emotion albeit it anger, love, or humour. The famous 'shower of arrows' scene in the film had to be especially created as in real life they could only fly 20-odd yards and scatter in different directions.[44]

As ever he was keen to work with his wife and approached the producer David O. Selznick about Leigh playing the French Princess Catherine in *Henry V*. He knew it would be a tough call and wrote caustically that the producer would no doubt want 'her tits, his balls, their three kittens … and all the takings' in exchange!'[45] Selznick would not budge and claimed the role of the French princess was too small for an actress of Vivien's status, believing it would harm her reputation. The powerful producer was also angry she had ignored her contract which stipulated she return to Hollywood. Leigh graciously turned down the role in her husband's epic so as not to infuriate Selznick into legal action.

Whether Olivier was ever weary with his own workload is hard to ascertain as his positivity and vigorous philosophy to live and learn through art regularly shines through in his correspondence especially when mentioning *Henry V*. Every time he faced and overcame a challenge he recorded it for his wife. (And for the censors of course who opened everyone's letters during wartime. He was after all officially still a Lieutenant in the Royal Naval Volunteer Reserve.)

One of his proudest moments as a director was the charge of the French cavalry scene. This involved not only large groups of men but the challenge of persuading horses to play dead in water for several minutes with 'dead or dying' men as French reinforcements thundered up from behind in a charge. Olivier proved a hero among the cast for plunging in the thick, muddy mire head down first of all. His leadership propelled the cast to go hell for leather at each other for realism and purpose. At times his character of Henry took over as a motivational force too.

This support from his own 'army' enthused Olivier even more as he began to know the hearts of the Irishmen around him. One day the Irish extras went on strike when they discovered their counterparts in England were earning more. Olivier immediately visited his Irish gallants to explain calmly and eloquently the financial situation would be equalled out to suit all. It worked and they picked up their props and returned to the set.[46]

The work of the composer William Walton was also seen by Olivier as 'the best ever'. However, the maestro did tell his friends how the film was a huge challenge and something of a 'bloody nuisance' as in 'how does one distinguish between a crossbow and a longbow, musically speaking!' Olivier recalled: 'The hail of arrows scene was a climax equally contributed to by visual image, sound effect and, above all, musical score – and composer William Walton's part in the success of the film was unique.'[47]

By the completion of *Henry V* the all-important Agincourt scene had taken 39 days to film – in between at least two weeks of rain. But while the actor was feeling optimistic about his masterpiece and had received great praise for its powerful imagery and performances in certain scenes which had successfully morphed into great propaganda, the producer Del Giudice was facing the wrath of the bankers. He had managed to raise £350,000 but it was soon clear he needed more and faced the prospect of visiting distributor and financier J. Arthur Rank. A deal was made but in return it meant the artistically unambitious Rank, a Methodist who believed film could help spread the Gospel, had gained a controlling interest in Giudice's film company, Two Cities.

With Leigh now back in London from her extensive tour of North Africa it was noted by friends she had lost 13lbs in weight and wasn't in the best of health and while her husband was busy finalising the details and another shoot of *Henry V* in Ireland she began preparing for *Caesar and Cleopatra*.[48]

It was Giudice who then persuaded Rank to show the new film only in a few London cinemas and in selected provinces for six months and in that way he hoped more of the total cost of the film – £474,888 – would be recovered. (The film went on to make £2 million – around £500,000 at the time – although Rank did not benefit financially until 1949). They believed the minority of art-lovers would adore it and then of course the majority of the population would be keen to join in the enthusiasm for it. It is an understatement to point out it was massively over budget but it was they deduced an absolute artistic masterpiece.[49] Although the film was deemed by some critics as a little too late as a propaganda piece it did do a tremendous job in relaying the ultimate importance of defending Britain in its hour of great need against an enemy.

The idea of *Henry V* being a raving success in the north of England was soon quashed as audiences fed on a diet of light-hearted, saucy Betty Grable films found themselves facing a very different type of experience on the big screen. In London, however, there was an 11-month run of rapturous applause but when *Henry V* galloped into the United States it ran up against the austere Hays Code of morality. Censors objected to the reference to 'God' in some of Shakespeare's speeches and felt the good name of the Deity should not be part of the film. Rank pointed out the significant cost of dubbing over the speeches to accommodate their rules. Eventually, it was Olivier who informed the uptight US censors that His Majesty King George had not complained about the film, nor had HM The Queen, the Archbishop of Canterbury, or President Roosevelt.

The distributors in Los Angeles decided to make savage cuts to the film, claiming the comedy scenes between Bardolph and Pistol and the Welsh captain Fluellen would not be comprehended by American audiences. Giudice was furious. The producer was also depressed about the way Rank was now running Two Cities Films and creating bureaucratic nightmares every time he wanted a decision about *Henry V*. Olivier was furious with Rank and confessed he was often tempted to break in to Rank's office 'to crack a few heads'.[50]

A fortnight after *Henry V* premiered at The Carlton Cinema, Haymarket, in November 1944 the war was moving in the Allies favour and the Russians had broken the German armies in the East and had moved steadfastly on from Stalingrad. It was also increasingly clear Hitler's attempts to wipe out London with V1 flying bombs and V2 rockets were about to cease thanks to the sterling work of the men and women of the Photographic Intelligence Unit based RAF Medmenham working in conjunction with Fighter and Bomber Commands.

Olivier was feeling exhausted. It had taken some weeks before *Henry V* had begun to attract large crowds and some reviews had not always been overly positive. Leigh was tired too. She had seen a doctor who advised her to take a rest from work for several months. She ignored this recommendation and began preparing for her role in Thornton Wilder's play *The Skin of Our Teeth*. Olivier knew this 1942 Pulitzer Prize-winning drama, labelled by its author 'a comic strip of mankind', had already proved a big hit on Broadway. He proposed to direct it with his wife playing the character of a siren named Sabina who was not unlike a woman Leigh knew well – Cleopatra.

By the time she took on the role the Hollywood mogul David Selznick had bought the rights to Enid Bagnold's play *Lottie Dundas* and he wanted her to star in it. He hoped it would revive Leigh's career and keep the big money rolling into MGM. Leigh refused and despite Selznick's decision to take her to court for breaking her contract she threw herself into her new role as Sabina, remembering too she had some excellent comedic tricks learned from her wartime touring friend Beatrice Lillie. Her determination and wilfulness to play Sabina as the eternal feminine, youthful, flirtatious sphinx was as admirable as her duty to what she perceived as her vocation as an actress.

Selznick's action came to nothing and even though Leigh was still eligible for war work, including employment in a munitions factory, it was deemed 'the play really was the thing' and once again she managed to slip away from any action which would damage her career. She managed to never work for Selznick again and her old contract became difficult for him to enforce.

The Skin of Our Teeth, described as akin to James Joyce's experimental novel *Finnegan's Wake* with its Biblical and Classical themes of Cain and Abel, Sodom and Gomorrah and the rape of the Sabine Women set in the modern day, opened in Edinburgh in April 1945.[51] According to Leigh's biographer Alexander Walker, the cast behaved with 'vaudevillian aplomb' and during the play's run in Blackpool Leigh encountered a stage-door caller, the actor Jack Merivale who had appeared with her and Olivier in *Romeo and Juliet*.

Walker wrote:

> Jack Merivale was now in the Royal Canadian Air Force and stationed just down the road. He had loved the play and Vivien was delighted to see him. 'What are you doing now the war is almost over?' she asked. Merivale told her he'd like to go back to the stage if it would have him. His family connections to the actor-playwright Robert Morley would come in useful.
>
> Vivien made him promise to keep in touch. 'I didn't need to promise,' he recalled and remembered Vivien still seemed to him the most exquisite creature he'd ever seen, although he thought her thinner than she should be.[52]

The Skin of Our Teeth, which opened in London in May 1945, marked the end of entertainment austerity. Firstly it was an immediate hit and secondly following the hearty VE Day celebrations to mark the defeat of the Nazis in Europe all the old style, grace and sparkle returned to the British theatre.

The wit of playwright Thornton Wilder struck home to audiences starved of professional theatrical guile and of course the winning combination of Olivier as director and Leigh as the star was just the tonic to revive survivors one and all. Not even the cynics could find fault with this play which was presented with aplomb by the 'royal duo' of the theatre.

For the Oliviers 1945 was extremely busy. Indeed just before the curtain went up on *The Skin of Our Teeth* the couple bought the mystical twelfth-century Notley Abbey at Thame which sat half-way between London and Stratford-upon-Avon in 56 acres of grounds. The habitable parts of it had been constructed in the eighteenth century. For Olivier the glories of Notley's historic home once ironically inhabited by Henry V, symbolised what he described as his 'baronial' period.

As decorators and builders descended on Notley, however, the actor was in Blackpool on VE Day with the Old Vic Company and by 19 May he had arrived in Brussels for a Victory Tour with his old friend and Fleet Air Arm colleague Ralph Richardson and the Old Vic. They visited stages in Antwerp, Belsen, Hamburg and then Paris and it seemed as if performing Shakespeare's *Richard III* was a catalyst for an actor exhausted to such a point it 'added an extra dimension' to the play.

He said:

> I was frightfully tired, and there was this audience, the whole audience were men in khaki with Sten guns between their legs, and I was absolutely dreading the performance I was so tired, didn't know how the hell I was going to get through it, and there was such a feeling from out there, expectation, expectancy, and feeling they were lucky to have survived the war, and saying, 'If you knew how we are with you boy. I hope we're making you feel alright.'
>
> I couldn't believe that I could have given a performance of such tremendous verve, and scaled the heights, feeling as I did when I walked straight on stage. I don't think I've ever done anything as good as that in my life. It's these boys, made me.[53]

In one of many letters he sent to Leigh he recalled seeing Belsen Concentration Camp where 'up to twenty people a day' were dying from typhus. In the meantime Leigh was told by doctors to go to Switzerland to rest and her ongoing cough was the start of tuberculosis. She refused and continued with the Wilder play. Olivier was in Paris performing *Richard III* when he was told by a friend about Leigh's ill health.

During the war the theatre director Tyrone Guthrie had worked hard to keep the Old Vic company in operation and despite the Luftwaffe's many attempts to blast London to pieces (with one bomb in particular almost destroying the historic Old Vic) the admirable Guthrie soldiered on. Not unlike the actor Donald Wolfit (1902–68) who during the Blitz had presented a programme of Shakespearean tragedies including *King Lear*. Wolfit's dresser Ronald Harwood based his successful play *The Dresser* on the life and theatrical times of the redoubtable Sir Donald. The play later went on to great success as a film starring the great Albert Finney (1936–2019) as 'Sir' and Tom Courtney as Norman the Dresser.

The play is set during wartime and shows how a theatre company struggles on throughout the Luftwaffe's reign of terror upon Britain during the Blitz to entertain dispirited communities – many of whom had lost their homes and livelihoods. (Incidentally a young Finney had worked with Olivier in 1959 in a production of Shakespeare's *Coriolanus* at Stratford so he experienced the full force of working with an actor/ manager at the height of their powers. No doubt elements of Olivier's behaviour may well have been woven into his performance as 'Sir'. In 1971 the veteran star tried to interest Finney in taking over the role as busy Chairman of the National Theatre – an offer Finney understandably declined owing to lucrative and creatively rewarding film offers.)

Meantime Olivier's triumph in a Chekhov play and other seasons of classics proved to be a roaring success. In January 1947 he went back to the film studio to direct and star in Shakespeare's *Hamlet,* his duties to the Bard forever uppermost in his mind and heart. The production, financed by Two Cities Films, won Olivier an Oscar for 'Best Actor'. Its box office took a whopping $3,250,000 in the US. By May 1948 when *Hamlet* hit the big screen the star had joined Ralph Richardson in resigning as a director of the Old Vic. Internal disagreements with its chairman Lord Esher had prompted them to step down. Weeks later Olivier was in Australia and New Zealand appearing as Richard III, also as Sir Peter Teazle in Sheridan's *The School for Scandal* and as Antrobus in Thornton Wilder's *The Skin of Our Teeth.*

When they returned to England both Olivier and Leigh discovered so many actors who had served in the armed forces were now joining in another fight – this time for work which would keep a roof over their heads and keep them connected to those in power in show business. The Australian/English actor Peter Finch was one such actor who joined the newly-formed Laurence Olivier Company. Finch had served with the Australian Army in the Middle East and during the bombing of Darwin was an effective anti-aircraft gunner. However, during his service he was often given leave to appear in propaganda films and in 1942 he was offered a role in *Another Threshold.* The following year he appeared in three more films and 1944 saw him on the big screen as the leading character of Peter Linton in *The Fighting Rats of Tobruk* directed by Charles Chauvel. The film centres on the siege of the Tobruk – the port city in North Africa which was held at first by the Italian army, then the British. The 'siege' came when the German Afrika Korps led by Field Marshal Erwin 'Desert Fox' Rommel surrounded and then captured it, then after the Battle of El Alamein the British reclaimed Tobruk. History reveals the whole of the area had been steadfastly defended by the Australians for 250 days.

By 1948 Finch had shaken the sand from his shoes and gone back to his life as a professional actor. Like many soldier-poets Finch had a great affinity with language and was a splendid character actor and great-looking too. After a performance in New South Wales both 'Larry and Viv' went back stage to congratulate him and offered him the opportunity to join their company in London. It was possibly then that Leigh decided she'd like to get to know Finch more and inspired a relationship between them. In his memoir Olivier admits 'he lost Vivien in Australia'.

Olivier had been knighted in 1947 and while professionally he seemed to be riding high, his personal life was proving difficult. He was lucky though to have some true friends around him including David Niven who recalled in his own autobiography he had 'helped Larry' when Leigh was experiencing severe bouts of depression and mental health problems. Years later her decision to leave Olivier came as a shock and after 20 years of marriage in 1960 the world's most famous star couple were divorced. Her close companion and long-term carer was the Canadian actor and former wartime pilot Jack Merivale. It was he who remained at her side until her death in 1967.

And for Olivier? Romance blossomed again when he met the female actor Joan Plowright during a stage production of *The Entertainer* by John Osborne in 1958. In 1960 and already missing his dear Joan, he appeared as Crassus – a Roman general, politician and the richest man in Rome – in the legendary epic *Spartacus*. Once again Olivier was working with the best, including actors who had served their country during the Second World War. Star of the film, was Amsterdam-born Kirk Douglas (real name Issur Danielovitch) who had joined the United States Navy in 1941 and served heroically as a gunner and communications officer aboard *PC-1139* which was a submarine-chaser in the Pacific. On 7 February 1943 Douglas was among the crew who detected via sonar a Japanese submarine heading in their direction.

Douglas informed fellow sailors of the enemy position and a depth charge marker was launched. By accident a sailor fired a live depth charge and when it hit the sea it blew up and sent the ship and her crew into the air. He recalled: 'The ship raised out of the water. I was thrown against the bulkhead, my stomach smashed into the equipment alongside of it. I found myself doubled up on the deck. Torpedo! Torpedo! There was confusion everywhere. But it didn't take us long to realise that we hadn't been struck by an enemy torpedo … we had blown up our own ship!'

The horrific accident meant Douglas suffered serious abdominal injuries and was medically discharged in 1944 as a Lieutenant Junior Grade. By the time he went on to forge a successful career in Hollywood his physical scars had well and truly healed as his muscular and near naked form as the slave Spartacus reveals on the big screen.

Politically and in real life Douglas went in to battle often. Having survived the war against the Japanese he thought nothing of taking on the might of Hollywood and the big shots of the late 1940s who were blacklisting any artist or writer suspected of communist sympathies. Douglas went against them all, risked his own career and chose the writer Dalton Trumbo (famous for the legendary film *Roman Holiday*) to write the screenplay for *Spartacus*. Trumbo was among many friends in show business who had been jailed for refusing to answer questions from the overly suspicious House Committee on Un-American Activities (HUAC). He was suspected of being a supporter of Stalin. During his imprisonment he continued to declare himself an isolationist when it came to politics. In 1960 during the filming of *Spartacus* in the US he counted Olivier among his friends.

Working with Olivier in the cast of *Spartacus* was the actor Tony Curtis who was cast as Antoninus. Eighteen years previously Curtis (born Bernard Schwartz) had joined the US Navy in 1942 aged just 16. He wanted to serve his country and was in uniform soon after the attack on Pearl Harbor. He wrote in his memoir *American Prince* how he had also been inspired by Cary Grant's role in the war film *Destination Tokyo*. Grant played the character of Captain Cassidy in charge of the crew of USS *Copperfin*. The film was based on a true story by former submariner Steve Fisher and has been hailed as a significant forerunner to the later classics in the submarine genre such as *Run Silent, Run Deep* (1958), *Das Boot* (1981) and *U-571* (2000). (By the time the US entered the war after the Japanese attack on Pearl Harbor, Grant, born in 1904, was too old to join the military but he did participate in a concert tour for troops and visited the wounded in hospitals around the US.)

But while Olivier was on the other side of the world flying military seaplanes around the Sussex Downs, a bright young and cheeky Jewish boy from New York was on his way to Manhattan to enlist. Curtis recalled how on a bright spring day he took the Lexington Avenue train from his home in order to reach Whitehall Street where there was a large building made of red granite. It was here he could enlist and where he met a group of young men keen to join the war effort.

He wrote:

A sergeant asked us all to fill out a form indicating what branch of the service we wanted to be in. I put down the Navy. The sergeant collected the forms and said: 'Oh, so sixty-five per cent of you want to join the Navy, thirty-five per cent of you want to be in the Army and just two of you want to be Marines. That means except for you two, all of you other guys want to live forever!'

'I almost took the bait,' explained Curtis, 'and switched my request to the Marines, but then I took a moment to consider whether I wanted to survive the war or not. I decided to take my chances with the Navy.'

From here the 16-year-old Curtis was told he needed his parents' permission and a signature was needed. Not to be deterred by any interference from his worried mother he took the form outside and forged her moniker. Having handed over the piece of paper he was told 'Welcome to the Navy'.

His prediction about his mother's concern turned out to be true as she anxiously quizzed him about why he'd joined up and where would he be sent?

The young Navy recruit told her: 'Mom, it's a great thing to be a sailor. You see the world. They'll be sending me everywhere, and don't worry about me. I'll be fine.'

'If you say so,' she replied to her son whose eyes sparkled with excitement.[54]

Curtis recalled returning to the Whitehall Street to pass a physical exam and then he was issued with a duffel bag, clothes and underwear and lectures and training about seamanship followed. His poetic description of that time offers us an insight into his character. He wrote:

The way I saw it, people are like leaves that have fallen into a swift-moving stream. As the leaves get carried downstream, some are caught in rocks and never get any further. Some are swept to shore.

Others – the lucky ones – keep going, missing the stones, staying clear of the shore, staying afloat until they reach the river delta and break free into open space. I was that sort of leaf when I joined the Navy. It was the happiest day of my life.[55]

After six weeks of watching documentaries and training films, enjoying dances and socialising, the young sailor felt free and described the Navy as his surrogate family. Already developing a charisma and style of his own, Curtis wanted to serve in submarines. He revealed in his memoir he was one of just a few selected for this job and after his rank as a Junior Seaman First Class, he was promoted to Signalman First Class. Curtis believed he received promotion because for the first time in his short life he received good grades. Known on the Champaign-Urbana base as something of a gigolo, he recalled always being happy to defend himself if any jealous sailors took a swing at him.

His next base was at New London, Connecticut – home of the main submarine operation. The training was tough and he listened intently to everything he was told. Curtis admitted this was quite unlike his behaviour at school which he said he 'hated'. But with the Navy he was treated well and he had a purpose.

The would-be young actor was dedicated to his duty as a submariner even though he felt the vessels themselves were 'intimidating' steel-plated monsters. It was only when he ventured into one and discovered how the crew were so tightly packed that he wondered if he'd made the right decision. His memory is clear as he describes how once amidships there was a tiny amount of space. He recalled:

The training officers took us into the control room, where we were told all about the submarine: what class it was, how much range it had, how deep it could go, etc. Then we went forward to the torpedo room. We saw the engine room, the mess hall and where the sailors slept. I couldn't believe how tight everything was. To get into a bunk I had to grab the bar above it and pull my butt and legs onto the mattress. It felt like I was resting in a chest of drawers.[56]

Curtis was given the option to change his mind as the Navy understood life close to the seabed for days and weeks on end wasn't for everyone. But feeling a strong sense of duty even though his imagination was working overtime at the thought of squeezing into those tiny bunks and lack of breathing space Signalman First Class Schwarz continued with his pledge – undoubtedly still inspired by Cary Grant in *Destination Tokyo*.

Able Submariner Curtis then took a train journey across country to San Diego, California where he was assigned to another base for more instruction. He recalled how one night he went to the famous Hollywood Canteen nightclub and saw the glamorous MGM star Gloria DeHaven entertain the troops. Days later and with his thoughts of Gloria helping to cushion any fears about the war he was aboard a transport ship for the journey to Pearl Harbor.

When he arrived in Hawaii he noted how Pearl Harbor 'looked like a massive naval junk yard'. He wrote: 'We could see the towering wreckage left from Japanese attack the year before. Oil was still leaking out of the sunken battleship *Arizona* and there was a tension in the air where thousands of American sailors had died so recently. There was also a sense of disgrace that America's Navy had been caught unprepared.'[57]

Over the next 12 months he felt confident he knew submarines inside and out. But his dedication to a life beneath the waves during a time of war was about to change direction as he was assigned to a submarine tender called USS *Proteus* which was a maintenance ship ready to transport supplies and haul submarines from the water.

So aboard this 9,734 long tons vessel with Captain Robert W. Berry in command, her crew sailed to Guam. Among them was not only future Hollywood star Curtis but comedian and future fellow film legend Larry Storch who after the war went on to appear in numerous classics and television shows with his US navy pal. Their names appear together on the credits of *Captain Newman MD* (1963), *Wild and Wonderful* (1964) and several more. In Guam in August 1944 and a few years before the pair were established as Hollywood favourites they recalled the island was a 'great place' to wait to be called for duty. Admittedly the majority of Japanese soldiers had been driven out by American forces although some were still in hiding in the middle of the island and would sneak about at night stealing food. When the war was over Curtis confessed how after all of his training he hadn't heard a single shot fired in anger. Back at Pearl Harbor he said he spent his days visiting the wounded in hospital. After more than three years in the Navy he was discharged and returned to New York. Days later he received a piece of paper in the mail saying he had served his country 'honourably'.

When the handsome Curtis was riding a wave of great success in 1959 he was to finally meet and work with his hero Cary Grant and appear in a film with him, *Operation Petticoat* which was a comedy about a submarine crew and their adventures in the Pacific during the Second World War. When they run out of grey paint the noble USS *Sea Tiger* is painted an awful shade of pink, with some of the screenplay including adventures which actually took place during the war years.

Curtis had some clout in the industry and got to choose the film and recommend Cary Grant as his co-star. It's sad Curtis didn't really describe in his biography what it was like to work with Grant at this time. Perhaps he was sensitive to the knowledge Grant was suffering from an addiction to LSD and was behaving strangely during various interviews with journalists like Joe Hyams. Instead of promoting the film Grant was talking to Hyams about how he was so relaxed he had a whole new view of the world and psychiatric treatment had made him face up to himself and tackle the darkness which was rupturing his soul.

Curtis' adulation of Grant was nonetheless evident in the film. He played Lieutenant Nick Holden and Grant was Lieutenant Commander Matt Sherman. Of course Curtis' ultimate tribute to his hero was when he starred in the legendary comedy that same year, *Some Like It Hot* with Jack Lemmon and Marilyn Monroe. His performance as the saxophone player Joe/Josephine/Shell Oil Junior reveals his awesome impersonation of Grant on so many levels.

In the following year of course he met Laurence Olivier on *Spartacus*. Ironically it was Curtis' wife the actress Janet Leigh who thought her honest, frank and boisterous husband should be more like Olivier and emulate his manners, charm and polish which by that time had become something of a badge of honour for the English actor.

The American actor claimed one of the highlights of making *Spartacus* was acting with Larry Olivier:

This was the first time we had acted together in a film. I loved Larry. He was a total character. He would sit and watch everything like a hawk. When things got crazy, as they often did, I would glance over at Larry, and the look on his face seemed to say, *I know what I'm doing, I know you do, too. Don't take the rest of it too seriously.* The film's editors cut the one scene we did together, the famous hot-tub scene where he tried to seduce me with his 'oysters and snails' line, but the scene was restored when the movie was reissued in 1991.[58]

It was to be eight years before Olivier was offered the chance to appear in a war film as the years in between looking after the management of the National Theatre and appearing in various Shakespearean productions had taken him away from the camera. But in 1969 audiences saw him on the big screen as Field Marshal John French in *Oh! What a Lovely War* a musical film which won him a BAFTA award for 'best supporting actor'. This story about the 1914–18 conflict began life as a radio play by Charles Chilton which was then transferred to the stage by Gerry Raffles working with the indomitable Joan Littlewood and her Theatre Workshop in 1963. Olivier's role as the veteran Field Marshal saw him as a typical military man of the time sporting a large white moustache, high leather boots and a no-nonsense swagger. In real life French, a hero of the Boer War, had been Commander-in-Chief of the British Expeditionary Force in France. Then in 1916 he became C-in-C Home Forces. This film featured a raft of stars who had cameo roles including John Gielgud, Dirk Bogarde, Michael Redgrave, Vanessa Redgrave, Ralph Richardson, Maggie Smith, Jack Hawkins, Kenneth More, Phyllis Calvert and John Mills who was cast as Field Marshal Sir Douglas Haig.

According to one of Olivier's biographers Phillip Zeigler, the director Richard Attenborough was only able to secure the sponsorship for the film from the US because he told them the greats like Olivier would appear in it. At that stage he hadn't even asked Olivier! Attenborough had served in the RAF Film Unit and Bomber Command during the Second World War and had amassed technical and production knowledge. Sponsors believed he could be trusted. He was fortunate Olivier did agree to appear in the musical as it persuaded the rest of the stellar cast to follow. The former RAF Sergeant Attenborough, as he had so often done filming from the gunner's seat in battles over Europe in 1944, had taken a gamble and won.

Olivier's awe-inspiring versatility as an actor appeared on the big screen again in 1969. It was a big moment and even a challenge for him to star as his own war hero Baron Sir Hugh Tremenheere Dowding GCB, GCVO,

CMG in the long-awaited full-colour film *Battle of Britain*. Olivier found himself among a starry line-up to be directed by Guy Hamilton.

As a former wartime pilot Olivier always had admiration for Lord Dowding as head of RAF Fighter Command who had stoically and resolutely masterminded the RAF victory over the Luftwaffe during the Battle of Britain in 1940. A deep thinking man who also saw his role as a 'guardian' to the young men (or his 'chicks' as he called them) Dowding (nicknamed 'Stuffy') stood against the odds and with perseverance won the day even though infighting among RAF leaders sparked ruthless changes to his career just days after the end of the Battle in November 1940.

Olivier's admiration of the quiet, sensitive Dowding, whose nerve was tested to the full during the aerial conflict over southern England in 1940, shines through in every take of him in the film with its astutely written screenplay by Wilfred Greatorex and James Kennaway. The musical score is memorable and rousing, composed by William Walton (who had worked with Olivier on *Henry V*) and Ron Goodwin. Wise, almost ethereal and other-worldly, it was Dowding who made the ultimate decisions over the actions of Britain's RAF fighter squadrons during an intense and ferocious battle to defend the country against the marauding German air force.

During the Battle of Britain a total of 1,542 RAF aircrew were killed, 422 wounded and 1,744 aircraft were destroyed. The number of civilians killed or injured totalled almost 35,000. The Luftwaffe, which fought with 2,550 aircraft against the RAF's 1,963 fighters and bombers, suffered a total of 2,585 killed and missing aircrew. More than 900 German airmen were captured and 735 were wounded. The RAF destroyed 1,977 of their aircraft – mostly in combat. The figures from this historic aerial conflict, arguably comparable to Waterloo or Trafalgar, are astounding. History reveals Britain's number of aircraft had been far lower than that boasted by the German Luftwaffe from May 1940, but collective human defiance combined with the Merlin-engine powered speed and stoicism of Spitfires, Hurricanes, Blenheims and Defiants pushed through an eventual and hard won victory for the RAF.

So who was Hugh Dowding? His personality remains just as memorable in the history books as his career in the RAF. Born in Moffat, Dumfriesshire, in 1882 and the son of a schoolteacher, his own education was at Winchester College before he went on to train at the Royal Military

Academy, Woolwich. The young Scotsman was then commissioned as Second Lieutenant in the Royal Garrison Artillery in the summer of 1900. It was 13 years later, a year before the outbreak of the First World War, that he expressed an interested in aviation and got his Aviator's Certificate having flown solo in a Vickers aircraft at Brooklands. From there he qualified at the Central Flying School and with his wings firmly and proudly sewn onto his tunic of the Royal Artillery he continued his life as an army man at a base on the Isle of Wight.

By August 1914, however, all changed and he became a pilot with the RFC and joined No. 7 Squadron, keen to take on the German air force. By October of that year he was with No. 1 Squadron spending time in France, then back in Britain he was made a flight commander and was in charge of the Wireless Experimental Establishment at Brooklands.

He was then appointed commanding officer of 16 Squadron and by June 1916 was near the front with 9 Wing at Fienvillers at the Somme. When the RFC became the Royal Air Force in April 1918 he continued to build his career in military aviation. In 1919 the dutiful aviator was appointed a Companion of the Order of St Michael and St George.

He served in several different leadership roles in the years between the wars and was a dedicated RAF man from the top of his ceremonial sword to the bottom of his polished boots. Dowding's expertise including a vast talent for technical matters saw him promoted to Air Marshal on 1 January 1933. By July 1935 he was appointed Commander-in-Chief of RAF Fighter Command. His contribution to the war effort was significant and yet after the Battle of Britain he always claimed he had been treated shabbily by the RAF thanks to Leigh-Mallory and Douglas Bader who had engineered his removal from Fighter Command in the November of 1940. He was never promoted to be Marshal of the RAF.

Dowding's personality was complex. He had been widowed not long after the birth of his son Derek, and in 1951 he married Muriel Whiting, who later became Lady Dowding. Having retired from the RAF in July 1942, he turned to spiritualism and wrote various books on the subject. As a middle-aged man he turned his back on Christianity and believed very much in reincarnation. His role in 1940 often haunted him as he wrote how he was visited by dead young pilots as he slept … young heroes who flew fighter aircraft into the clouds and yet bore him no malice for his decision-making during the war. A theosophist, vegetarian and spiritualist, he often attended the House of Lords and ignored those who chided him for being crazy for acknowledging the existence of fairies and the afterlife. (In the 1956 film *Reach for the Sky* starring Kenneth More, the role of Air Vice Marshal Dowding was played by Charles Carson. In the recent war film *Darkest Hour* he was portrayed by Adrian Rawlins.)

When Olivier came to play Dowding he no doubt recalled his own youthful desire to be a fighter pilot. Whereas the actor knew all about the theatre of Shakespeare, the great Dowding's knowledge of the theatre of war was just as vast, just as passionate and intense. The combination of such talents absorbed within Olivier's performance offered a magical quality to the character of Dowding he presented to us on screen. By the time the film of the Battle of Britain was made, almost 30 years after the real-life conflict, Olivier would have had access to various people who had known Dowding including the former pilots who the director Guy Hamilton had appointed as consultants on the film.

He was of course to meet again his old school acquaintance Sir Douglas Bader who had been the legendary Commanding Officer of 242 Squadron at firstly Tangmere, West Sussex then RAF Duxford. Bader had also been CO of 12 Group and as a Hurricane pilot had taken part in not only the Battle of France from the autumn of 1939 and until the early spring of 1940, but in the Battle of Britain and the Blitz. It was Bader, famous too for his boisterous personality and artificial legs (his own having been amputated after a flying accident in 1931), however, who joined with Air Vice Marshal Trafford Leigh-Mallory in a debate against a strategy devised by Dowding and 11 Group Commander Sir Keith Park.

Both men had decided the best way to out-fox the Luftwaffe would be to use 11 Group to 'husband' the RAF fighters. But Mallory and Bader were all for sending up large formations as defensive walls. They believed the battle would be won by a 'Big Wing' of squadrons and 11 Group in counties like Kent and Sussex was stationed too close to the Luftwaffe and therefore would take too much time to get into action. This friction between Park and Leigh-Mallory led eventually to the controversial transfer of Dowding and Park out of Fighter Command by November 1940.

The challenge to Dowding's authority during a crisis meeting is pertinent and the savage scene in the film is no doubt made even more authentic by the expert gathering of consultants. (Although how much influence Bader had over this is worth considering as he was, according to Dowding, instrumental in orchestrating Dowding and Park's eventual removal from Fighter Command.) It's worth questioning how much Olivier knew about this reality as he attempted to step into Dowding's shoes in the film. He may have recalled how Bader's rebellious personality had first shown itself to Olivier when they were schoolboys.

In the film, as tensions grow, the audience watch Park fly in and land a Hurricane on the airstrip at Bentley Priory in Hertfordshire, the Headquarters of Fighter Command. The role of Park had been offered to the celebrated actor Rex Harrison who had served with Park and 11 Group during the war as a young RAF Flight Lieutenant. The director believed Harrison would fit the role well as he'd admired Park and knew in real life the struggle his CO had faced against the 'big wing' brigade. Then apparently and quite suddenly owing to bad weather which led to the filming being put back, Harrison was unable to take on the role due to other commitments. Trevor Howard was given the role of the great Sir Keith Park GCB, KBE, MC, DFC, DCL. But when Park then living in Auckland, New Zealand, discovered Harrison had suddenly withdrawn from the film he was furious – an anger still chafing all those years after Dowding had been 'sacked' straight after the Battle in 1940. Park shouted loudly and the press agency Reuters ran a story about his accusation that the truth of what happened in the higher echelons of the RAF in 1940 'was being swept under the carpet'. Harrison, he claimed, was kicked out because he knew too much about Park and would play him with honesty. The Reuters press report read:

Air Chief Marshal Sir Keith Park, Commander of 11 Fighter Group covering London and South East England during the Battle of Britain, and now a city councillor in Auckland, has some serious doubts about the film *Battle of Britain*, now in production.

He charges it will cover up 'a dirty little wartime intrigue' which led to the sacking of Lord Dowding, Chief of the RAF Fighter Command then.

'It is very strange that an actor taking one of the leading roles in the film should at this late hour throw in his hand. It is possible he doesn't agree with the script and its interpretation of the part I played in the Battle of Britain,' said Sir Keith. 'There was a dirty little intrigue going on behind the scenes among the Air Ministry staff and the Group immediately to the rear of No. 11. As a result, just after the Battle of Britain was won, the Air Ministry sacked Dowding and I was sent off to a training command'.[59]

In the film Park flies in and explains to a fellow officer who greets him that the situation is bad as Kenley and Biggin Hill have been hit, and hit badly 'all because Leigh-Mallory couldn't get 12 Group up to defend the bases'. Park says: 'Big wings! They might as well stay on the ground for all the use they are … '

When Park and Leigh-Mallory (played by Patrick Wymark) stand before Dowding in the film they begin to argue their cases. Olivier as the seasoned RAF statesman sits at his desk and listens. The audience can imagine Dowding's expression is fixed and remote as if they aren't there.

In his protest to Dowding we watch Leigh-Mallory: 'We *were* up, sir, trying to knock out the enemy air mass. It takes time to assemble forty or fifty aircraft at … '

He is cut shot by Park who says firmly: 'It takes far too long! By the time your "Big Wing" is up, the enemies have already hit their targets and are on their way home.'

Leigh-Mallory replies with: 'All that matters is to shoot them down in large numbers. I'd rather destroy fifty after they've hit their targets than ten before.'

At this Park responds sternly: 'Don't forget, the targets are my airfields, Leigh-Mallory. And you're not getting fifty. You're not even getting ten!'

Then with a presence only afforded to great actors Olivier as Dowding removes his glasses, exudes solemnity and says quietly, calmly and wisely, pausing cleverly for dramatic effect: 'Gentlemen you're missing the essential truth. We're short of two hundred pilots. Those we have are tired, strained and all overdue for relief. We are all fighting for survival. We don't need a big wing, or a small wing, losing. We need pilots. A miracle.'

An air raid siren is heard in the background. Then Dowding puts on his glasses, looks down and says quietly to Park and the bristling Leigh-Mallory: 'Goodnight … gentlemen.'

Trevor Howard reputedly reported that 'crafty editing' of this scene covered up for the fact Olivier was not actually present during filming and the characters of Leigh-Mallory and Park are actually talking to an empty chair.

The other consultants on the film included heroes of the Battle such as Group Captain Hamish MacHaddie who organised twenty-seven Spitfires including the former Gate Guardian Spitfire Mk II at RAF Colerne in Wiltshire, twelve of which could still fly, and six Hawker Hurricanes, three of which could still get airborne including a rare Hurricane Mk II flown by its then owner, a Canadian by the name of Bob Diemart.

The set designers worked hard to conceal the fact the flying fighters had to look like early Mk Is, Mk Ias and Mk IIs which were the only types available in 1940. Many of the dramatic aerial sequences were filmed from an American B-25 Mitchell bomber which had been converted to carry cameras on frames and equipment to assist the crew on the aerial shoots. Spanish-built versions of German Heinkel He 111s were used along with twenty-seven Hispano 'Buchon' single-engined fighters which looked very much like the Luftwaffe's Me 109s after they'd been re-built here and there to carry mock guns.

The filming itself was spread over several authentic locations which had seen action during 1940. These were the famous airfields at Duxford, North Weald, Debden and Hawkinge and Bovington. Picturesque villages in east Kent like Chilham, and The Jackdaw Inn in Denton appear too. The beachfront in Huelva, Spain supplied the stunning blue skies of Dunkirk for the moment Hermann Göring is seen looking through a telescope at the White Cliffs of Dover. At this point he is arrogant and buffoonish in his determination that 'Adler Tag' (Eagle Day) will mean the end of the RAF.

In London the cameras, directed by the dedicated Hamilton, moved to St Katharine Docks, where old houses were being demolished and would look perfect for the image of a war-torn London. Aldwych Tube Station is included in the film and night-time scenes of Berlin were actually filmed in the Basque Country.

One of the most ardent and determined men often at the shoot was the producer Ben Fisz – a large, fleshy Polish man who had flown Hurricanes with the RAF during the Second World War. The film meant everything to him and he described it as 'his life's work'. He was something of a veteran in the genre of war films as in 1965 he completed

Audie Murphy

Audie Murphy – the war hero.

The Hollywood star Gary Cooper was greatly admired by Audie Murphy. Cooper is pictured here in 1926 in the film *The Winning of Barbara Worth*.

American troops and the tank 'Eternity' on Red Beach 2, Sicily, July 1943.

American armour and infantry in Coutances, Normandy, France in July 1944.

US infantry including Lieutenant Audie Murphy fought in freezing conditions in 1944.

Audie Murphy's 3rd Infantry Division in Nuremberg, in the spring of 1945.

Audie Murphy in 1951 in the American Civil War film *The Red Badge of Courage*. It was directed by John Huston.

The writer and director John Huston served with the rank of Major in the US Army during the Second World War. His breathtaking documentaries explored the lives of men in battle. Huston became one of the few men Murphy respected in Hollywood.

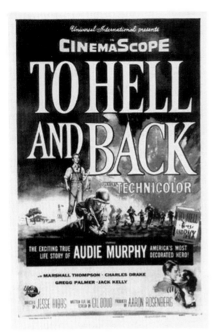

A poster of *To Hell and Back* in 1955.

Audie Murphy's grave in Arlington National Cemetery.

The actor Tony Curtis, a US Navy veteran, who worked with Murphy in several Westerns including *Kansas Raiders* in 1956. At first Murphy wanted Curtis play him as the heroic GI in *To Hell and Back*.

Laurence Olivier

Laurence Olivier in 1939. (*Carl Van Vechten*)

The British star David Niven first served as a Lieutenant in the Rifle Brigade (Prince Consort's Own) then transferred to the Commandos. He was with Olivier in the USA aboard a yacht in 1939 when he first heard Britain had declared war on Germany. Niven returned to England and was sent to France just after D-Day in June 1944 to carry out secret reconnaissance missions. He is pictured here in 1948 as the star of a wartime film, *Enchantment*.

The twin-engined Airspeed Envoy aircraft of the type which appeared in *Q Planes* (1939) – the British propaganda comedy spy thriller starring Olivier as the pilot Tony McVane.

'Churchill's Man in Hollywood', the director and producer Alexander Korda.

Olivier as Admiral Nelson and Vivien Leigh as Emma Hamilton in Churchill's favourite propaganda film directed by his friend Alexander Korda – *That Hamilton Woman* (1941).

The trusty Fairey Albacore in 1943 was an aircraft often flown by Olivier during his pilot training at HMS *Kestrel* (RNAS Worthy Down) near Chichester, West Sussex.

Olivier's favourite Fleet Air Arm aircraft to fly was the Supermarine Walrus seaplane.

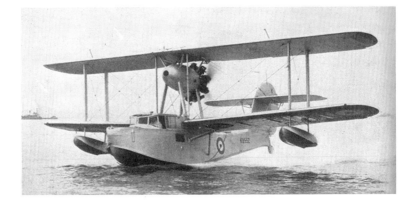

Lieutenant (A) Laurence Olivier RNVR, on the wing of a Fairey Albacore at RNAS Worthy Down with the first ever troop of Air Scouts (from St Paul's School) on 5 August 1942. (*Courtesy of Royal Navy Fleet Air Arm Museum*)

Olivier in 1944 as the fifteenth-century warrior king in his film version of Shakespeare's *Henry V*. (*Getty Images*)

Sir Laurence Olivier starred as Air Marshal Hugh Dowding in the 1969 film *Battle of Britain*.

The American actor Lieutenant Commander Douglas Fairbanks Jr KBE DSC was known as the 'Father of the US Navy Beach Jumpers'.

Foreign newspaper correspondents visiting the Denham Film Studios in Buckinghamshire, England. They are inspecting a beer barrel and tent 'at Agincourt', part of the set built for the 1944 film of *Henry V*.

Dirk Bogarde

The young British Army officer Derek 'Pip' van den Bogaerde in his uniform of The Queen's Royal Regiment. This photograph was taken by his father Ulric van den Bogaerde. (*Photograph and copyright of the Dirk Bogarde Estate*)

RAF Medmenham (Danesfield House before the war) where Lieutenant van den Bogaerde learned the secret art of aerial photographic interpretation. He was promoted to Captain in 1944.

The cap badge of the Queen's Royal Regiment proudly worn by wartime British Army officer Derek 'Pip' van den Bogaerde.

Women's Royal Auxiliary Air Force Section Officer Constance 'Babs' Babington Smith, a journalist and photographer specialising in aviation, was recruited by Churchill to head up the Central Interpretation Unit at RAF Medmenham where Lieutenant van den Bogaerde was based during his training as an Intelligence Officer.

Captain 'Pip' van den Bogaerde, left of the photograph, with an army pal somewhere in Europe in 1944 or 1945. They seem to be promoting Peak Freans biscuits! (*Courtesy of the Medmenham Collection*)

As a young intelligence officer Lieutenant van den Bogaerde is pictured here at work examining aerial photographs taken over enemy territory during the war. (*Courtesy of the Medmenham Collection*)

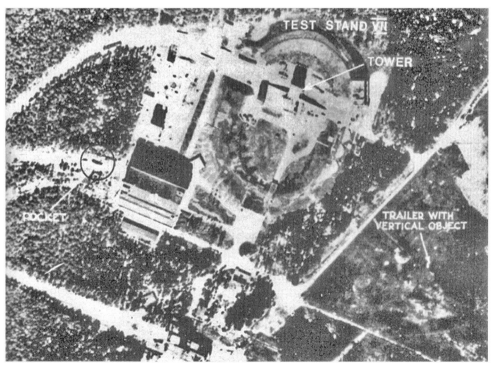

Operation Crossbow – the aerial photograph of Peenemünde in Germany which alerted RAF Medmenham and Bomber Command to the exact whereabouts of Hitler's deadly V1 and V2 missiles.

Ever aware of his father Ulric's terrifying experiences as a serving officer during the First World War, a young Derek van den Bogaerde, already a talented artist, was inspired to create this poignant image entitled 'Satyrs Wood 1918' of a dead soldier after battle. (*Photograph and copyright of the Dirk Bogarde Estate*)

Dirk Bogarde, left of the picture, as Captain Hargreaves and Tom Courtney as Private Hamp in the court martial scene in *King and Country* (1964). (*Getty Images*)

Joseph Losey, the director of Bogarde's favourite war film – *King and Country* (1964). (*Getty Images*)

Sir Dirk Bogarde being interviewed by the author Melody Foreman in 1991. (*Photograph – Author's collection*)

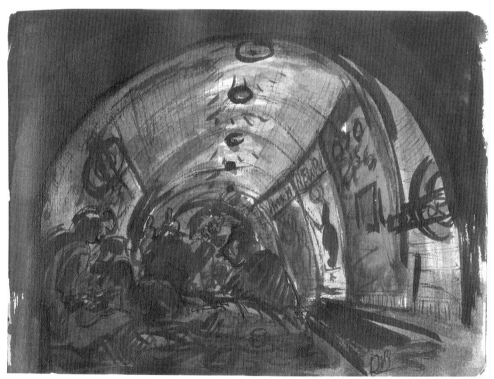

This painting of Piccadilly Tube Station was created in 1941 by the young Derek van den Bogaerde just before he was called up to join the British Army. (*Photograph copyright of The Dirk Bogarde Estate*)

10. June. '92

Thank you so much for thinking
to mail me your report in the
paper, Kent Today — it was very
good of you.

I have no idea if (what?)
came to light about was of any
use: but one must hope that —
                              Verso.

Perhaps ONE person understood — in
the audience?

I was very fortunate to be
invited to view —
                    Thank you —
Sincerely
        Si [Dirk Bogarde]

Dirk Bogarde's 'thank you' letter to the author following the publication of their groundbreaking interview which appeared in *Kent Today* newspaper in 1991. (*Author's collection*) to great acclaim *The Heroes of Telemark* – the story of resistance fighters in German-occupied Norway.

Fisz had been inspired to produce *Battle of Britain* after watching a Spitfire and Hurricane fly over Hyde Park, London. At the time he was out walking near his office and still reeling from the news a recent project would now no longer go ahead. When he heard the roar of Merlin engines and the sight of two legendary fighters above him on 13 September 1965 it triggered an enormous surge of creativity. The aircraft had been rehearsing for the 25th anniversary flypast over London which was to take place on 15 September – Battle of Britain Day – a turning point in 1940 when the Luftwaffe finally conceded defeat to the might of the RAF.[60]

The excited Fisz quickly contacted Freddy Thomas at the Rank Organisation and told him he believed a film about the Battle of Britain would be a perfect tribute to Churchill's 'Few' and 'the Many' of 1940. He then talked extensively to the acclaimed screenwriter and playwright Terence Rattigan about a script. He wanted the German characters to speak German in the film and this would be subtitled in English. After more talks with Rattigan, however, he discovered the writer was still heavily involved in another project and unable to quickly complete a draft screenplay for *Battle of Britain*. Rank executives then wrote to Fisz and suggested the film be called *The Thin Blue Line* and sent a cheque to buy the rights. At this Fisz became defensive and accused Rank of trying to steal his idea. He was told, however, that with so much money at stake it was vital Rank bought the rights to make sure all was above board. They promised to send Fisz more cash but the feisty Pole said he would not be treated like a 'B' producer.

After several weeks passed a new writer was appointed – James Kennaway – who began work with an agent tracking down fighters and bombers and researching aircrew stories, and by the spring of 1966 the famous producer of the James Bond films, Harry Saltzman, contacted Fisz.[61]

Both men were very different despite their Jewish backgrounds. Fisz grew up in an anti-Semitic environment where the brutal atmosphere of Russian Pogroms invaded the Polish communities. He discovered the only way to get what he wanted was not with his fists but with charm and persuasiveness. Saltzman was brought up in the calm of Cleveland,

Ohio, in the US and during the Spanish Civil War in 1936 helped a circus flee the country. By 1940, as air battles took place in the skies of southern England, he had arrived in Hollywood and was working on his first film. Later in the war he was in France having joined the US Air Force and War Office of Information. Saltzman, a charismatic and artful man, joined the US Psychological Warfare Bureau and after the war he began to build his career in showbusiness.

He'd met Olivier in 1957 when he was involved in the film adaptation of the award-winning hit *The Entertainer* by John Osborne which starred Britain's legendary actor in the role of Archie Rice. When Saltzman joined forces with the American producer 'Cubby' Broccoli they had realised the idea of the kitchen sink drama was fast becoming unfashionable and so they hit on the idea of turning Ian Fleming's spy thrillers into the legendary series we know today as the Bond films.

It was the 1960s and the appetite for adventure in films was fast-growing. When Saltzman met Fisz for dinner in a Soho restaurant in 1966 he decided there and then he wanted 'in' on *Battle of Britain* and he promised to raise extra money for the project. Whilst Fisz realised he now had a 'big daddy' as a business partner at least he knew for sure his baby would get off the ground.[62] Rank put up more than £1 million towards the project and agreed the film should be billed as a Harry Saltzman and Ben Fisz shared production. But within a few weeks Rank's big noise John Davis got involved and wanted to change the terms of the contract between them all.

There had also been some hold-ups with the script as James Kennaway had writers' block during the process and was overwhelmed with the amount of interviews he had typed out and piled up on his desk. Also Saltzman had appointed Guy Hamilton as director. This was a decision which at first was not to Fisz's liking as he was unsure Hamilton was the right choice. Saltzman was a big fan of Hamilton's though, and he especially liked the director's latest film *Funeral in Berlin* which starred Michael Caine who was a veteran of the Korean War of 1950–3.

Poor Fisz had even more despair to cope with when Saltzman stuck to his guns about the original contract and Rank decided to pull out of the production. Studio bosses at Paramount were at once approached. They took shook their heads in a large, loud 'no'. Saltzman, who had other projects to get up and running, sat back and shelved the film while Fisz worked frantically with Kennaway to get a full script completed.

Then, as the film's biographer Leonard Mosley reveals, 'a funny thing happened as soon as it became public the *Battle of Britain* film would not be going ahead. Hundreds of letters started to pour into Fisz's office in Hyde Park. And not just encouraging correspondence but donations of money and offers of funding from many interested parties keen the film was made as a tribute to the men and women of the Battle. Even the Air Ministry agreed to be prepared to assist in any way it could to ensure the picture went ahead.

The charming Fisz began to approach his friends in political circles and the Minister of Defence in the Labour government Denis Healey wrote to Saltzman explaining how the British Government was tremendously grateful he had agreed to make *Battle of Britain*. The Deputy Leader of the House of Lords. Lord Shackleton also got together with the RAF and the Air Ministry and a committee was formed to discuss a financial contribution.

The ever-artful Fisz then wrote to a senior man at Rank and explained how there was now an opportunity to come back on board. He wanted to arrange a lunch to include Lord Shackleton. Rank agreed. Whilst no terms were agreed with Rank the meeting went well. In the meantime in 1967 Saltzman had been working hard to secure a deal with United Artists and Spitfire Productions. The film, announced Saltzman, was not cancelled. It was very much going ahead and he set a date in 1968 when shooting would begin.

By now the director Guy Hamilton DSC (Royal Navy) was working on the screenplay with James Kennaway and it had begun to take shape. Hamilton had a dislike of the German military which came from his wartime service in the Royal Navy. Hamilton was with a crew on the 15th Motor Torpedo Boat Flotilla tasked with transporting agents into France and rescuing downed RAF pilots and returning them to Britain. When he knew Fisz had recruited the Luftwaffe fighter ace Adolf Galland to the project as chief German consultant he wondered 'if there would be trouble'. Galland was a hero of the air and had won the Knight's Cross with Oak Leaves, Swords and Diamonds. The proud Luftwaffe ace insisted from the start during a lunch meeting with Fisz that 'there had been no Battle of Britain … !'

'All that happened,' he said pugnaciously, 'was that we made a number of attacks against England between July and September. Then we discovered we were not making the desired effect and so we retired.'[63] Fisz had flown a Hurricane in combat against the likes of Galland in 1940 and was forced to listen to the German fighter ace argue about certain facts including the German use of radar. It was realised soon after the war that the use of radar in Britain played a major role in Britain's aerial victory in 1940. While the Germans had their own system it is claimed they failed to utilise it correctly thus giving the RAF the upper hand. After Fisz got home from his heated meeting in Bonn, West Germany, the ruffled Galland wrote him a letter of apology and yet most meetings between the German fighter ace and later with Hamilton turned out to be a lively, often disagreeable experience. Galland went on a hair-splitting spree whenever he made notes on the script in his role as a consultant. He claimed the 'English always smile' but the Germans 'always grin!'. He was determined to uphold the honour of Germany and expressed his opinion more often than not that *Battle of Britain* should be about bravery and not about a British victory.[64]

In his autobiography *The First and the Last* (1953) Galland, who was credited with more than 100 aerial victories including the aircraft he downed during the Spanish Civil War when he served as a Legion Condor pilot in 1936, wrote his opinion of the film script.

One gets the impression here that again the chance is spoiled to make a true fliers', or better still, the fighter pilots' film. What is planned is one of the usual solemn hero-worshipping films on the war with which the public is so fed up. The only attraction in the film might be found in the planned fights in the air, if they can be realised.

It was to be expected that this film would give a one-sided picture of the Battle of Britain purely from the British point of view. This battle has become a myth but also a kind of trauma to the misty-eyed Englishman ...

The film is not even very English, for no attempt is made to toy with the famous English understatement, but it is simply heroics from beginning to end. The characters in the film do not know what fear is!

He criticised the early representations of men he knew in 1940 including Osterkamp (Kesselring's Chief of Staff) and the bomber commander

Fink. Galland (who is the character of 'Falke' in the film) wonders why the character of Göring comes across as knowing nothing about the actualities of the battle. He thought the young fighter pilots came over as too dim and similar in their only reason to fly was to win more medals. Galland pointed out the scene showing German pilots shooting at parachuting RAF airmen was degrading and incorrect. He too wanted more emphasis on the fear of flying over the Channel and being shot down.

And he warned the film was in danger of being too kitsch and sarcastically suggested the Warsaw Concerto accompany it throughout. His notes on the script towards the end continued: 'I do not think this screenplay could be altered to a great extent. Its tendency would have to be changed completely in order to make it acceptable also to a German. Let the British have their Battle of Britain, but spare us.'[65] When Hamilton and Fisz read Galland's comments they agreed to 'take another look at the script'.

While the script was prepared and the facts artistically manoeuvred to make for great camerawork and the kind of cinematic interpretation which would appeal to audiences, Saltzman had set the budget at £8,500,000. Freddie Young OBE was made lighting cameraman in chief and had already won Oscars for his work on *Lawrence of Arabia* (1962) and *Doctor Zhivago* (1965). Fisz and Saltzman had recruited the best in the business including Art Director Maurice Carter and aerial cameramen like Skeets Kelly and Bond film ace Johnny Jordan (who died in May 1969 after an air accident in Mexico).

The art director Maurice Carter decided upon Huelva in Spain for the Dunkirk scene. Saltzman (producer of the Bond spy thriller films) had been chided by the locals for not knowing the corpse of the 'mystery naval officer' ('The Man Who Never Was'), floated in the sea by British Intelligence to fool the Nazis during the war, was buried in Huelva Churchyard! Hamilton introduced some fictional characters like the WAAF officer Maggie Harvey (Susannah York) into the mix. The story of the character's personal life added another depth of humanity to a film examining the personal effects of the deadly battle which was raging over Britain in 1940.

During the filming Galland, who hadn't flown a Messerschmitt for 26 years, suddenly found some overalls and flew again to show the crew how a dogfight should be carried out. Sure enough he succeeded in carrying out a barrel roll in mid-air. His friend and former RAF fighter ace Wing Commander Bob Stanford-Tuck (also a consultant on the film) watched in awe and said: 'That is the famous Galland roll. He used to do that every time he shot down a British aircraft during the Battle of Britain. You wouldn't think he was 56 years old would you?!'

By 1969 another hero of the Battle, Group Captain Peter Townsend CVO DSO DSC, famous for his royal connections, went on a publicity tour to promote the film, often having to deflect questions about his doomed romance with HRH Princess Margaret. The society photographer Anthony Armstrong-Jones (later Lord Snowdon and husband of the Princess) was also allowed on set to capture the images of the day. Relations between the men were cordial and Townsend the usual epitome of politeness.

The willing consultants on this ground-breaking film included the awesome Group Captain Tom Gleave who himself had baled out of a burning Hurricane in 1940; Squadron Leader James 'Ginger' Lacey, one of the top-scoring fighter pilots of the war; Wing Commander Bob Stanford-Tuck; 303 Squadron Leader and the Polish fighter ace Bolslaw Drobinski; Squadron Leader Robert Wright who had served as Lord Dowding's personal assistant and later biographer; and Wing Commander (Women's Royal Air Force) Claire Legge. The German technical advisors listed on the film credits are Galland, Colonel Hans Brustellin and Major Franz Frodl, although many historians have suggested there were in truth many 'silent' advisers from the German side. Some of the expert advisors and veterans of the Battle wrote books about their experiences so undoubtedly the director would have been fully informed of authentic events which would prove of great use to the film. Their expertise was vital and such authenticity provides gravitas and power in every scene.

Olivier's old friend, actor and Fleet Air Arm colleague Ralph Richardson appears in *Battle of Britain* as Sir David Kelly, the British Ambassador to Switzerland, and Kenneth More, who had served in the Royal Navy during the Second World War, appears as Group Captain Barker (Bader), Station Commander at RAF Duxford. Other war veterans taking part included Nigel Patrick (Group Captain Hope), formerly a lieutenant colonel in the King's Royal Rifles. Patrick fought in battles in North Africa and Italy. The actor Robert Flemyng OBE MC who played

Wing Commander Willoughby was a hero of the Royal Army Service Corps and won the Military Cross in 1941.

Appearing as Germans were actors like Curd Jürgens who played Maximillian Baron von Richter. In 1944 Jürgens had been sent to a Hungarian labour camp because he was an opponent of the Nazi regime. Hein Riess, who played the head of the Luftwaffe Reichsmarschall Hermann Göring, told Galland he had once met his character. It was Galland who reported that Riess was a great actor who could sound just like the domineering and bumptious Göring he had known during his time in the Luftwaffe during the war.

When the cast list was finalised the actor Robert Shaw (who had been in the RAF during his National Service) played a character based on the mighty South African fighter ace 'Sailor' Malan – another hero of the Battle. The actor Christopher Plummer landed the role of Squadron Leader Colin Harvey. A young Ian MacShane plays Sergeant Andy Moore – a Londoner who is shot down and survives by parachuting into the Channel. He returns home on leave and his young family are killed in the Blitz. This was an important role for MacShane whose character showed how many of Churchill's honoured 'Few' of the Battle of Britain were working-class sergeants but just as brave as any middle-class grammar-school educated officer. A languid Edward Fox with his fair moustache was cast in the role of Pilot Officer 'Archie' not dissimilar to that of the real life RAF prince 'Ginger' Lacey. A young Michael Caine appears as Squadron Leader Canfield. It was Caine who asked Lacey: 'Exactly who was Leigh-Mallory?' Lacey replied: 'He was a clot!'[66]

Invited to Duxford airfield to watch the aerial action were a number of the greats who had been in the RAF in 1940 – pilots like the awesome Air Commodore Al Deere and Group Brian Kingcome DSO DFC, Group Captain Johnny Kent DFC AFC who led the victorious 303 Squadron of Polish pilots, Tom Gleave, Stanford-Tuck, 'Ginger' Lacey and Douglas Bader.

Before the visit to Duxford Lord Dowding had been introduced to Olivier at Pinewood Studios. Olivier, who had grown a moustache for the role, portrays him with utter sobriety and a voice of quiet calm to quell the monstrous realities of noise and death going on in the skies above. Olivier admitted his own moustache wasn't perfect. He recalled:

'Dowding had a more definite type of face than mine. I tried to imitate Dowding's voice but there was nothing very remarkable about it'.[67]

What is so commendable about Fisz, Saltzman and Hamilton was a determination to make sure there was vindication for Lord Dowding who had according to evidence released over the decades been treated appallingly by the RAF and the British government after the Battle of Britain. (Originally in 1966 Fisz had wanted Alec Guinness to star as Dowding but delays over the film's production meant the actor had taken on other commitments by the time casting was finalised.) His departure as Head of Fighter Command had been orchestrated by factions working against him during 1940 which included Trafford Leigh-Mallory, who was supported by Douglas Bader, and Sholto Douglas – the man who took over Dowding's job in November 1940. For decades Dowding got little thanks for his work leading Britain to victory in the skies and he retired in 1943 a disappointed man. When Lord Dowding was invited to appear on the film set at Duxford on 26 May 1968 he was 86 years old, frail and his arthritis had left him in a wheelchair. However, since learning about the making of the film he found the necessary energy to make it known how he had been so badly treated. He wasn't amused though when Bader approached him, grabbed the wheelchair handles and began to push him around to view the aircraft on the ground. Dowding was overheard to say to a small group 'the Battle might have gone considerably better if junior officers had not exercised undue influence on their seniors at critical moments …'.

One of the key locations was of course the magnificent Bentley Priory in Hertfordshire – the very place where Dowding made the decision to send hundreds of young RAF aircrews into action in the skies over southern England in the summer and early autumn of 1940. During a recent visit to Bentley Priory I spoke to one of the guides about the film. He said Olivier had approached Dowding after the special screening of the film and gently wondered if his performance had at all resembled the real Dowding! At this, the elderly Dowding frowned and said 'Not at all!' It's doubtful Olivier was deflated by the comment as Dowding knew the actor well enough to pull his leg and at one time had wondered if Olivier's moustache was 'too gingery'. Also, it's on record that Dowding's quiet appreciation of the film was confirmed when he wept silently at the end of a special screening. Olivier's performance also helped to persuade

Dowding to reassure Sir Keith Park the film had done a decent job in putting the record straight over the internal battles which took place in 1940. Robert Wright was a former RAF navigator during the war and had been Dowding's personal assistant during 1940. He had been on the set as a consultant and said Olivier's performance was an 'authentic' one and the producers to their credit had gone to great lengths to ensure Dowding was happy with the film.

One day during a scene shot at the former Hawkinge airfield from where some of Sir Keith Park's 11 Group would take off to fight in 1940 over the nearby Folkestone coastline, the former head of Fighter Command got talking to Trevor Howard who played Keith Park. In his book *Dowding and the Battle of Britain* (1969) Robert Wright recalled:

One summer's day in 1968 both men were sitting beside a Hurricane aircraft while filming was going on a short distance away. The summer had been just as it was that September day twenty-eight years before: a sparkling clear, hot summer's day.

From the direction of the Channel, no distance at all, two Spitfires which appear in the film came hurtling in to land, the singing of their Merlin engines awakening strong memories in the minds of those who had known what it had all been like. The two fighters, of that slim beauty that no fashion can decry, slid easily through the air over the airfield, turned, and came in and landed on the grass in a style that marked them as part of a golden age of flying.

Although Dowding watched the aircraft with intense interest, his thoughts were on the subject that we had only just been talking about. He turned to Trevor Howard, and he said: 'If it hadn't have been for Keith Park's conduct in the battle, and his loyalty to me as his Commander-in-Chief, we should not be here today ... '[68]

It was a tense day for the production team and the cast in 1969 when David and Arnold Picker, then heads of United Artists arrived to see the rough cut of the film which had until then cost $10 million. After the screening they left and were obviously impressed as they gave Saltzman another $3 million to finish it, 'but that was it!'.[69]

As a vehicle for Sir Laurence Olivier's career it's arguable *Battle of Britain* cemented his reputation as one of the greatest actors of all time.

His performance of gravitas and sincerity as Air Chief Marshal Hugh Dowding was seen at the premiere of the film at the Dominion Theatre in London on 15 September 1969. Lord Dowding himself was also in the audience among the VIPs including 350 brave men who had taken part in the real Battle. The reviews, however, were mixed. The *Evening Standard* described it as 'absorbing rather than stirring' and the American press couldn't decide if had documentary value or fictional might. One reviewer claimed it didn't match the energy of the epic war film *The Longest Day* (1962).

Four years later in 1973, the voice of the great Olivier was chosen to narrate the legendary 26-episode-long documentary series *The World at War* produced by Thames Television in conjunction with Noble Frankland of The Imperial War Museum. It was originated and directed by Jeremy Isaacs and its now-legendary soundtrack was composed by Carl Davis. It was Episode 4 which brought Olivier back in touch again with the Battle of Britain of 1940 and the extraordinary evacuation of British troops from the beaches of Dunkirk that same year. In the excerpts about the aerial conflict of that year we hear the consultant on the 1969 film Adolf Galland talking about the Luftwaffe, and an RAF fighter pilot of the Battle Sir John Aitken (2nd Baron Beaverbrook) is introduced by Olivier. Beaverbrook goes on to describe the scene of Dunkirk and the aerial conflict which he recalled well as a pilot with 601 Squadron. He said: 'I hated the Germans. They were trying to enslave us.' Sergeant Pilot Roy Holmes said: 'You put the idea of being killed out of your mind.' The grave and measured voice of Olivier sounding like the character of Lord Dowding he had played so well in the 1969 film, told viewers of this remarkable series how 103 airmen of the RAF lost their lives in 1940 and 128 were seriously wounded. Britain had lost more than 500 aircraft in two weeks and the last days of August saw Fighter Command on its knees. Many airfields had been pounded to pieces by Luftwaffe attacks. Just when Britain braced itself for an invasion the Luftwaffe turned its attention on London. 'It was,' narrates Olivier solemnly, 'their biggest mistake.' Fighter Command re-grouped.

The World at War series ran for almost a year and was hailed as a major achievement of British television. Its footage of humanity in conflict, its grainy images of death and destruction reminded audiences throughout Britain and the world of the damage inflicted by war. The faces of soldiers, airmen, sailors, concentration camp inmates and civilians sparked a renewed interest in military history.

Its narrator was now associated with a major feat of televisual communication. His voice described the fifteen main campaigns of the war. Other episodes focused on the Home Front and a massacre in a French village. In Episode 26 Joseph Haydn's *Missa Sancti Nicolai* can be heard and the famous *'Dona nobis pacem' (Grant Us Peace)* is a rousing tribute to the dead. As the series ends we hear Olivier say 'Remember …'.

For the actor there would be another war-related film to add to his credits. This time in 1976 he was to appear alongside Dustin Hoffman in *Marathon Man* – a suspense thriller with a plot showing a student (Hoffman) getting mixed up in a Nazi war criminal's plan to find stolen diamonds. The old Nazi Christen Szell is artfully played by Olivier and the film itself directed by the legendary John Schlesinger proved a box-office hit in its theme of endurance in the hunt for Nazis of the Second World War. Olivier was nominated for another Oscar and this time it was for Best Supporting Actor. (That year the award went to US Navy war hero Jason Robards for *All The President's Men*. Robards served as a radioman aboard the USS *Northampton* in 1941 which was hit and destroyed by Japanese torpedoes – a carnage from which Robards was to swim for his life. Later he served aboard the USS *Nashville* at the invasion of Mindoro in the Philippines.)

Two years later in 1978 Olivier appeared as the Nazi hunter Ezra Lieberman in *The Boys from Brazil*. He was as busy as ever and his career was heading skyward. He was back on a roll. The character in this science-fiction film was loosely based on the acclaimed writer Simon Wiesenthal who spent much of his life hunting down surviving members of the Third Reich. The star Gregory Peck was cast as the evil butcher of Auschwitz Dr Josef Mengele who in the film was to be hunted down in Paraguay. Based on the book of the same name by Ira Levin, the film was described by its producers as not about Nazis but about cloning, 'a logical extension of existing facts. And it's about the hatred that two men have for each other.' When the executive producer made this comment to the press he was referring to the film's plot which involves a collective of Nazis who are shielding various children all over the world whose mothers had been injected with zygotes which gave each child Hitler's DNA.

In *The Boys from Brazil* we see Olivier as the Jewish Lieberman track down Mengele who then taunts him that Hitler will now live on and on. When Mengele is killed the Nazi hunter removes a list from him and on it finds the names of all the children cloned from Hitler. Olivier plays the role with aplomb. When his character realises there is a plan to kill all the children on the list he decides to destroy it because they should be given a chance to live.

The actor shot some of his scenes in London and often there were scenes created in Portugal, Austria and Pennsylvania, USA. Olivier was nominated for the eleventh time as Best Actor at the 1979 Academy Awards. There was much talk he was favourite to win and it is recorded he even wrote an acceptance speech. At the time he was told by the Oscar committee he was to be presented with the 'Special Lifetime Achievement Award' but it wouldn't affect his chances of winning Best Actor.

It was then Olivier had a flashback to the time he felt he'd been cheated out of the Best Actor award for *Henry V* (1944). He wanted to know if the 1978 Oscars committee had come up with another plan to avoid him taking the top prize? They assured him they had not and explained the Lifetime Achievement Award and Best Actor were not related and if he turned down the latter then it wouldn't look good. When Best Actor went to Jon Voight for the Vietnam war drama *Coming Home* it's fair to say Olivier was disappointed. He did, however, gracefully accept his Lifetime Oscar statue. He was cheered in 1982 when he received the award of the Order of Merit from HM The Queen. This honour is only given to a select few and is regarded as the supreme accolade. Olivier was the first actor to win such a medal. The OM put him in the ranks of Graham Greene, Earl Mountbatten of Burma, Benjamin Britten and Winston Churchill.

To try and discover the true personality of the man often hailed as 'the greatest actor' of all time is difficult. He has been described as mercurial, an introvert and yet an exhibitionist when needed. Some of his friends including his wife Joan Plowright likened him to a lion.

The brilliant theatre critic and writer Kenneth Tynan once wrote of him:

Larry has this bottled violence, which is what gives him this great authority on stage and gives his acting a sense of danger. You quite often feel that with immense effort he is being civil to people that he would like not to just walk away from, but to kick very hard. That is why, when he is prevailed upon to make a speech, he puts on a pose of elaborate humility which embarrasses anyone who knows him. He pretends to be such a wilting violet. And you know he would quite enjoy seeing those people blown up!

Others who knew him described a kind and sensitive person including the actress Athene Seyler who brilliantly thought him 'A Man for All Seasons'. To so many he was the actor who had achieved after a lifetime of hard work an exceptionally brilliant balance between narcissism and self-criticism. He could get angry, he could be gruff, he liked to have authority over his projects and lead from the front. Whoever he was to whoever wanted to know him it's true to say Olivier's important wartime role as Henry V had stayed with him throughout his long and multifaceted life. The young wannabe fighter pilot had succeeded in creating a theatrical and film career which took him to the heights known only to so few.

Dirk Bogarde

'It is a story of imagination, devotion and courage... '

Lord Tedder speaking in praise of intelligence officers including Lieutenant Derek van den Bogaerde and RAF Bomber Command who served at RAF Medmenham.

I was 15 years old when I first became aware of proud British Army officer and film icon Dirk Bogarde. It was an early summer morning in 1979 and I was gazing out of a window at a school games field as it sparkled with dew. Waiting at my desk alone in the classroom I listened out for my rabble of schoolfriends to come clattering down the corridor and arrive with their frivolity and chatter. Some reeked of fresh bubble gum, others carried the acrid whiff of yesterday's sweat on their blouse, and some, usually those in specs and more subdued, made their way to the front so they had an easy view of the blackboard.

When seats had been taken, desk lids had stopped crashing and chewed pencils were at the ready for note taking, most of us were prepared to begin our two hours of history. This was always a favourite on my timetable owing to the narrative gifts of a worldly teacher we knew as Mr H – a middle-aged, portly man and undoubtedly a veteran of the Second World War. He was properly dapper in many ways and always, always carried a yellow silk spotted handkerchief which frothed out the top left-hand pocket of his tweed jacket. He walked with a brisk military deportment. More a distinguished 'Major' type really than a boisterous gung-ho type with a bushy moustache.

And so he arrived in the classroom that morning with a bright shine bouncing off his brown lace-up shoes. He closed the door with the old brass handle tight shut and announced we didn't need our books as he wanted to talk about a film. He then added there would be something else he'd like to tell us towards the end of our lesson too but that could wait. He knew no one could resist a surprise story and it might help us remain alert.

Our history lesson of that day was to focus on the 1914–18 conflict. I was keen to listen to his voice – a voice which might help explain the eye-watering horrors pictured in our dog-eared study books. Pages and pages showing exhausted men in the mud and slime of shell-ravaged trenches. These unforgettable images needed some sort of present-day human intervention ... even explanation.

Realising the benefits of listening to Mr H was probably shared by a handful of other girls including those usually more interested in munching cheap meat pies they'd stolen from the local shop that morning. We believed this teacher's own reportage of a film would be far more entertaining and so we slapped shut scruffy textbooks and became an audience to this seasoned, grey, balding man who engaged us with his conversational style. We secretly congratulated ourselves on being so attentive to him especially as he was in our eyes some ancient soul from another planet. And also what was this 'other story' he'd promised us? We were all ears.

'To start with I want to tell you about probably the greatest film ever about the First World War. And that film, a masterpiece really, wouldn't have been so great without an actor named Dirk Bogarde who played a British Army officer facing the moral dilemmas of war brought about by the class system. That film is called *King and Country*. It also starred Tom Courtney who plays a beleaguered soldier named Hamp,' announced Mr H, now leaning back in a battered old leather chair which creaked in sympathy. Briefly he glanced out of the window, pondering no doubt how best to describe the film in a bid to keep our attention. Even if just one person listens, he thought to himself before asking us: 'Has anyone seen *King and Country*?' He wasn't surprised by our silence and shaking of heads. Teaching teenage girls about war? It had always been a challenge, but he believed so necessary.

Then he reached over to a bookcase behind him and withdrew what looked like an old film annual. As he held up the required page there came a flash of awe. There was a close up photograph of an actor with the sophisticated name of 'Dirk Bogarde' looking magnificent in a trim dark suit in a 1960s' style pose. I stared into Dirk's soulful eyes for as long as I could before Mr H closed the book and placed it on the desk. That day having seen Dirk, albeit in a photograph, I felt I had met a long-lost friend.

And that is mostly why I want to start this section about Dirk's military career and his war films with firstly a nod to the memory of a culturally astute history teacher who introduced me to what became a lifelong interest in the legendary Dirk, and secondly to *King and Country*. Dirk had always said it was the film which made him most proud – a fact that was confirmed by his official biographer John Coldstream.[1]

It was no surprise to learn the actor sincerely believed this, as to watch him in the film as he passionately exposes the hypocrisy in the army's court-martial process makes for Oscar-winning stuff. The director Joe Losey described this film, made in 1964, as 'a class conversation in which the officer is educated by the boy Hamp's simplicity'.[2] I hope Dirk would have been pleased to know his enlightening performance had ensured *King and Country* was remembered, and remembered well by not only our history teacher but also by the teenage girls who sat in that dusty classroom that day. I had no idea at that time I would get to meet him by chance 12 years later in circumstances I explain further on in this book.

Dirk's decision to star in *King and Country* was arguably inspired by his own family history. His father Ulric van den Bogaerde had served gallantly in the 1914–18 conflict.[3] Initially as a gunner in the Royal Horse Artillery (RHA) he would have trained at Woolwich for several weeks and learned to live with and understand the importance of good equine management. Fitness was a top priority and recruits would have to spend hours in the gym to build up their muscles to enable them to manage heavy artillery. More often than not they'd be required to lift heavy shells and weaponry at great speed. As a gunner Ulric's role was vital and yet seriously dangerous as there were always great risks involved in the loading process. At times men died because of a 'premature' – a name for the shells which had exploded too soon.

British gunner Tom Brennan of the Royal Horse Artillery described how:

There were four kinds of shells. There was a DA, direct action; there was a shell they used for blowing up billets and which didn't go off for a minute or so, it sunk in the ground before it went off, delayed action; then the third one was shrapnel; and the fourth was poison gas. They were all painted a different colour so that you'd know which one was which. At night time, if it was dark, you would know which shells you were going to fire.[4]

In a howitzer battery there were daily programmes of destruction of earthworks; portions of trenches which had to be carefully ranged on and subsequently annihilated. While heavier guns were demolishing earth constructions the men of the field artillery were busy cutting dense wire protecting the German front line, endeavouring to cut paths through for the assaulting British and Allied infantry at zero hour. 'We fired usually about 800 to 1,000 rounds per day. It was not incessant; we had broken periods during the day. It took 12 men to man an 8-inch howitzer, the shell of which weighed 200 pounds and the matter of manpower and the preservation of manpower necessitated careful reliefs which took place approximately every four hours,' explained W. Walter-Symons who served in a howitzer battery on the Somme.[5]

Ulric van den Bogaerde would have witnessed such regular ear-splitting counterbattery operations which aimed to knock out the enemy guns. Imagine the noise, imagine the suffering. The war wasn't just killing men, the regimental horses were dying in their thousands too. Artists including the great Italian-born painter Chevalier Fortunino Matania were also working close to the battles and capturing the ever-changing scenes before them. One of Matania's masterpieces is the famous 'Goodbye, Old Man' depicting an unhappy British soldier tenderly holding the head of his dying horse and saying farewell. At times, when briefly away from the front line, the artistic Ulric found solace in sketching – rather like his own son Derek van den Bogaerde who some 25 years later occupied his own free time in the same way during the Second World War.[6]

By April 1917 as a Second Lieutenant with 106 Battery of the 22nd Light Brigade Royal Field Artillery at Croiselles, Pas-de-Calais, France, Ulric was among so many tens of thousands of men who suffered shell shock after three months of raging, crashing conflict at the Somme. One RHA officer who served at Ypres said:

Our job at that time was counter battery work. If there was a German battery in action, we had to engage it – helped at times by aeroplanes. But the weather was so bad, the planes couldn't fly very often and we had to rely on visual observation from the ground. Well that was done by one of the junior officers in the battery which in most cases was me! We lost most of our young officers a very short time after we got there. That left just the captain and myself to fight the battery. So I often had to go up to Sanctuary Wood (10km from Passchendaele) which was as far as we could go for observation purposes – and get what information I could and control the fire from there. I went up with two telephonists who ran out wires as we went and they connected their telephones and communicated with the battery. Well it was all visual and it wasn't very, very nice.[7]

Years later when Ulric mentioned his own experiences of the trenches his son Derek (later Dirk) listened intently. In a volume of his memoirs Bogarde reveals that his father Ulric was born into a strict Catholic family and his faith was firmly at his side when he strode off to war in 1914.[8] Bogarde wrote:

> My father's belief, like that of so many other young men of that time, was shattered on the Somme, in Passchendaele, and finally for all time when he pulled open the doors of a chapel, after the Battle of Caporetto in Italy, and was smothering in the rotting corpses of soldiers and civilians who had been massacred and stuffed high to the roof. He once told me, many years later, 'Jesus does not have his eye on the sparrows. But you follow whatever faith you wish: it is your life, not mine.'[9]

Some of those memories shared by Ulric van den Bogaerde helped no doubt add gravitas to his son's performance as Captain Hargreaves in the film *King and Country*. The character of Hargreaves is described in the novel as a man in his twenties whose worries made him look nearer to 40 years old. Bogarde was aged 41 when he starred as the serious minded Captain Hargreaves who 'uses his controlling nature to hide a ruthless nature with a taste for violence'. He plays the 'gentleman always responsible for his retainers' and is yet 'moved by Hamp's faith in him to a new awareness of that responsibility'.[10]

King and Country is based on a play by John Wilson who had been inspired by a particular chapter in a novel by war correspondent James

Lansdale Hodson. The film is set in the muddy, slimy, rat-infested trenches of Passchendaele – a battle which in reality lasted from July 1917 to November 1917. The budget was a tiny £86,000 and it was shot in black and white over 18 days at Shepperton Studios. The distributors were Warner-Pathé (UK) and Allied Artists (US). The actor had been keen to be part of it ever since the director Joseph Losey had first offered him the chance to read a television script entitled *Hamp* back in 1959. Losey had also decided to direct *King and Country* because of Bogarde's own experiences of war.

In the meantime though Bendrose – the film company he had set up with his partner and manager Tony Forwood – Bogarde had bought the rights to *Covenant with Death*. This is a novel by John Harris about three friends serving in the army during the First World War. Bogarde showed the book to Losey and advised him to carry out some historical research and visit the Imperial War Museum. The actor came close to starring in *Covenant with Death* but sadly it was never made. (In 1986 however Bogarde did think seriously about adapting the novel into a screenplay for the well-known producer David Puttnam. But when Bogarde realised the book contained 400 pages and he discovered how in the first great battle of the Somme on 1 July 1916 60,000 men were killed or wounded between the hours of 7am and mid-day he was understandably overwhelmed. 'How can I write a film which requires so many bodies in the green corn of the Somme valley above Serre?' asked Bogarde).[11]

It's true to say however his deep interest in films with a military theme was justifiable and completely commendable. He grew up looking at his own father's artwork depicting the 1914–18 conflict and Bogarde, himself a veteran of the Second World War, experienced the stress that comes with front-line action. Any film that explained, challenged and examined warfare had his attention especially if the futility of conflict was exposed. Bogarde applied his interest in the subject even though much of the British population in the 1960s were keen to forget about war, move forward and turn their minds to a future of sunnier times.

The actor's official biographer John Coldstream wrote: '*King and Country* was forever a source of pride for Dirk, both in playing Captain Hargreaves and his input in the film based on his own military experiences and his father's in the First World War. His father had been gassed in the trenches and Dirk saw the results of that. The anti-war message matched

Dirk's own abhorrence of war and killing.' In 1964 many of those who believed in the film and its controversial theme had taken political and financial risks to make sure it was made, mostly because they had a deep respect for Losey as a director and they believed wholeheartedly the story should be told.

King and Country pivots around Private Arthur Hamp who is accused of desertion. A martinet officer – Captain Hargreaves – is tasked to defend him during a biased court martial. While building up a defence for Hamp who is a humble cobbler and father of one small boy in civilian life, Hargreaves learns his charge has experienced a litany of personal trauma.

Firstly Hamp receives a letter from his wife to say she'd found another man. Secondly the dejected soldier reveals too he is the last surviving member of 'A' Company and had joined up three years previously 'as a dare to his wife and mother-in-law'. The worst tragedy for Hamp was when his last friend from 'A' Company was blown up and the body parts of the man landed all over him. Hargreaves takes this information on board with a quiet look of sincere pity.

In the film we watch how well Bogarde at first acts out his irritation during conversations with Private Hamp and then later his understanding grows about why the honest, simple soldier had a good reason to take an innocent few moments to walk in the opposite direction from the front line. Bogarde's own script reveals a handwritten contribution undoubtedly inspired by Ulric van den Bogaerde's own First World War experiences.

It focusses on the part in the film in which Hargreaves questions Hamp about his motives for running – or wandering – away, and the private replies how he had been blown into a deep shell hole where he thought he would drown until he was rescued by two of his comrades who pulled him out with their rifles. In Bogarde's copy of the script is a passage in his own hand: 'I saw it happen to a bloke once before – he just slipped off the duckboard – wasn't pushed, just fell – into the hole, he went bobbing up and down in the mud like an egg boiling in water – with his pack and everything you know. The egg and the water: just as Lally described Ulric's recurrent waking nightmare.' (Lally was the much loved van den Bogaerde family nanny when Dirk was growing up near Alfriston, East Sussex).[12]

As the court martial scenes take place we witness the gruff Australian actor Leo McKern playing the army doctor Captain O'Sullivan declare how the solution to all medical conditions including shell shock is to take a dose of laxatives! One cure suits all. And yet in spite of Captain Hargreaves' eloquent speech defending Hamp which persuades the court to recommend mercy the judgement is overruled. The top brass sitting in judgement on the case deem that an example should be made of men like Hamp who is sentenced to death by firing squad. On the day he faces the execution squad he is not killed outright and Hargreaves, as his only friend, has to finish him off and therefore 'end his own life as well as that of the boy Hamp'.[13]

Coldstream described *King and Country* as a 'devastating indictment of war'. For the cast and crew working on this extraordinary film each day was intense and conditions reflecting those in the trenches were obviously desperately unpleasant. Everyone was always glad to leave Shepperton Studios after a long day among rotting horse carcases, rats and all the gruesome muck of authenticity which in reality had been suffered by the heroes of the 1914–18 conflict.

Once *King and Country*, with its script adaptation by Evan Jones and music by Larry Adler, was in the can there was a struggle to find a distributor owing to its sombre and sobering subject. There were also murmurings about it being anti-establishment but fortunately for the cast and crew there was a key supporter, namely the leading producer Lord John Brabourne – son-in-law of Earl Mountbatten – who helped ensure the film was officially released. On 3 December 1964 and in spite of mixed reviews *King and Country* was shown at a limited number of screenings in cinemas across the UK. When it got to the US, *The New York Times* hailed it 'an impressive achievement,' noting 'As usual, Mr. Losey has drawn the best from his actors,' and concluded that 'Some of its scenes are so strong they shock. Those who can take it will find it a shattering experience.' In October 1965 the *Life* magazine reviewer wrote: 'Losey has the ability to make each frame a matter of conviction and feeling, to make the screen seem darker, like an etching.' However, the public relations chief at Landau Films claimed 'the rats had a negating effect' on audiences. But the judges at the Venice Film Festival of 1964 were impressed enough to award the Volpi Cup for best actor to Tom Courtney for his compelling portrayal of Private Hamp. However, although

Losey believed the award should have been shared with Bogarde, the ever-gracious Courtney admitted he had been shown great kindness by Bogarde. 'Tom, who is an extremely good actor, would be the first to acknowledge he could never have given that performance if Dirk hadn't been that generous,' explained Losey.[14]

After the film was released, Bogarde was invited to give a lecture to an audience at the Philharmonic Hall in Liverpool on Friday, July 14, 1967. He decided to talk about *King and Country* because out of the forty-seven films he'd made so far it was the one he found had satisfied him the most – even though it had been shown to so few people and it had been a commercial disaster. *The Liverpool Echo* reported how Bogarde noted there was a clear majority of girls among his listeners, and he hoped that the screening which was to follow his talk would not be so horrific as to result in aisles full of the fainted. However, no one did pass out. But the newspaper article made it clear his young audience were much moved by what they saw and heard.[15]

Twelve years later my history teacher Mr H had chosen well to highlight to us the great power of the film which successfully reveals the brutality of the military top brass of the time who dismissed those suffering from shell-shock or mental breakdown as cowards deserving execution. Bogarde was described by Mr H as 'an astoundingly good actor'. And who could disagree? Mr H then told us the 'surprise' story he'd promised us at the beginning of the lesson. He was feeling especially pleased with himself, so he said, because he'd only recently been on BBC radio talking about a mysterious real-life experience which can only be described as 'a ghost story'.

He told us he had just returned from a holiday in Devon when he'd heard the radio appeal for 'other-worldly' tales. Enthusiastically he explained:

> I contacted the BBC because while on my holiday I witnessed what I believe to have been a strange uncanny moment when the past and present meet. I was on my own and taking a walk along a country lane in Devon. I was enjoying the peace, the sound of birdsong and the general ambience of the countryside in summer. Suddenly I heard the sound of men marching, boots crunching along the dusty road. Left, right, left right, left, right … It was a noise which grew

louder until finally I looked behind me and could see clearly what looked like a battalion [500–1,000 men] come around the corner some half a mile away.

I stepped onto a grass verge and watched and waited as they marched towards me. Some were whistling, some were singing the old song about Tipperary. When they reached me I noted they were in First World War uniforms. How smart they were, their green tunics looked fresh and crisp, their rifles caught the sun, and I could even smell a whiff of gun oil and boot polish as they went by. I seem to recall one or two of them acknowledged me with a slight nod and for what seemed like several minutes I stood still watching them as they marched and marched down the long road until they disappeared around a right-hand bend at the end of the road in the distance.

Then there was silence and I started my walk again. The sky was still the same cobalt blue, the birds were still twittering, rabbits were rustling about in the hedge. Even the dust thrown up from the weight of the men's boots was still drifting about in the air. I then wondered if there was some sort of military tattoo or a festival taking place in the vicinity. These sort of events were popular in the 1970s so I told myself to ask around when I got back to the village. It did occur to me I should have made a note of the soldiers' cap badges as I had no idea what regiment they belonged to. Any information would have helped. I wanted to see them again as they'd made such an impressive sight.

Later that day when I was having a pint of beer in the village pub I asked the regulars about any festivals in the area involving troops of the First World War. I was met with blank stares. Nobody knew anything about that. So I bought a copy of the local newspaper and yet there was nothing in it advertising a military festival. For several days I tried and tried to discover just where those soldiers were going and who they were but came up with nothing. One chap involved in such events said there would never be enough uniforms left from the First World War to outfit a replica battalion. But I know what I saw and I can't change my memory.

Mr H then asked his class full of intrigued teenage girls if they had any ideas where the soldiers came from?

'Maybe you imagined it?' replied one. 'Or fell asleep and dreamed about some book you'd read!' suggested another girl. I'd listened to his story but was still thinking about the photograph of Bogarde. 'No,' he said softly retaining the magic of the moment. 'I think I just happened to have been stood, albeit briefly, at a place where time overlapped and maybe, just maybe that very moment had proved to be some kind of anniversary of a day the youth of Devon marched off to war … ' And then he gathered up a folder from his desk, looked up at the clock atop the blackboard and said it was now break time. He made for the door and left us all thinking about his 'other-worldly' experience.

Today and so many, many years later I can easily recall the sight of him striding down the corridor towards the staff room where his colleagues smoked and grumbled and slurped tea from chipped green china teacups. He'd done a good job, educated us so brilliantly about the First World War and I began writing 'Dirk Forever' on my workbooks whenever I could. As an adult it seems to me some things never change!

While researching this section of this book I spotted a poster of *King and Country* published in a 1964 copy of *Newsweek* magazine – this was the year the film opened in cinemas. The image was far more startling than my schoolgirl introduction to Sir Dirk Bogarde. There was a bold headline taken from a review in the *New York Herald Tribune* screaming 'A SHOCKER!' and a harrowing photograph of a hand belonging to Bogarde as Captain Hargreaves holding a gun to the mouth of Private Hamp (Tom Courtney). 'Go ahead … kill him … you're the only friend he has!' is written in bold beside it.

*   *   *

On a bitingly cold day in London in 1947 Bogarde was thinking to himself: 'Hang on! This isn't me! I've just finished a war and I've got seven medals. So I walked out … in the snow with holes in my shoes … on the idea of going to Hollywood. I wasn't signing THAT contract!'

And who could blame the 26-year-old Queen's Royal Regiment Captain Derek 'Pip' Jules Gaspard Ulric Niven van den Bogaerde for refusing to be turned into a puppet by American screen bosses. Inwardly he seemed even more appalled at the Studio representative's claim they 'had been building stars since Noah left the ark!' 'That may well be', he thought but he wasn't going to sell out on his talent even though his meagre life savings were rattling around in an Oxo tin.[16]

His medals were a source of great pride to him. He had a 1939–45 Star, a Burma Star, France and Germany Star, 1939–45 Defence Medal, a War Medal for full time military service, a General Service Medal for recognition in British Army and RAF operations, and a SE Asia 1945–46 Medal. This list was confirmed by Dr Barbara Siek (The Dirk Bogarde Estate) after lengthy research carried out by Micky Ojeda. What the medals prove was how Bogarde was a man of valour and courage. During his life he had seen the atrocities of war close up and he knew the importance of duty and standards. Any sudden realisation he'd have to push to one side his formative years in the military which aligned to his own artistic sensibilities of self-sacrifice, courage and sincerity, was all too alien to him especially so soon after the war. His medals were awarded for genuine battle experiences which he would eventually successfully re-craft into the characters he played in a dramatic list of war films and of course his memoirs and novels.

During his storming career his films in the war genre include: *Appointment in London* (1953), *They Who Dare* (1954), *The Sea Shall Not Have Them* (1954), *Ill Met by Moonlight* (1957), *The Wind Cannot Read* (1958), *Libel* (1959) – not strictly a military film but there are scenes of Bogarde in the Army – *The Password is Courage* (1962), *The High Bright Sun* (1964), *King and Country* (1964), *Little Moon of Alban* (1964) in which he appeared as a recovering soldier but not on active duty, and of course as Lieutenant General 'Boy' Browning in the epic *A Bridge Too Far* (1977).

His six novels and eight volumes of memoirs are full of critical observation and insightful comment. Some of his fiction contains characters based on his wartime experiences and his autobiographical accounts include important reportage of military action. Such authentic evidence of his own battle scars meant then he was in no mood in 1947 to entertain the repressive psychological demands inflicted upon actors in return for the fickle sense of 'star' status. He soon discovered expectations in Hollywood at that time included not only a ridiculously punishing work schedule to please greedy studio bosses but a monopoly over his life in exchange for having his face on the big screen. At a young age he had absorbed the war-survivor mentality and realised the worlds of film and theatre, although he took them seriously as a career, were NOT matters of life and death.

When he did finally take up the challenge of working in the US in 1959 he was the one with at least some of the power to agree a specific salary and any adjoining benefits. Much of the finance he earned from any US venture including *Song Without End* (the story of Franz Liszt) for Columbia Pictures enabled him to take up the opportunity to star in what were then professionally risky films including *Victim* (1961), the first English-language film to use the word 'homosexual', and *The Servant* (1963) with the notable director Joe Losey.

But back in the mid- to late 1940s and early 1950s and while some of his acting contemporaries like James Mason had joined Hollywood's dictatorial star system, the young former army officer known in pre-war theatrical circles as the actor 'Derek Bogaerde' immediately decided he wasn't going to be told which blonde starlet he should marry and when he could get divorced! Two years after the end of the war in Europe he rebelled too against any Hollywood-style plan to transform his 'scrawny chicken figure' into that of a 'beefcake' and then to have his name changed to Ricardo in order that he ride the cloud of superficiality surrounding the hills of Los Angeles. Forget it. Arguably it all sounded a little too familiar to the attitudes of Hitler and his delusions of creating a superior race. 'And the boys who became "beefcake" actors? Where are they now?' asked the actor who became international film legend Sir Dirk Bogarde. In a televised BBC interview in 1961 he admitted Britain's own Rank Studios had some thoughts about him being 'Billy Biceps' and even sent him weights to 'build up his muscles'. This equipment, confessed Dirk, sat in the same place for six years. 'I wore two jumpers to build me up!' he quipped.[17]

* * *

Derek Jules Gaspard Niven van den Bogaerde was born on 28 March 1921 in West Hampstead, London. His mother Margaret, a lively Scot, was an actress. His father Ulric, who had Belgian ancestry, was a graphic artist and photographer. By the end of 1918 Ulric had found himself in Italy after the Battle of Caporetto with his sketchpad as ever by his side. By January the following year he was back home in Britain and had replaced his army uniform with a dark suit and tie to join Lord Northcliffe's team as Art Editor of *The Times* in London.

His eldest son Derek, as with so many children born after the First World War, arrived with recent family memories of soldiering and warfare very much in their DNA. Derek grew up with a sister Elizabeth and a younger brother Gareth in the idylls of the Alfriston countryside in East Sussex and were cared for by a nanny called Lally. His early life full of childhood adventures was encapsulated in sketches and watercolours, all heartening memories which he happily recorded in later life in the first of his memoirs, *A Postillion Struck By Lighting*.

But the joys of those childhood years were to change rapidly when the teenage Derek was sent against his wishes to Glasgow to stay with his mother's relations. Here in a tough city and an urban street so alien to him he was made to understand at school that life was 'not all cushions and barley sugar'. He hated every minute of his time there and wrote extensive letters to his sister Elizabeth about his desperate unhappiness.[18]

A few years later and with any 'sharp edges' supposedly rounded off by a Glaswegian world of hard knocks he returned, to his eternal gratitude, home to rural Sussex. At first he attended University College School and then was accepted into the hallowed classrooms of the School of Art, Chelsea Polytechnic, London where his teachers included the sculptor Sir Henry Moore. Derek was a fine artist. During his time in military service during the Second World War he sketched many scenes including people sleeping in the underground during bombing raids, fashion and other subjects of note. His artwork from the Second World War was exhibited in London and his much praised poetry of the time appeared in the *Times Literary Supplement*. Some of his beautiful drawings were published years later in his volumes of memoirs

In 1938, however, Derek exhibited his stubborn streak and broke the news to his father that he wouldn't be following in his footsteps to join the art department of *The Times*. Instead the handsome young man with the dark soulful eyes was determined to be a drama student. Still known then as 'Derek' he had already had some experience as a scenic designer and commercial artist and had enthusiastically joined in performance events organised by theatrical students at art school.

His enthusiasm for acting began to flourish thanks to Lionel and Winifred Cox who were theatrical acquaintances of his mother Margaret.

The Coxes put on a series of plays and pantomimes in Newick, near Milnthorpe in Cumbria, and it was in these little productions he made his first appearances. His artwork for the Newick Amateur Dramatic Society (NADS) poster was dynamic and declared *Journey's End* by R.C. Sherriff about the First World War, as 'a play the rising generation must see'. (Laurence Olivier had been the first to play the character of 18-year-old soldier James Raleigh in *Journey's End* in 1928.) Derek van den Bogaerde's performance as Raleigh was saluted by the local newspaper as having the right amount of shyness and deference.[19] He also assisted a no-nonsense elderly woman by the name of Elissa Thorborn who had her own theatre in Uckfield, Sussex. Miss Thorborn gave him his first wages for appearing on stage in a play called *Glorious Morning*. Her young protégé earned 5 shillings for each performance.

So exactly what sort of world was the aspiring actor expecting to conquer in the late 1930s? At this time the British theatre was flourishing and scores of repertory companies (groups of actors and backstage staff and management often resident at one venue) were presenting plays by Shakespeare, Marlowe, Henrik Ibsen, Anton Chekhov, George Bernard Shaw, Noel Coward, J.B. Priestley and Oscar Wilde. A whole programme of comedies, tragedies and musicals were on offer to local communities fortunate enough to have a theatre on their doorstep. Performers including Sybil Thorndike and Gertrude Lawrence continued to wow the audiences both at home and abroad. In 1936 Lawrence received ovations and resounding applause for her performance in Noel Coward's hit play, *Tonight at 8.30*. Many repertory venues were remembered fondly by actors who made it to the London theatres and the big screen.

Working in the provinces provided young performers with a good experience of dramatic technique, vocal experience, stage awareness and honed the qualities which fed into the audience expectation of good character representation. Repertory companies fostered a wealth of talent in Britain and taught their cast members the true craft of acting. They also provided a training ground for many of the professional set and lighting designers and stage managers. Within such communities of artistes professional productions could flourish.

Only recently Bogarde's friend, the Oscar-winning film star and former MP Glenda Jackson, took up the complaints from television audiences about young actors who mumble their lines. Jackson, who worked in repertory in the 1950s for six years after training at the Royal Academy of Dramatic Art, said the demise of rep or stock companies had led to a modern crop of performers who didn't have the training to adjust their voices to the requirements of television performance.[20] Bogarde, a former repertory actor who had received the best of stage training from notable names of the 1930s and late 1940s, had appeared with Jackson in *The Patricia Neal Story* in 1981. He described her performance in the film as 'sheer magic'.

The wonders of rep were also embraced by other award-winning names we know today including Dames Judi Dench, Maggie Smith and Eileen Atkins, and Sirs John Gielgud, Ralph Richardson and Ian McKellen. Also Jeremy Brett, Peter O'Toole, Arthur Lowe and many more all learned their craft from the hurly-burly demands of the live stage.

The long apprenticeship to qualify to be a great actor was a serious business. Thanks to repertory companies many actors became just as skilled as doctors, journalists, scientists, teachers and lawyers and yet they stood out on their own as magical in their own right. The stage was the ultimate foreground to present a cultural and social bond between communities. Its raw power to communicate knew no bounds.

By the time young Derek van den Bogaerde had arrived on the dramatic scene the great Russian theatre practitioner Konstantin Stanislavski (1863–1938) had written his famous book *An Actor Prepares* (1937). For many would-be performers this became a bible as Stanislavski explained his 'system' of performance (now known as 'method acting') which went on to greatly influence European and American theatre with his ideas of naturalism and realistic techniques. As a co-founder of the Moscow Art Theatre the Russian actor and director wrote enthusiastically about how the actor should inhabit authentic emotions while on stage and use feelings developed in their own lives to add depth to a character in order for realism to take place on stage. Motivations and reasons behind a character's behaviour were also the order of the day and much of Stanislavski's 'system' was absorbed by Hollywood acting tutors including the famous Lee Strasberg.

Years later Bogarde revealed he never believed in method acting and this didn't change over the years. In his memoir *Snakes and Ladders* he discusses director George Cukor during the filming of *Justine*. 'There were some incredibly awful bits of original casting which Cukor was powerless to change, and half his vibrant energies were spent in bullying, cajoling, pleading and encouraging performances of one kind and another out of these wooden, self-indulgent method actors.' He also admitted though to the terror he always felt about stepping out on stage before a live audience.

> The noise of that curtain going up and the hush of the audience is a sort of prelude to 'you're on' and your heart races and the adrenalin flows and that's it you're there to entertain for two hours or so and it is one of the most extraordinary experiences you can have providing you don't see the audiences' faces – that was death if you caught a face. Acting on stage was much more perilous than anything I went through during the war and I had six years of that! Acting is terrifying and it never gets better. At the risk of sounding pretentious without that fear you cannot perform and you do not expose your soul.[21]

When it came to post-war theatre performances Dirk Bogarde, a gallant young veteran of the 1939–45 conflict, braved the crowds at the Q Theatre in London to star as a blind RAF pilot in a play called *Sleep On My Shoulder* by Michael Clayton Hutton. It was one of three war-themed stage plays he was cast in. The others were *The Shaughraun* by Dion Boucicault and *Foxhole in the Parlor* by Elsa Shelley. He said: 'I hated the star thing though. It stopped me doing theatre. I lost my nerve in the theatre because of the sweet fans who came to see me. They'd shout "we love you Dirk" and throw meat pies at us on stage. Of course it ruined the play and what we were trying to do anyway. I hated not being in control of myself.'[22]

In interviews about his acting technique Bogarde described how the intensity of getting to know and then act a realistic representation of a character is an exhausting experience. It is, he admitted, upsetting too when the play or film is over. He was especially sad when the making of the epic 1971 film *Death in Venice* was complete. In this beautifully shot and internalised film set to the emotionally loaded music of Gustav Mahler's Third and Fifth Symphonies we see the mature Bogarde as the silent, tortured, ascetic and disciplined character of Gustav von Aschenbach. For eight long months the robust Italian director Luchino Visconti had demanded the best of Bogarde in order to achieve a performance which not only revealed an actor arguably at the peak of his powers but one which was to confirm his status as a true icon of European cinema. Bogarde said later in a television interview: '*Death in Venice* nearly did for me. The intensity was so great.'

So who taught him to act before the camera? Did he find it so very different from the stage? Years after he had retreated from regular film appearances in order to concentrate on his writing he revealed more secrets about his creative life. He said he was taught more about film acting and technique by the notable camera operator Bob Thomson than any director. Thomson, a red-haired Scot, had shown great bravery during the Second World War as a cameraman in the Royal Navy. He spent much of his war hanging over the side of a creaking Fairey Swordfish biplane with his trusty camera above enemy territory to film German positions. A few years after the war and tremendously lucky to have survived such a precarious act of duty, he worked with Bogarde on one of the *Doctor* comedy films and also in *A Tale of Two Cities* (1958) and *Victim* (1961).

When interviewed for a BBC *Omnibus* programme in 1983 a razor-sharp Bogarde revealed how Thomson had asked him if he knew what a 75 was or how the film went through the gate? Thomson then told him where the boom went and where the lights were, and about the 'dinky inkie' which is a brand of 100-watt incandescent spotlight. Bogarde explained: 'I learned how my left side was the best side of my face. In fact it was Bob (Thomson) who told me everything I needed to know about the making of a film – my technicians, my mates, not my directors because they didn't know and I never met an English director that did.' He learned too from Thomson to inform film technicians they would need to be aware of 'Dirk's Bar', a special look in his eyes that left the onlooker beguiled by Bogarde's characterisations.

But long, long before he worked with Thomson the young actor known as 'Derek Bogaerde' still had ambitions for the stage. It was through *The Times* newspaper that his father Ulric managed to talk to London theatre managers about his son's ambitions and by the early autumn of 1939 Derek nervously walked along the busy Waterloo Road towards the Old Vic to audition for the fee-paying drama school whose adjoining company was directed by the famous actor Tyrone Guthrie.

It was a big step for the young man who had with the help of his mentors meticulously prepared his Shakespearean speeches ready to impress his examiners. He need not have worried as his audition was a success and he won his place with credit, but the acting school at the Old Vic never got to open its doors that year. It was 1939 and on 3 September the Second World War erupted. Derek's hopes of working for the great director Tyrone Guthrie were cast aside.

Soon afterwards with the passion to become an actor still dominating each waking hour Derek, somewhat disappointed, joined a club of theatricals in Cambridge. Here he met the multi-talented Peter Ustinov (who went on to serve during the war as batman to the famous actor Lieutenant David Niven in the British Army). The avuncular Ustinov made a big impression on Derek and advised the young actor (before the threat of war clouded all stage ambitions) that 'total dedication' was required for a successful life in the theatre.[23]

When the film cameras came calling in 1939 for Derek Bogaerde he appeared as an extra in *Come on George!* – a production starring George Formby who was to later help the war effort by joining ENSA and entertaining the troops with his ukulele and cheerful songs. Derek got the part because his mother Margaret was an acquaintance of the director's family. On the set of *Come on George!* he met Basil Dearden and Ronald Neame – two members of the crew who would later direct a few of his greatest and most challenging character portrayals as an actor. Films like the 1961 pioneering classic *Victim* (Dearden) allowed a by-then seasoned actor like Bogarde to reveal any personal knowledge of alienation he may have felt himself as a homosexual. In *Victim* he plays a married barrister called Melville Farr who was being blackmailed for being photographed with a rent boy known as 'Boy Barrett'. In the 1950s any whiff of such a scandal would have destroyed the careers of all sorts of professionals including actors, judges, lawyers, teachers and journalists. The film reveals them one by one paying the blackmailers until Farr exposes them, thus destroying his own life in doing so. It's a story of truth and the pains some go through to reveal it. The character of Farr realises prison comes in many forms but the truth has the power to release a person from the bars around the soul. It's all that matters. The decision to take on such a controversial role at the time showed just how committed Bogarde was to his work as a serious artist. His own secret personal life may have inspired him to use the medium of film to support the homosexual community. Homosexuality was only partly decriminalised in 1967. (In 2017 Sarah Wooley's play *Victim* was broadcast on BBC Radio 3 as part of the Gay

Britannia season marking the fiftieth anniversary of the 1967 Sexual Offences Act. The drama depicted how Dirk took the gamble of his career and changed public attitudes to homosexuality. The play reveals how those involved in the making of the film exuded a brilliant mixture of bravery and pragmatism in getting this ground-breaking enterprise off the ground. It must be praised for providing a fascinating glimpse of Britain at a tipping point of social change.) The director Ronald Neame went on to work with Bogarde in 1963 in *I Could Go On Singing* starring Judy Garland whose sensitive and emotional performances were and still are worshipped by millions today.

But back in 1939 and Derek (Bogarde) was in need of work. He was helped by his father's contacts and it was Jack De Leon at the Q Theatre who offered him work, mostly as a set designer. Situated near Kew Bridge the venue had hosted the early talents of many who went on to forge lasting careers on the big screen including Vivien Leigh, James Mason, Bernard Miles (later Lord Miles) Trevor Howard and Anthony Quayle.[24]

Derek got his break in the West End not working with his paintbrush but by playing a minor character in J.B. Priestley's play *When We Are Married*. Then came another walk-on role in another Priestley drama, *Cornelius*. His stage name became 'Derek Bogaerde' and at the Richmond Theatre he worked with the gifted Bernard Miles and began to network to find out which theatres and companies could offer him a job in rep. He appeared on stage at The Playhouse, Amersham, Buckinghamshire, in a production of Ibsen's *The Master Builder* and by the spring of 1940 he had widened his network of contacts who included another young actor by the name of Paul Scofield who was later honoured with a CH and CBE. (When Scofield went to enlist for the army during the Second World War he was horrified to be turned away because he had crossed toes therefore deeming him unfit for military service. He lamented: 'I was unable to wear boots. I was deeply ashamed.' But there was an important role for Scofield with ENSA which was presenting classical theatre to the troops in many quality and morale boosting productions.)[25]

Still at the Amersham Playhouse and attracting a regular crowd of female fans, Derek went on to appear in Somerset Maugham's *The Painted Veil* as the character of Charles Townsend. It was in this play he appeared alongside 21-year-old actress Annie Deans. According to his memoir he proposed marriage to Annie on a warm summer's day in 1940 just as the

British Expeditionary Force was being evacuated from the beaches of Dunkirk.

In later life he wrote:

> Did I lose my cool and control simply because of war hysteria? It is impossible, all these years later, to remember. Perhaps, and it is quite possible I was simply in love with her, and with the army looming at my side, so to speak, military service was beyond avoidance. (I had tried to be a conscientious objector, at her suggestion, but found that the questions which were asked at a tribunal at High Wycombe were so idiotic that I simply had to abandon her idea). With the beckoning terror before me, I suppose that I decided, as so many did, to marry before I was thrust into oblivion![26]

The marriage did not take place although he appeared in several productions with Annie in 1940. In the outside world and far from the greasepaint and glitter of the Amersham Playhouse an actual theatre of war was in full horrific flow. From 31 May to 31 October 1940 the Battle of Britain was raging across the skies of Kent and the south-east of England. Each hour and each day young aircrews were in battle, and at times sacrificing their lives for the sake of liberty. The armed forces of the British Empire and Commonwealth were massing. The only thing that mattered now was to defeat the Nazi hoards – at any cost.

Many actors with a passion to boost the morale of Britain's armed forces had already joined Basil Dean and Leslie Henson's Entertainments National Service Association (ENSA). Performers including Margaret Rutherford, Vivien Leigh, Anna Neagle, Gertrude Lawrence, Dora Bryan, and Terry-Thomas were among them. Later on in the war popular stars including Laurence Olivier and Ralph Richardson were made honorary lieutenants in ENSA having successfully presented morale-boosting productions of Shakespeare to the troops.

By January 1941 Derek was stepping out on stage in revue with Peter Ustinov at The Wyndham's Theatre in the West End, but only matinees were being performed because of the bombing raids which tended to occur in the evening. Both young actors were also nervously awaiting their call-up papers to join the armed forces. They knew their lives were about to change and change very quickly. One day as smoke from a Luftwaffe bombing raid billowed out across London and St Paul's Cathedral, Derek and his pal Ustinov got out their tin hats and tried to get through the rehearsal of a revue which government propaganda chiefs had declared a definite 'morale booster'.[27]

In the first volume of his memoirs, *A Postilion Struck By Lightning*, Bogarde described how despite his growing popularity on the stage and his wages reaching £5 a week he still felt a 'strange guilt' about not wearing a uniform. Soon enough he received a letter informing him to go to Brighton for an army medical and then while in London he joined a friend and enlisted at Charing Cross. Some of his companions in the theatre world tried to protect him. They encouraged him to work in particular productions which would guarantee him a deferment. But any idea of him becoming a 'conchie' and digging ditches, hauling logs in the frozen depths of Scotland and awaiting sinister envelopes full of white feathers didn't appeal and so he decided to sit it out and wait for notification to report for training.

In the meantime he discovered the ENSA troop based at Drury Lane, London, was in need of an actor to join the cast of Arnold Ridley's famous play *The Ghost Train*. He was informed the production would tour for six months and if he was deferred from active service because of his role in it then maybe the war would have finished by the time he had to join the Army.

Still feeling stuck between two worlds as he awaited instructions from the military he auditioned and got the role in the production. It's likely the actor knew how the author and director (Ridley) of the play was already a hero of both world wars, and the majority of the audiences were going to be made up of servicemen and women. (Ridley of course went on to find great fame as Private Godfrey in the 1970s hit comedy show, *Dad's Army*.) Whilst he got to play the juvenile in *The Ghost Train* Bogarde recalled how it wasn't the happiest of times performing in 'cold, dreary barns of theatres', and enduring 'long bus journeys in rain and fog, miserable hostels and endless stations'.

I felt even guiltier playing to uniformed troops than I had felt walking the streets of London, and by the time we got to Amesbury I welcomed a telephone call from my father, to say that I was requested to report for Military Service at Catterick Camp, Yorkshire. I wanted no further deferments. When the final curtain came down for me, in my performance in *The Ghost Train* I felt a surge of joy. Someone had made a decision for me; I'd just do as I was told from now on … until it was over.[28]

On 8 May 1941 a theatrical friend named Vida Hope (Vida, incidentally went on to appear as a WAAF officer in the 1952 war film hit *Angels One Five*) accompanied him to King's Cross Station where a train was waiting to take him and many other nervous young recruits to Catterick Camp, south of Richmond, North Yorkshire. There they would be trained in and around the austere grim barracks on a windy 2,400-acre site now known as the largest British Army garrison in the world.

The history of Catterick Garrison goes back to 1908. Its inception was instigated by Lieutenant General Robert Baden-Powell, the creator of the Scouting movement. The actual camp (originally known as Richmond Camp) was built at the outbreak of the First World War in 1914 and was made ready to house 40,000 men in 2,000 huts. Its name changed to Catterick Camp the following year.

It's mind-blowing to think of the amount of men who have passed through its gates over the decades. During the Second World War a young actor and soldier named Daniel Thorndike, the nephew of theatrical legends Dame Sybil Thorndike and Lewis Casson, was working in the administration office. No doubt he checked recruits in and out of the camp and was involved in other necessary duties to ensure smooth management of such a large operation. Thorndike had been declared unfit for front-line duty following a collision with a motorcycle in which he was seriously injured. However, according to The Wartime Memories Project website, he played his role in keeping up the morale of wartime audiences by performing excerpts from Shakespeare at the Georgian Theatre Royal in Richmond. Decades later many remember him as Lord Whiteadder in the hit satirical television show *Blackadder*.

Back in 1941 Derek van den Bogaerde had no option but to put his theatrical dreams on hold as like so many other young passengers on the train with him that day he was about to be introduced to Catterick Camp's rigorous military training methods of physical and mental discipline. Life was about to become deadly serious.

The day the young actor went to war was recorded in his diary:

Train Crowded – Soldiers, old women. Conscripts like self. Journey awful – gaze at receding Country – wonder if I'll die, and never see London again, hope not. Awful old Bitch in the Compartment says she'll vomit if I smoke – have to stand in the Corridor – feel like going back to School.

Arrive at Richmond Yorks at 6.45pm. Bundled into Army Lorry with 22 others. Arrive at Camp – bleak, barren and horrible – have awful supper – Sausages. Get Shown to bunk-room – sleep on floor on Straw Biscuits – 4 blankets – lights out at 10.30. 25 of us here, all homesick dead tired – feel life has ceased for ever – weep four bitter tears under my blankets. Feel much better when find my neighbours doing same – fall into a troubled sleep, full of train journeys – Soldiers – Far East all mixed up with pathetic glimpses of home ...[29]

The following day Derek, along with a crowd of shivering bewildered young men, was given a service number. He was assigned, most bizarrely he thought, to the Royal Signal Corps. His number was 2371461 – a fact which he used when describing a fictional military character in his first novel, *A Gentle Occupation* (1980), a story inspired by his own wartime experiences in South East Asia in 1945.

Now known only by a number he was also confused by the army's initial decision to turn him into a Signaller especially as he admitted he had 'the co-ordination of a bursting dam'. And while he was exceedingly proficient at bringing boots to a high shine, sewing on badges and focussing on the aesthetics of army life, his accomplishments with Morse Code proved sadly dismal.[30]

In Coldstream's authorised biography of Bogarde, we learn how he volunteered to help in the cookhouse in a bid to keep his head down and get through each day possibly in the hope no one would really notice his ineptitude at operating anything technical or indeed mechanical. He wasn't alone in experiencing a feeling of displacement as despite the smiles and laughter of the men around him most of them were crying inside. Only the unity of comradeship, the strict regular kit inspections, drill training and other rigours of military training which became so embedded in the fabric of their lives kept them sane. Such activities, revealed Coldstream, were to prove useful and effective time-killers.

All life was there at Catterick, death too as Derek and his comrades, some still in their late teens, discovered when they saw one unhappy acquaintance known as 'Palmers Green' hanging dead from a lavatory ceiling. Derek was one of the pallbearers at the funeral – an event which began well but ended in chaos after one of the young soldiers tripped and got entangled in a flag and they dropped the coffin. Later on the pallbearers were reprimanded by a tetchy red-faced Regimental Sergeant Major (RSM) who told them they were a 'disgrace' to the regiment.[31]

In between his general duties as a rookie soldier at Catterick Derek applied to join Officer Cadet Training. He opted to sign up with the Royal Engineers as he hoped his previous experience in stage design and technical art might offer him a wartime experience more fitting to his skills. Soon enough he was posted to the 1st Officers Training Battalion where he was promoted to lance-corporal and promptly joined the OTB dramatic society. After more than a year with the Signals a decision was made to send him not to the Royal Engineers as he'd wished, but the Royal Artillery. It must have seemed as if he was following, albeit briefly, in his father Ulric's regimental footsteps – without the horses though.

He said:

Although everyone was delighted the war had made me into a man, implying that I had returned from ten months in the trenches and the Battle of the Somme. Everything, so I began to believe, was applied to their war of twenty-two years before.

I was quite unable to tell them, nor did they wish to hear if I tried, that all I had seen of war was the inside of Catterick Camp and a few acres of the Yorkshire Moors.[32]

He then recalled how he was quickly posted away from Catterick and his memories of officer training at Wrotham in Kent reveal a young man determined to be the absolute best. It was tough and often physically hard going being put through the rigours of soldiering day after day. The army was looking for not only the super-fit but the mentally astute too – men who could lead and take command.

One day on manoeuvres in woodland Derek discovered he'd 'killed a man' with a dummy bullet of red paint – he was horrified. It began to dawn on him war was going to be all about killing and he began to question, even philosophise his way around surviving it and all the brutalities which lay ahead.

So far so good until Major C.E. Lumb criticised him for being too young to dish out orders. Major Lumb's opinion on Derek's technical training was grim and claimed the officer cadet had 'no mechanical aptitude and himself feels unable to cope with technical training'. Lumb did however acknowledge an enthusiastic approach to the military and Officer Cadet van den Bogaerde was intelligent and of the type who would make a useful officer if trained for an army corps of less technical difficulty than RA (AA) – Infantry, Parachutists or Airborne Division are suggested.[33] So a future with the Royal Artillery wasn't looking too bright. For two months he found himself posted to the 148 Independent Brigade Group where he could further enhance his aircraft recognition skills. Derek then received orders to report to 161 OCTU at Mons Barracks in Aldershot.

Lieutenant Colonel P. L. Bowers graded him with a 'C' and wrote in a report: 'Has it in him to be a good officer if he will take himself in hand and realise his responsibilities. Will need firm handling at first if he is to make proper use of his natural advantages. Could have been graded higher if he had extended himself more.'[34] The road to becoming an officer had not proved too easy for the artistic Derek van den Bogaerde. There's little doubt the military top brass he'd encountered during his training had begun to wonder in earnest just what role might suit him best.

On 1 April 1943 he was proud to line up with his pals from D Company at Sandhurst Military Training College in Camberley, Surrey to pass out as a fully qualified officer. He had a new rank of Lieutenant and was officer number 269237 and the proud wearer of a uniform and cap badge representing the Queen's Royal Regiment (West Surrey). Finally his military career was moving forward although it wasn't long before he found he was considered something of a spare part in military life and became known as a 'draft of one'.[35]

His life as an officer began in earnest with the 7th Battalion of the Somerset Light Infantry in Redruth, Cornwall. From here it was a posting to 214 Independent Infantry Brigade where he became a liaison officer and learned to ride a motorcycle to fulfil his duties. In Cornwall Lieutenant van den Bogarde found his new commanding officer, Brigadier Hubert Essame MC, more easy-going and definitely more approachable. Brigadier Essame was a short, sandy-haired man who was a veteran of the Somme. He believed his men should cultivate their minds with good conversation and quizzes to exercise their brains. Any top up to their military training could be dealt with by various educational courses available at the time. (And while in later life as a novelist Bogarde claimed his characters were fictitious there are certainly elements of the unconventional Essame which ring true to the descriptions of his CO in his factual memoirs. The brigadier in his novel set in the war-torn Far East of 1946, *A Gentle Occupation*, shares similar attributes with Essame. The same can be said for General Douglas Hawthorn to whom Bogarde acted as ADC in Indonesia in 1946).

But life wasn't all gin slings and games in the Officers' Mess. Brigade records of 1943 show the young Lieutenant and his comrades were transported to Inveraray, Argyllshire in Scotland as part of a top secret plan involving an Allied invasion of Portugal's Azores Islands. Working with the Royal Navy and Marines the brigade took part in a multitude of dangerous exercises with live ammunition and fighter aircraft. Eight men were reported to have been killed during the mock invasion along parts of the Scottish coastline.

But just as the men had fine-tuned their battle skills for the real assault (Operation Alacrity) they discovered the mission had been called off because the Portuguese dictator Salazar had agreed that some ports and airfields could be used by the Allied forces. By 1943 the growth of military strength among the American forces during the North African campaign had led the Germans to defer any plan to occupy the Azores. The Allies knew the islands would provide essential bases for aircraft monitoring German U-boat activity.

Meantime Derek was promoted to full Lieutenant and by then was known as 'Pip' to his close friends including a heroic Royal Navy commander called John (Tony) Francis Jones. 'Pip' was, explained Bogarde, a reference to the day a signaller irritated by his lack of progress with Morse Code shouted at him 'You bloody give me the pip!'[36]

By the end of 1943 the lieutenant's military life was quiet and straightforward. There was even time to write poetry and feel confident about his days. Also he had successfully returned from Smedley's Hydro at Matlock in Derbyshire after taking a special course from which he had emerged as official Brigade Intelligence Officer. In December of that year he was examining 'Enemy Documents' and by February 1944 he undertook more training to become an interpreter of aerial photographs. Ironically the job was to prove not unlike that carried out by his father Ulric who was working with images as Art Editor of *The Times*.[37]

Brigadier Essame, somewhat proud of his protégé's progress under his command was furious to hear about Derek's new posting to join Second Army Headquarters in London as an Aerial Photographic Interpreter. Bogarde explained in his memoir *Snakes and Ladders* how his future was now out of Brigadier Essame's hands as the order had come direct from General Bernard Montgomery himself.

*   *   *

On a day in early 1944 Lieutenant Derek van den Bogaerde arrived at the door of a rambling mock-Tudor style stately home ready to play his role in the dark and complex world of secret intelligence. Being posted to RAF Medmenham, which sat close to the River Thames bordering Marlow and Henley, meant he could now make a serious start to his military career which had until then been difficult for him to define beyond answering the compulsory call of military duty.

It was only when his superior officers recognised his keen intellect, remarkable attention to detail and brilliant observational skills that he was classified as a 'draft of one' and trusted to fulfil his potential, whatever that might truly be, for the good of the war effort. His father had always advised him to 'observe, notice, compare and keep silent'. It's arguable his son, the epitome of stylish serenity and personal camouflage, was guided by such words for much of his life.

Before the war the rambling property where the 23-year-old lieutenant would find himself was known as Danesfield House. It had belonged to an ostentatious groceries millionaire who had a hand in its lugubrious design. Along the road from the property (also known as 'The Wedding Cake' because of the abundant shape of the building) sat the ruins of a spooky eighteenth-century abbey and many dark stories about ancient witchcraft and mad monks were embedded into local folklore. It seemed the Central Interpretation Unit (CIU) had moved to a place with a colourful history tinted with a little black magic too. While on the outside the house was somewhat architecturally gauche, on the inside its large windows in each room provided valuable light for its new residents and their war work which demanded the ultimate in precision and magnification techniques.

Since late 1939 the work of the Photographic Interpretation Unit (PIU) had been carried out from a building in west London, but as the importance of the work increased along with staff numbers the RAF made the move to Medmenham. Days later PIU became known as the CIU and closer ties were established with RAF Bomber Command. The records of raids over Germany were logged and analysed by the CIU. By 1941 the Nissan huts in its grounds had been turned into something of a friendly village accommodating an assortment of military intelligence personnel.

At RAF Medmenham the Lieutenant discovered how the results of magnified camera work proved to be key in directing bomber aircrews to enemy targets in Germany. Indeed his new occupation was described by the founder of the Allied CIU, Constance Babington Smith, MBE, Legion of Merit, FRSL (1912–2000), as 'a vital and unique style of photographic reconnaissance which provided an accuracy which had never before been envisaged'. This remarkable woman, a journalist and writer, also let it be known to the military top brass how the war's images taken from high in the sky provided vital and detailed information which could be extracted and understood only by those who could interpret a secret language. She certainly had an eye for detail as she had worked as a milliner before the war and knew all about the importance of being exact and precise. One of her most popular creations was a fez-style hat which had a small model aircraft on top pointing skyward. A photograph of the attractive fashionista Babington Smith wearing her latest fashion headgear was taken at an aerodrome garden party at Hammondsworth, Middlesex on 8 May 1938. By this time she had also written articles for *Vogue* and *Aeroplane* magazines.

By the spring of 1941 now Flight Officer Babington Smith (known to many as 'Babs') of the Womens' Auxiliary Air Force (WAAF) found herself at RAF Medmenham with Winston Churchill's theatrical daughter Sarah Oliver and the actress Pauline Growse. Her brother Bernard brought his sharp mathematical skills to the top-secret base and his department focussed on aerial photographs taken at night. Also on the staff was a man called Bertram Rota who in 1923 had established his London bookshop, specialising in first editions and rare manuscripts, as one of the best in the world. His meticulous cataloguing skills proved to be of great use to Babington Smith who asked him to put together important briefing files of aerial images before each bombing mission.

In charge of Technical Control was Douglas Kendall – a softly-spoken man who was the go-between who was the go-between each committee of the armed forces involved in an operation. Dropping bombs on the right target needed to be cohesively co-ordinated between a range of military operators including the Royal Navy, the Royal Air Force and British spies on the ground in enemy territory.[38]

In 1941 Babington Smith appeared before the cameras in the propaganda documentary *Target for Tonight* which focusses on the crew of a Wellington bomber during a mission over Nazi Germany. (Much later, in the 1965 film *Operation Crossbow* about the outstanding intelligence work carried out at RAF Medmenham, Babington Smith was played by Sylvia Sims who in 1961 went on to appear with Bogarde in the ground-breaking film *Victim*.)

The meticulous work carried out by Babington Smith led to her detecting and recognising the launching site of the enemy's deadly pilotless aircraft (Doodlebugs) at Peenemünde on the Baltic coast in Germany. A photograph supplied to her by Mosquito pilot Squadron Leader John Merifield revealed the Germans had built a ramp holding a tiny cruciform shape on rails. Such an important find via the use of intense magnification, indicated and confirmed Britain was about to become the target of thousands of flying bombs. (This breakthrough occurred just before Lieutenant Derek van den Bogaerde joined the ranks of the bright and the brilliant at RAF Medmenham.)

The need to wipe out the Germans' new launch sites was paramount and under the codename 'Crossbow' Babington Smith provided Bomber Command and its Pathfinders with enough information to begin the decimation of Hitler's deadly 'secret' weapons. The V1 assault on the southern counties of England had started in June 1944, with the V2 ballistic missiles striking the capital city in the autumn of that year. Babington Smith, who was by now leading a vast team of interpreters, made a lasting impression on the inventor of the jet engine Group Captain Frank Whittle. Those working at Medmenham at the time remembered jovially how his interest in her perfume caused much mirth among his friends. When he enquired what it was Babington Smith, who incidentally never married, told him she wore Guerlain's L'Heure Bleue as its 'light, refreshing scent detracted from the square cut of her uniform!'[39]

But she puts all sense of whimsy aside when in in her excellent memoir *Evidence in Camera* Babington Smith describes how more than ninety launching sites for the German doodlebugs had been constructed in the Pas de Calais area of northern France close to the coast. After a months of hard work by the men and women of CIU, the RAF aircrews taking part in Operation Crossbow had precise information and prepared to bomb V1 launch sites and locations housing deadly V2s which had begun raining down in London and parts of south-east England. She wrote:

> The immeasurably vast and complex undertaking of planning for the D-Day landings depended in many ways on photography. Years before the final choice of beaches was made, for instance, interpreters had been watching the whole shoreline of northern France. The cycle of effects caused by seasonal storms, the size and shape of underwater reefs and sandbanks, the positions of breakwaters and beach exits – all were carefully recorded so that when the time came the planners would have the information they needed.[40]

Around this time Medmenham's photographic section was turning out seven million prints a month. Such were only a few of the contributions to the planning for D-Day on 6 June 1944. Both the Americans and the British took part in what was a fully Allied achievement.

For Lieutenant van den Bogaerde, now working within the hallowed instructions of a genius like Babington Smith, it was the aroma of words like 'secret' which captured his lively imagination and he set about his new job with relish. Spying was attractive and all very hush-hush and he very much appeared to be the right man for the job. It's worth noting by this time Bogarde had a supremely vivid imagination, and also his enormous gift for secrecy went on to play a major role in the fabric of his personal life. Perhaps too his early years interpreting images at RAF Medmenham sharpened his talent for character analysis when it came to his success as an actor.

If Babington Smith had bumped into him on the stairwell at Medmenham there's little doubt she would have noticed him. Who wouldn't look twice at such a handsome man? He would have certainly been aware of her and may well have caught many a whiff of her famous perfume as she strode about the corridors with a furrowed brow at the thought of another deadline looming ahead. The keen lieutenant was a charming young man who turned anyone's head. He did for sure get to know Babington Smith's WAAF friend from Medmenham, a photographic interpreter called Eve Holiday. They got to know each other even better in Calcutta, India in the summer of 1945 – a period of the war which is discussed later in this book.

But of his time at RAF Medmenham Bogarde wrote:

I loved the detail, the intense concentration, the working out of problems, the searching for clues and above all the memorising. It was, after all, a very theatrical business. How many haystacks had there been in that field three weeks ago? Look back and check. Six. Now there were sixteen ... did the tracks lead to them and now away from them? Were they made by tracked vehicles or wheeled ones? Guns, tanks or radar maybe? Or were they, after all, only haystacks, it was June ... [41]

It is important to point out that he took his work as an aerial photographic interpreter tremendously seriously and although he was often described by some in the military as something of a dilettante he retained utmost focus on any task required of him.

The thousands of images which landed on the interpreters' desks were supplied by RAF aircrews who risked their lives each day. They'd fly wooden-framed twin-engined De Havilland Mosquitoes. The specially equipped photo-reconnaissance Spitfires were often painted in a light pink colour to blend in with the clouds.

Military aerial photo-reconnaissance began in the First World War. In 1917 No. 70 Squadron of the Royal Flying Corps took off in flimsy Sopwith two-seaters to obtain images of enemy positions. Perhaps flying too low to accommodate the camera technology of the time they soon ran into trouble. Not one member of the crew of the final sortie of six returned. Within days the RFC realised the height, speed and range of the trusty Airco DH4 bomber with its Rolls-Royce engine and 42ft wingspan was more suited to aerial photography. The importance of aerial photography during warfare was now established and its benefits had silenced the deluded military commanders who during the early part of the conflict had seldom listened to 'flyboys' who had only words to report what they'd seen going on from the air. It was the DH4 that secured the role of bombers for photo-reconnaissance and in 1939 it was the Bristol Blenheim which was tasked with this important work. They were usually flown by the RAF's No. 21 Squadron at Watton, Norfolk. One of the most famous photographs taken during the squadron's first successful mission in 1939 shows the giant German battleship *Tirpitz* being fitted out at Wilhemshaven dockyard on Germany's North Sea coast.

Within months other heavy aircraft including the Short Stirling were being considered just as or even more suitable for the role. RAF crews often flew over enemy guns and flak in order to provide the Night Photographic Interpretation Section of No. 3 Photographic Reconnaissance Unit with important target information. Most special operations were carried out from RAF Oakington in Cambridgeshire (home of Short Stirling Squadron No.7) at first and then later from nearby RAF Alconbury where surface conditions were deemed more suitable.

Two years before Lieutenant van den Bogaerde joined Medmenham the expanding workload included almost every aerial operation which required military intelligence and strategic activity. Such important tasks were carried out by 1,400 personnel and by 1945 records reveal 25,000 negatives and 60,000 prints were dispersed among specialist interpreters for considered reports and proceeding actions.

The raid carried out on the night of 16/17 May 1943 by the Dambusters of Bomber Command in 1943 resulted in the destruction of three key dams in Germany's Ruhr Valley. The mission was known as Operation Chastise and successfully utilised bouncing bombs designed by Barnes Wallis. The CO at RAF Medmenham at the time was the popular Peter Stewart who had met many Bomber Command heroes including Wing Commander Guy Gibson VC, DSO, DFC of 617 Squadron. Up to 125,000 aircrew flew over Germany day and night in various types of heavy aircraft including of course the four-engined Lancaster. By the end of the European war on May 8, 1945 the library at RAF Medmenham had archived a total of five million prints and 40,000 reports.

By the time Lieutenant van den Bogaerde joined the CIU the Americans had already been closely involved in order to ascertain accurate target information for bombing missions over Germany carried out from British airfields. In 1944 the CIU briefly changed its name to ACIU (Allied Central Interpretation Unit) then reverted to its former name when the Americans left in August the following year. In Taylor Downing's book *Spies in the Sky* the social life at Medmenham is described as 'lively – especially as it was staffed with so many artists'. The evening entertainments 'were of a very high standard' and included concerts and theatrical events starring the interpreters themselves. Musical composers including Robin Orr – the organist at St John's College, Cambridge – and Humphrey Searle took part in the fun. And any choreography was often created by Royal Ballet genius Frederick Ashton who too spent his war years at Medmenham. 'Drinking was an important part of RAF culture and the local pubs, The Dog and Badger and The Mace and Hounds, were popular haunts. But of course no one was ever allowed to talk shop in the local for fear that enemy informers were listening in. Everyone was told not to talk about their work and to "Keep Mum" as the wartime phrase had it,' writes Downing.[42]

Shirley Eadon was a WAAF who worked in the Press and Publicity section at Medmenham. She remembered the place as 'a bunch of nuts'. 'They were all distinctive characters and individualists,' she recalled and noted that a certain Lady Charlotte Bonham-Carter carried her umbrella and a bag full of breakfast remnants everywhere. Once she was told off by a groundsman for walking across the playing fields to get to work instead of using the driveway. Lady Bonham-Carter promptly told him she'd paid her RAF Medmenham sports subscription and never played games so walking on the grass was one way of getting her money's worth![43] Lady Bonham Carter, however, was taking part in the frenzy of activity at the secret base especially once the Allied invasion of Normandy (Operation Overlord) was heading towards actuality. Without a doubt the best efforts of every man and woman were required. As a member of General Bernard Montgomery's 21st Army Group, Lieutenant Derek 'Pip' van den Bogaerde, said: 'We were clever little fellows planning D-Day and were all BIGOTS. A splendid code name for 'top secret'.[44]

Among the aircraft used frequently to assist the RAF Medmenham staff were camouflaged Spitfires which carried no guns, only cameras and a pilot. With a top speed of 400mph at around 30,000ft accurate photographs were taken by five heated cameras. The only big problem of an aerial photographer's life was fog which could cloud the camera lens. Many images were three-dimensional thus providing more detailed accuracy for CIU staff like Lieutenant van den Bogaerde to process and investigate. When quizzed on a television show about his wartime experiences he once admitted: 'Yes I did indirectly kill people through my decisions over which targets we should strike in Germany.'

Other notables of RAF Medmenham who became successful in the film world after the war included former ACIU personnel who were snapped up by Hollywood seeking excellent cameramen and women. One of them of was Xavier Atencio who became one of Disney's top creatives. The famous archaeologist Dorothy Garrod CBE FBA, a specialist in the Palaeolithic period, worked at RAF Medmenham as one of the 150 women photographic interpreters. Glyn Daniel – the host of the post-war television *Animal, Vegetable or Mineral?* show – was also part of the Buckinghamshire intelligence personnel.[45]

Memories of RAF Medmenham are only briefly recorded in the memoirs of the intelligence officer who became the iconic actor Sir Dirk Bogarde. No doubt he'd signed the Official Secrets Act and didn't want repercussions, even imprisonment. However, in *Snakes and Ladders* he does painfully describe a time how terror such as 'dive-bombing' and 'women delivering a child induced by shell-shock' was 'so completely incomprehensible'. From here on we begin to understand how war changed him, and he wrote how he had not realised so much horror 'strewn along our victors' path' was what 'growing up entailed'.[46]

After several months learning his craft at RAF Medmenham the highly skilled officer was ordered to report to RAF Odiham, near Basingstoke which was home to 39 (Reconnaissance) Wing of the Royal Canadian Air Force. This posting was to last almost a year and his life as a 'Draft of One' led him directly into the world of the aircrews who acted upon his work and that of his colleagues at CIU. He'd certainly never worked with the Canadians before but he soon found out that he began to fit in rather well. His association with the Queen's Royal Regiment had begun to fade somewhat as he married himself to his solitary kind of specialist job as an aerial photographic interpreter and made himself ready to go wherever he was sent and to work with whoever was in charge of the unit.

In 1957 Marshal of the RAF The Lord Tedder GCB said:

From 1931 – 1941 the Blenheims had to struggle for PR [photo-reconnaissance] until, despite the insatiable demands of fighter defence, sufficient Spitfires had been made available, modified and developed for this highly specialised task. If ever the need arises again it is hoped we have been wise before the event.

The story of the development and achievements of the twin arts of photo-reconnaissance and photographic interpretation is to me the most fascinating aspect of the Second World War; a story of British genius at its best, the genius which can weld into a perfect team a wide variety of highly individualistic individuals, and harness to the common cause their widely differing temperaments and skills while allowing full scope for their individual originality, enthusiasm and initiative. It is a story of imagination, devotion and courage whose contribution to the ultimate success of the Allied cause was quite incalculable.[47]

Lieutenant van den Bogaerde was an individual just as Lord Tedder described and had obviously flourished at RAF Medmenham. He admitted often to friends he would have stayed in Army Intelligence if he hadn't have been demobbed. It's interesting to note that having found his metier in the military, he also felt the security of spiritual absolution to write a will. Just before D-Day he expressed his wish for the silver ring from his little finger to be given to Jack (Tony) Jones who 'shares my life' along with a photograph of Ypres Tower in Belgium.[48]

By now his sister Lu was in the Women's Royal Naval Service (WRNS) where she served at HMS *Lizard* at Hove near the family home in Sussex. His parents Ulric and Margaret helped American troops stationed nearby feel welcome by hosting teas and organising mail deliveries. Many of these men were waiting to be sent to Normandy.[49]

On 5 June 1944 Lieutenant van den Bogaerde found himself in a briefing room at RAF Odiham. During the war North American Mustangs and Hawker Typhoons flew out of RAF Odiham and were mostly operated by the men of No. 2 Squadron. By the end of June 1944 the Spitfire Mk IXs of No. 4 Squadron could be seen on the airfields. Also in the room that day was Flight Lieutenant Christopher Greaves, a commercial artist and photographer who Bogarde described in his memoirs as 'calm, quiet and funny'. They became friends and often discussed artistic representations of war – endeavours which were never far from each other's minds. In the room that day the CO soon informed them Operation Overlord (D-Day) had started and the ships had left harbour. But while most of the men of RAF Odiham were scrambled immediately to be part of the 6 June assault Lieutenant van den Bogaerde was ordered to remain at his post as there were photographs to examine, most of them containing images of German Panzer divisions in Caen, Normandy. That day the 24-year-old lieutenant stood alone in a wooden hut listening to the deafening roar of aircraft 'thundering overhead' towards France. He recalled how the windows rattled and an overwhelming sense of doom made him weep.[50]

But his orders finally arrived for him to head for Normandy and as he flew across the Channel in a Dakota he wondered what he'd find. Records show Lieutenant van den Bogaerde arrived in Sommervieu (B8) near Bayeux, in the Calvados region, on 1 July. The area had been liberated on 7 June 1944 by the 2nd Battalion Essex Regiment, 56th Independent Brigade, and by The Royal Engineers 24th Airfield Construction Group.

Between 14–22 June, the men of the Royal Engineers constructed an aerodrome called 'ALG B-8' located to the west of Sommervieu. Two parallel runways were installed, one of compacted soil and the other covered with Square Mesh Track (SMT) used in particular by the Recce Wing, 123/136 Wing and the 145 Wing (74 Squadron, 329 Squadron 'Cigognes', 340 Squadron 'Ile-de-France' and 341 squadron 'Alsace' – Free French). The airfield was operational until August 1945.

Lieutenant van den Bogaerde landed at the Royal Engineers' clever air base to meet the Canadian squadrons tasked with bombing Germany. The airfield at Sommervieu (B8) also hosted the Mustang fighter aircraft whose pilots of 430 and 414 Canadian Squadrons depended on CIU photographs to carry out low-level strafing missions against enemy railways and shipping convoys. Their commanding officer of 39 Wing was a popular Aerial Photographic Interpretation Service (APIS) officer, Captain Sydney Allen.

For Lieutenant van den Bogaerde and his CIU friend Christopher Greaves work took place from the back of a lorry full of specialist equipment which was parked near the base. Home was in a tent in an orchard prone to be rained on by pieces of shrapnel flying around from anti-aircraft guns defending the Mulberry Harbour at Arromanches. In his memoir *Backcloth* Bogarde described the truck as our 'office' with a couple of desks and lamps and not much else. 'In this, plus a jeep, we drove across Europe in the wake of our Forward Recce Squadron who had taken the photographs.' Both men had to be ready at the double to examine photographs for enemy troops and tank movements whatever the cost.

Soon enough their skills were required beyond Sommervieu. In August 1944 they were sent on towards the bombed-out city of Caen, Normandy which had been the centre of a series of brutal battles from June to August that year, including the famous and bloody battle for Pegasus Bridge. Indeed records reveal that to ensure victory against the might of eight German Panzer divisions, seven infantry divisions and three heavy tank battalions, the Allies commanded by Generals Bernard Montgomery and Miles Dempsey sent three armoured divisions, eleven infantry divisions, five armoured brigades and three tank brigades to the area. While Operation Overlord eventually led to a German retreat it came at the cost of thousands of lives including the French civilians of Caen and its environs. Most of the destruction of the medieval city had been inflicted that summer by Allied bombing. It took until 1962 for the town to be completely rebuilt and regenerated.

Life on the battered roads of northern France was to prove very different to the enclosed classroom-like intensity of RAF Medmenham and Lieutenant van den Bogaerde found vital resources were at a minimum. Deadlines were of the greatest importance and had to be met at all costs. At first Montgomery's troops had failed to take Caen and the resulting aerial battles over B8 between Spitfires and Me 109s often left the men on the ground running for their lives. In *Backcloth* we learn of that time when 'the air trembled' and 'the blazing town was a monstrous cathedral of flame'. The horrendous sight of death and destruction witnessed by the young officer along the Falaise Gap in Normandy was not reported by him to his family. Secrecy was the rule of the day. But a multitude of poignant sketches he made of the area exist in an album. Some are now on show in the British Museum, and others remain in the Bogarde family archives.

A young Canadian pilot by the name of Richard Rohmer recalled his own experiences in one of his many books written after the war.

On August 1, 1944 I was flying back to Sommervieu in my Mustang in fading light when I saw a flash of a gun. I went into a gentle bank to see what was firing. To my astonishment I found I was sitting over dozens of tanks, probably the greatest number I had ever seen in one place in a battle situation. It was an incredible sight, and extremely exciting for a young bloodhound. The long guns hanging way out over the front of the tanks signalled only one thing to me. They were German Tigers!

Rohmer flew back to base and on his way he broke the rules of radio silence and revealed what'd he'd seen on the ground below him. He also quickly took photographs as evidence. When he landed he was met by angry superior officers who told him he faced a court martial for making a transmission in mid-air. He was also told the tanks were no doubt 'British!'

The pilot recalled the only proof they were Tiger tanks would be in the photographs. He explained:

Bursting in on the startled APIS (Aerial Photographic Interpretation Service) duty officer (Lt van den Bogaerde), who was unaccustomed to seeing a pilot in his place of business at that time of night I quickly explained the situation, produced my photographs and asked him to make a judgement. What were those tanks?

With no great haste he took the films, put them together in front of him, picked up the main tool of his trade, a pair of stereo lenses which when placed over two in-line photographs gave him a three-dimensional view of the objects in the photographs. By this time I was in a terrible state of anxiety. But still he was in no hurry. Studying the images below him he emitted two or three contemplative grunts. Then, laconically, and without even looking up, he said: 'They're Tigers'. Thank Christ! I could have kissed him![51]

Richard H. Rohmer DFC had already proved by then that he was no ordinary pilot. On 17 July 1944 as he flew over Normandy in his P-51 Mustang his sharp eyes spotted on the road below him an open Nazi staff car carrying Field Marshal Erwin Rommel. Whilst he was forbidden to strafe the vehicle he was able to report its whereabouts by radio to the Group Control Centre which then dispatched two Spitfires to carry out the attack. Rommel was badly injured and unable to ever play a significant part in the war again.

Just like Lieutenant van den Bogaerde the heroic Rohmer took part in the liberation of France, Belgium and the Netherlands. Post-war he remained with the Canadian Royal Air Force and by 1978 he had been promoted to Major General, Chief of Reserves of the Canadian Armed Forces. As Canada's most decorated citizen he retired from the armed forces in 1981. From there he became a distinguished lawyer, successful author, and was chairman of the 60th Anniversary of D-Day celebrations in 2004. On 6 June that year he was honoured to escort Her Majesty The Queen around the exhibitions at The Juno Beach Centre.

In a recording made for the Veterans' Voices exhibition at the Centre he said: 'My motivation was to defeat the deadly enemy and liberate Europe. Looking back over 65 years, we veterans of D-Day can now see that we had a strong role in an enormous military assault that was the beginning point of massive changes in the future of Europe, and indeed of the entire world. Our costly D-Day success at Juno Beach laid the unforeseeable foundation for the betterment of mankind.'[52] On 24 January 2021 the Hamilton-born hero Richard Heath Rohmer celebrated his 97th birthday.

After Bogarde's memoir *Snakes and Ladders* was published in 1980 he received a letter from Major General Rohmer OC CMM OOnt DFC CD QC about that day in the late summer of 1944 about how 'someone in APIS saved his life'. Bogarde replied he remembered the photograph well and from there on Rohmer hailed him a hero!

Back in 1944 and not long after Rohmer escaped court martial the sounds of battle and aerial dogfights began to fade as Montgomery's Second Army successfully drove back the Germans from Arromanches. Lieutenant van den Bogaerde recalled how he was 'constantly on the move', unlike his father's generation of soldiers who often remained in the same spot day after day fighting for yards of land. Work too was non-stop as army chiefs demanded to know where it was safe for their men to walk. Information supplied was as detailed as the width of streams and minefields.

39 Wing including Lieutenant van den Bogaerde and his pal Chris were moved to Ste Honorine de Ducy and within days the brutal battle for the Falaise Gap had been won by the Allies. By now the Germans had lost control of Paris and 39 Wing arrived at another new base – this time at Évreux. They couldn't help but note the horrific sight of hundreds

of dead Germans along the roads and in the hedgerows. The rows of fallen horses made too for a sad memory. The aircrews of a Typhoon squadron nearby had been busy. Both men made their own way to Paris and then they continued their journey towards Belgium. Here in Brussels they were due to meet up again with the rest of 39 Wing. A foray to the van den Bogaerde ancestral home in Izegem is described in his memoir *Cleared for Take Off* (1995).

On 17 September 1944 the Allies' Operation Market Garden erupted at Arnhem in The Netherlands in an attempt to create a bridgehead over the Rhine. At this time 39 Wing was grounded because of heavy rain. The aircraft were stuck out in a 'soggy airfield' in nearby Diest.[53] Nine intelligence officers were required to visit Arnhem at General Montgomery's behest. Lieutenant van den Bogaerde was among them.

The Battle of Arnhem lasted nine brutal days. It involved Allied airborne troops who would be dropped in the area to take possession of key bridges and towns along the Allied axis of advance. In the north of the country the British 1st Airborne Division, the men of the Glider Pilot Regiment and 1st Polish Parachute Brigade had been led to believe Operation Market Garden would be a 'walkover'! These hardy souls were then planning to meet with British XXX Corps in two days. However, they had landed some way from the bridges and within a short time met the full force of the Germans' 9th and 10th SS Panzer Divisions. Many men found themselves trapped by the Germans who battled hard to maintain their hold on The Netherlands. Some had no choice but to surrender and live out the rest of the war in Germany in a prisoner-of-war camp.

As the battle raged through the north of the country the British 1st Airborne Division lost almost all its men with the Glider Pilot Regiment finding its numbers depleted by almost 20 per cent. Indeed the British and Polish casualty list was horrendous – approximately 1,984 killed and 6,854 captured. The Germans suffered the loss of 1,300 and had 2,000 wounded.

Arnhem veteran Victor Gregg, co-author with Rick Stroud of the memoir *Rifleman*, recalled how there was

noise all over the place, blokes screaming, machine guns, and if people wanted to find each other you've got to locate those who've landed, the area where all your gear had landed, get yourself in some sort of group, and then make your way over the Dropping Zone. That was when a lot of blokes didn't make it.

Organisation failed because the bloke in charge of it all, [Lieutenant-General] Browning landed on the opposite side of the river Rhine, and then the bloke who took his place went walkabout, got trapped in a house for two days and in the meantime the Germans had sent an armoured force and cut the route to the bridge in two so that was it – operation finished!

All we could do was re-form and create a perimeter. I was on a machine gun so I was stuck on the outside of the perimeter. I wasn't with my original team by then. I was just lucky I survived. On the sixth day an officer went off to find some more ammunition and he came back and said there was nobody there. We thought the Germans had been behind us. It was a couple of days before the they found us and we were taken prisoner. [Gregg was sent to a labour camp in Dresden.]

We found out there were just eighty men left of the six hundred that were dropped with us in Arnhem that day in September 1944.[54]

At the time Montgomery appears to have been fed a heap of 'scapegoat' style information about Arnhem – now known as an immense British military failure. He claimed he had been given misleading details about how the Polish forces had 'fought very badly' at Arnhem. Thus the blame was laid at the feet of the Polish General Stanislaw Sosabowski (1892–1967) who was accused of being an argumentative and tricky personality and impossible to deal with when it came to attack procedures. It was alleged he put his own men first and wasn't prepared to follow orders given by Lieutenant General Frederick Browning. Exactly who used Sosabowski as a scapegoat for the disaster remains a mystery.

However, Sosabowski (played by Gene Hackman in the 1977 film *A Bridge Too Far*) had influential supporters in the military and the press who informed Churchill of the significant Polish contribution to the Battle of Arnhem. He was believed and Sosabowski was made commander of rearguard troops and was demobbed in 1948. A bust commemorating his bravery during the Second World War was unveiled in Krakow on 1 September 2013.

Lieutenant van den Bogaerde described Arnhem as a 'catastrophe' and experienced 'dreadful days of fury, frustration, despair and defeat which followed'. Many military historians argue Operation Market Garden was weak and doomed from the start. On paper it may have looked feasible and General Montgomery knew the German army was by now much weakened. Its troops in Arnhem were mostly made up of either teenagers or wounded veterans.

But it appears not enough thought went into the logistic demands. Many of the Allied troops were stranded without equipment, fuel, food, water and military transport. Many were hemmed in by German troops hiding in the woods around them.

Secondly the RAF, concerned about conditions on the ground at Arnhem, dropped British paratroops at least 13 miles from the all-important bridge. The RAF had taken this decision despite an earlier protest by I Airborne Corps' intelligence officer, Major Brian Urquhart, who knew the vital element of surprise to the enemy associated with paratroopers would be lost. The essence of his force had relied on a quick attack with light machine guns and then they'd make a quick dash to a place where they'd wait for backup from an armoured unit. Why, however, the RAF deemed it okay to drop General Sosabowski's Polish paratroopers right next to the bridge remains an interesting question to this day.

More than three decades later the talented 'individual' intelligence officer of RAF Medmenham had become film star 'Dirk Bogarde' and was cast as the old Etonian Lieutenant-General Frederick 'Boy' Browning in the 1977 war film *A Bridge Too Far*. As he studied for the role he recalled having met the real 'Boy' Browning at Arnhem during his service with 39 Wing.

During the Second World War Lieutenant-General Browning was known as an ambitious soldier. He was a Grenadier Guard with Sandhurst training, a veteran of the First World War in France and had been awarded the Croix de Guerre. He was regarded as the 'father of the British airborne forces' and had been promoted to deputy commander of the First Allied Airborne Army during the battle for Arnhem (Operation Market Garden).

Colleagues described Browning as 'nervy' and 'high-strung'. His career was blighted when he was criticised for over-estimating the amount of

Allied troops at his disposal at Arnhem. Records of the time reveal he was ordered by Montgomery to hold the bridge for two days but allegedly he wrongly suggested his men could hold it for four days. Later on Browning had admitted that four days might be going 'a bridge too far'. It was a line that inspired the author Cornelius Ryan to pen his famous book of the same name. For the film a replica of Browning's original uniform was made in Bogarde's measurements. This military attire was on display for years in the Parachute Regiment and Airborne Forces Museum. It was moved to the Imperial War Museum in 2008.

Browning's wife (Lady Browning) was the novelist Daphne du Maurier who when the film came out in 1977 declared her husband had been portrayed in a less than flattering light. National newspapers carried stories expressing her wrath about the production's 'unforgivable treatment' of him. According to du Maurier's biographer Margaret Forster, her attitude towards the film was completely different to that of the book it was based upon. Its author Cornelius Ryan (who also wrote *The Longest Day* about the Normandy Landings) had visited du Maurier in the early 1970s to gather research on Browning and when the book was finally published in 1974 she felt it depicted her husband as a fine soldier. She liked the description of him as 'lithe, immaculately turned out with the appearance of a restless hawk'.

When the film's director Richard Attenborough began casting he believed his friend Dirk Bogarde, a former army intelligence officer, was a perfect choice. (Attenborough and Bogarde had known each other for decades. In 1949 they had appeared together as rebellious Borstal inmates in a film called *Boys in Brown*.) But the inconsolable du Maurier was not happy at all about Bogarde playing her husband. She said Lieutenant-Colonel Browning shouldn't appear in the film as 'effete and mincing' and she made herself ill with fury about Bogarde's portrayal of him.[55]

Bogarde's authorised biographer John Coldstream writes how the actor seemed 'fine' with the film until he read du Maurier's furious comments. Bogarde hated any form of criticism and to be so publicly humiliated was in his opinion 'monstrous'.

The novelist's rant had touched a nerve in the actor who strictly and unreservedly concealed his private life as a gay man. She said Bogarde came over on screen as a Guards Officer more concerned about shining boots and buckles than the hard business of combat. She stressed how her husband 'certainly was not a homosexual'. Bogarde was hurt by the sting of du Maurier's comments and then looked around and pointed the finger at the director Richard Attenborough, deciding that 'Dickie had set him up'. Their friendship was never the same again. In Richard Attenborough's autobiography *Entirely Up to You, Darling* there's also a suggestion Bogarde had felt his friend, recently knighted, had tried to ruin Bogarde's own chances of a title.

Playing Major-General Roy Urquhart, a more substantial role, requiring three weeks' work – and, to Bogarde's fury, triple his own fee – was another tax exile, the macho Sean Connery. These two stars had never worked together and, unsurprisingly, did not exactly hit it off. With so many layers of barely concealed animosity, the atmosphere on set that morning was decidedly edgy and the scripted confrontation between Urquhart and Browning took Richard a very long day to shoot, recalled Diana Hawkins who co-wrote Attenborough's memoir.[56]

Connery, who was chosen by Attenborough because he looked like the real Major-General Urquhart as a young man, had almost pulled out of the film when he discovered Robert Redford was earning much, much more than him for just two weeks' work. (It has been suggested on the IMDB website the figure was more than $2 million.) Redford starred as Major Julian Cook DSC who during the real battle was commanding officer 3rd Battalion 82nd Airborne. His job was to seize the main bridges over the Maas-Waal canal and the river assault crossing the Waal canal.

The huge star-studded production was fraught with internal struggles and Bogarde felt he'd been horribly exposed by du Maurier's damning remarks which somehow in his mind had been validated by her status in society via her marriage to top brass. By then Bogarde had begun to show signs of snobbery himself and felt appalled about what might happen because he had offended Lady Browning. Coldstream suggests, an opinion shared by others, that perhaps Bogarde should have 'ignored' du Maurier's comments and just got on with the production. Those who knew Browning thought the portrayal was 'genuine and precise'. Indeed Lord Mountbatten supported Bogarde's performance wholeheartedly, much to the fury of du Maurier who had apparently already complained bitterly about it to him.

Eventually and after days of the angry novelist putting pressure on Attenborough the film includes Bogarde as Browning saying a line about Arnhem being 'a bridge too far'. Du Maurier was still fuming that

Browning's role at Arnhem had been reduced to a mere cameo in the film. Bogarde too had his issues with the script. He didn't like the way the American screenwriter William Goldman had made Browning appear like a 'cross between Terry Thomas and Ralph Reeder'. The actor insisted he wanted to 'cast historical accuracy to the wind' and play Browning as a 'brave, courageous, wise gentleman' even though he confessed 'the more I play Browning the more of a prick he emerged'.[57]

Attenborough had the foresight though to consult with the real veterans who were being played by a raft of cinema's biggest names. Michael Caine starred as Lieutenant Colonel J.O.E. Vandeleur, CO of 3rd Battalion (Infantry), the Irish Guards, the Guards Armoured Division, XXX Corps. The real Vandeleur was on the set one day when Caine asked him how he delivered a particular line. The retired army officer told Caine he said quietly during the battle, 'Well get a move on then'. And that's how Caine delivered the words in the film.

Notable veterans of Operation Market Garden employed as military advisors included Brian Horrocks (played by his friend Edward Fox who was desperate to portray Horrocks as the man he knew and trusted), James M. Gavin (Ryan O'Neal), John Frost (Sir Anthony Hopkins), and Roy Urquhart (Sir Sean Connery). On the German side actors included Hardy Krüger who was cast as Generalmajor der Waffen-SS Karl Ludwig. The character was based on the real life Heinz Hamel of the 10th Panzer Division who did not want his name mentioned in the film. The famous Maximilian Schell appeared as General der Waffen-SS Wilhelm Bittrich of II Panzer Corps. Civilians included Sir Laurence Olivier who arrived on set in his battered gardening clothes and shoes to play the part as the war-beleaguered old Dutchman, Dr Jan Spaander. The young Dutch woman Kate ter Horst was played by Liv Ullmann.

The production itself required a raft of Civil Aviation approved aircraft including Dakotas and replica Horsa gliders. This important element of the film was organised by the specialist staff of the Joseph Levine Production Company who worked closely with the Danish Air Force and Finnish Air Force. In a bid to keep general traffic moving across the real Arnhem bridge, the Dutch government gave Attenborough permission to film some scenes in Deventer where there was a similar bridge situated over the River Ijssel. The overall budget for the film was set at $25 million. In total the box office made $50.7 million.

The reviews in general were mixed. Pulitzer Prize winning critic Robert Ebert wasn't overly impressed and wrote:

Such an exercise in wretched excess, such a mindless series of routine scenes, such a boringly violent indulgence in all the blood and guts and moans they could find, that by the end we're prepared to speculate that maybe Levine went two or even three bridges too far. The movie's big and expensive and filled with stars, but it's not an epic. It's the longest B-grade war movie ever made.

The Washington Post was more positive and its reviewer described *A Bridge too Far* as a war epic with an unusually conscientious theme: '... in terms of careful period recreation, visual spectacle (the sequences depicting paratroop landings are particularly awesome), the mixture of exciting combat episodes with vivid human interest vignettes, an effort to establish a coherent, many-faceted view of a complicated and ill-fated military adventure, and a generally superior level of film-making intelligence and craftsmanship.'

A Bridge Too Far was to come closest to Bogarde's real-life wartime experiences as his involvement in Operation Market Garden at Arnhem in 1944 included of course his vital work with the aerial photographic interpretation unit. Sadly, it was also to become the film which dropped the actor into the centre of a tide of negative publicity. So much so he couldn't be blamed for thinking about leaving the cinema for good.

A damning letter had appeared in *The Times* by General Sir John Hackett who declared the actor had played Browning as 'unkind and untruthful' and a man who was 'superficial, heartless, petulant and uncaring about the men in his charge'. Letters of support to balance out the huff and puff of the discontent did get written though, including one from a veteran of Operation Market Garden. He agreed Browning was debonair and dapper and yet no army was any worse off just because its lieutenant general had shiny boots and looked after his appearance. He mentioned Admiral Nelson and Lord Mountbatten as examples. Mountbatten told the press he couldn't find anything 'really detrimental to Boy' from Bogarde's portrayal and one must remember that Operation Market Garden had been a failure and Browning was one of the men responsible for that. Despite his comments du Maurier continued to complain and even approached the Royal Family. She was told by HRH Prince Philip that 'Boy' would have 'laughed it off as tripe!'.[58] So who was the real Lieutenant-General Sir Frederick Arthur Montague 'Boy' Browning GCVO, KBE, CB, DSO (1896–1965)? According to his son Christian he was a 'strict disciplinarian' and always very smart and well dressed. But when it came to the film the Americans who had financed it 'wanted a fall guy'. Bogarde's biographer John Coldstream, speaking on YouTube WW2 TV, said:

I think Dirk regretted making the film because he became the subject of derision and that would be something really he would never ever tolerate. But he had a script, an original script that I saw that has Browning saying to Roy Urquhart, 'We just tried to go a bridge too far.' And then that was changed largely as a result of campaigning by Dirk, and the pressure being put on Attenborough by Daphne du Maurier, Lady Browning, to: 'well as you know I've always thought we tried to go a bridge too far.'

Those are the words that resonate off the soundtrack when the original line was what Browning actually said to Monty – I think we might be going a bridge too far.' So if that had been portrayed faithfully, the actual line, was in the film there would have been none of this fuss I'm absolutely sure as the whole thing would have been structured in a much different way. What happened of course was the top tier, the Ikes and the Montys were stripped out of the action of the film and so one was left with tier two so then it became this dialogue, this difficulty between the commanding officers on the ground and what was happening at headquarters was ultimately not being faithfully portrayed. So again, and also to satisfy the American audiences and so on all sorts of compromises were made, but the bottom line is when the film was premiered and incidently Patrick Gibson in *The Daily Telegraph* wrote that this general (Browning) as portrayed by Dirk was a not one I would have trusted to run a cocktail party!

Well that's a fantastically unfair thing as it was based upon what he had seen and heard in the movie so there was a fantastic furore in The Times and that was hugely affecting Dirk because of course The Times was his father's paper so to be derided on the pages of the great Thunderer was no way Dirk could tolerate it.

It's sad that the last film of Dirk in uniform should be remembered in this way.

It's interesting to note the film marked a time in Bogarde's career when he began to take a break from the camera. After *A Bridge Too Far* he made only one film in 1978 (*Despair*), and waited three years before appearing as Roald Dahl in *The Patricia Neal Story* in 1981. Then a full five years passed before we saw him in 1986 in a film version of Graham Greene's *May We Borrow Your Husband*.

* * *

In early October 1944 and as soon as they could take off 39 Wing made for Eindhoven. Then came the orders to join the 50th Northumbrian Division between the Waal and Nederrijn bridges. CIU officer 'Pip' van den Bogaerde had been promoted to the rank of captain. His photographic interpretation skills were much in demand as the Allies continued to advance towards Berlin. In a letter to his parents he grumbled about being back with the army again and how he was sorry to leave his trusty Canadian friends at 39 Wing.

By the end of November however came the good news he was to return to his pals of 39 Wing who were a stark contrast to the depleted and sad faces of his former unit the 214th Independent Infantry Brigade. When he chanced upon them in the village of Elst in the Netherlands he discovered they'd been smashed by the hell of D-Day and many men he once knew had either been killed or wounded.

His old boss Brigadier Hubert Essame, who had once accused him of leaving to take up a 'cushy job', met him in the Mess one day towards the end of the war in Europe with a chilly stare and the comment: 'Won't find anyone you used to know here now; all gone. We lost more than half the Brigade. Bloody lucky for you that you got out when you did.'

At this time the young officer was able to strike up contact with the touring ENSA troupes playing at small venues nearby. Ever aware of the difficulties finding work as an actor he rightfully realised they would prove useful to him after the war which he knew must be rolling towards a conclusion in favour of the Allies.

By January 1945 he had been posted again. He travelled to Nijmegen and crossed the town's bridge in his jeep as German bullets cracked by him. But the Allies were forging powerfully ahead towards Berlin and following the hard-won victory at the Battle of the Bulge Captain van den Bogaerde was en route and crossing the Rhine. 39 Wing had made it to Lower Saxony. The 24-year-old captain and his colleagues in CIU had by now became all too familiar with photographs of concentration camps. He studied them in detail while peering through the vast magnifications offered up by the specialist equipment he'd been trained to use in his role as an aerial photographic interpreter and inspector. The aircrews of course were snapping photographs of the panoramas below which contained evidence of the camps like a 'pox' on the landscape.

On 15 April 1945 Bergen-Belsen in North Germany was liberated by Lieutenant Colonel Bob Daniell and his men of the Royal Horse Artillery. He described it as the 'nearest thing to hell on earth'. A few hours later 39 Wing arrived at nearby Wunstorf.

*   *   *

At this point in the story of Bogarde's military career I recall the day 30 years ago that I met and interviewed him. I can report in detail a conversation I had with him about Belsen. It was what he wanted to talk about.

To me Sir Dirk Bogarde was the epitome of style and grace. He was a man of great dignity and had successfully blended his acting career into the labours of a superb novelist and diarist, showing readers he was a man of acute emotional potency and had a searing wit. And yet beyond his effortless elegance and sophisticated manners was someone who carried the deep scars of a war which ever shaped his creative life.

When I met him as a young newspaper reporter in September 1991 the great man himself was dressed in a crisp grey-blue suit of the finest cut, Saville Row, no doubt. His silk tie in a perfect Windsor knot matched a handkerchief which fell in delicate ruffles from the top left-hand pocket of his jacket.

We sat opposite each other at a polished table made of walnut, in the headmaster's study at Kings' School Rochester, Kent. Bogarde, a youthful 70, focussed his deep, dark soulful eyes on me. I am embarrassed to recall I might have blushed. I was a gauche young newspaper reporter with pencil and notebook at the ready to hear what I thought would be tales of his friends like the late Judy Garland or Ava Gardner, and the glitterati of the film studios.

But any prospects of lively repartee about his career on the big screen was definitely not to be. Bogarde, who within weeks of our interview was to be at Buckingham Palace to receive his knighthood, took complete control of our conversation and quietly made it clear he was on a serious mission to talk about a time in his own youth as an army intelligence officer – brutal days, he said, which had led him to become one of the first British soldiers to help liberate the skeletal inmates of the Nazi concentration camp, Bergen-Belsen.

Chit-chat about his fame and all the paraphernalia surrounding his cultural status did not belong in the conversation that day. He explained in that lovely chocolate velvety voice of his how he felt compelled to talk to young people and put straight recent and disturbing claims that the Holocaust in which six million Jews had died during the Second World War was a 'cartoonish hoax'. Bogarde, it appeared, was quietly yet determinedly pretty fired up and ready to present the real facts.

What I didn't know at the time was he had recently reviewed four books about Nazi atrocities for *The Daily Telegraph* and he was now determined that any potentially corrupting and outlandish claims of denial should be banished from the public consciousness. His fervour to rebel against the pro-Nazi lobby was further enhanced after the newspaper received ugly anti-Semitic letters which were nothing but savage and despicable rants of a certain few. 'The hatred still exists,' he said at the time.

'No one can tell me the Holocaust didn't happen because it bloody well did,' he said quietly. 'I saw it with my own eyes.'

'What did you see?' I asked the actor. He began telling me how in the spring of 1945 he was with the Second Army (39 Wing) choosing ground targets for the Second Tactical Air Force and RAF Bomber Command to attack.

He said the weather was extremely cold and the date as 'one could never be sure during the war' was 17 or 18 April. He was with a pal driving along the road near Belsen in a jeep. They knew the Germans had pulled back and had abandoned a large concentration camp.

'I recall me saying I wanted a pair of German boots if there were any laying around the place,' he said. 'German boots were much better than ours. That was all I had in mind really that day.'

What he described next was a vivid and horrifying story of how he 'lost his boyish laughter forever'.

We rode towards the camp and as we reached the entrance we stopped the jeep. We had arrived in hell. I particularly recall a young girl and I only knew she was a girl because her breasts hung from her chest like a puppy's ears. She spoke English. She pointed to our sandwiches on the dashboard of the jeep and of course we quickly gave them to her. She kissed me.

What she did next I will never forget. She threw the food away and ran off with the piece of *Daily Mirror* newspaper in which they were wrapped. It was just as well she didn't eat the food as we were told soon after if starving people eat too quickly they could die within minutes. Later we asked where the girl had gone and were told she was Estonian had been an English student and the words on that piece of newspaper had been the first English sentences she'd seen for a long time. This girl was then found dead, curled up in a corner of a disgusting hut and clutched in her palm of her bony hand and folded into the size of a postage stamp was the piece of newspaper.

At the time of our interview Bogarde had already become a supporter of voluntary euthanasia and disliked the Roman Catholic religion for its opposition to it. He repeated the words he had written in a letter, 'When I was standing among 60,000 dead and dying at Belsen just where was God or Jesus?'

At the camp and in utter shock as a young man he 'walked through mountains of dead people, so slushy and slimy, you tried not to but it was the only way to move forward'. Quickly he was informed to stay clear of the camp as the area was riddled with typhus. He admitted it was many, many years before he could even speak of that day but the memory of that girl in filthy striped rags often visited him in nightmares … usually during a thunderstorm. Seeing a camp like Belsen on the ground had provided him with an atrocious reality and a serious contrast to the images of the simple wooden huts he had seen during his war work as an aerial photographic interpreter.[59]

When he had told the story of Belsen to the boys of Tonbridge School in 1991 many had wiped away tears. Most of them had never heard of the Holocaust. The Roffensians at Kings School, Rochester, Kent, not known for displays of emotion, found the speech desperately 'harrowing'. He asked me to send him a copy of my article about our interview which appeared in the next edition of the *Kent Evening Post/Kent Today* . I did so and within a couple of days he replied on a personally monogrammed blue-grey postcard. I still have the card and the envelope showing his bold handwriting in dramatic black ink. On the card he'd expressed his hope that 'at least one person had understood.'

This talented man, cryptic as ever, seemed to imply he liked my description of our meeting that day. I just wish I'd had another chance to talk to him more fully having now researched him, watched his films and read his books. Today and when I recall my treasured memory of that interview with him it is so much easier for me to seriously appreciate the life of the elegant man I'd met so long ago.

But way before we met in the elegant surroundings of the headmaster's study at King's School, Rochester, he had taken part in a BBC radio broadcast in 1966 in which he discussed his social conscience. He mentioned first his army career and then described his experiences of Belsen as a young man of 24 as a 'kind of adjusting thing' to have done. In all sincerity he said:

> Nothing has really very much mattered after Belsen to me and nothing has really been significant except Belsen. And so from that point onwards I've always had that at the back of my mind, a determined conscience that minorities must not be persecuted and that life is for living. Because if you've seen twenty-thousand bodies in a heap, just lying glistening in the sun like wax you begin to really wonder what life is for and I think basically the very simplest way I can put it is that it's for living and for enjoying and sharing and for teaching and learning and assisting and basically living.
>
> Today [1966] I am concerned too about everything. That blasted bomb for instance. I've seen the results of such a thing in Hiroshima. Also I remember Belsen and the persecution of the Jews and the persecution of the coloured people and the persecution of anything whether it's a homosexual or a housewife with three legs. Anything that is persecuted I have a violent urgency to go and assist and I don't know why.

By 2015 Bogarde's official biographer John Coldstream secured absolute proof Bogarde had indeed witnessed 'hell on earth' at Belsen.

At first during the writing of the biography he doubted if the creative Bogarde had seen the concentration camp as the young officer's letters home never mentioned it, some people he had known were cynical of his claims, and there was no real record of Bogarde needing to stray far from his military base nearby in April 1945. He would have been tremendously busy interpreting the thousands of photographs taken by 39 Reconnaissance Wing of the Royal Canadian Air Force.

However, new and resounding evidence came to light and in 2015 Coldstream wrote on the official website devoted to Bogarde:

Dirk was a fine teller of stories. His six novels are evidence enough of that. So too are his memoirs. The record he compiled of his personal life and of how he secured a unique place in the world of the arts, with his 15 books and more than 60 films as a 'name above the title', is a fascinating, often brilliant, exercise in literary embroidery by a born writer; a highly-coloured tapestry, which amply proves the axiom that all autobiography is merely a version of a life.

However, I was contacted by Canadian scholar Mark Celinscak who informed me how his own research into the RCAF 39 Wing confirmed it was 'highly unlikely that Bogarde did NOT go to Belsen'. And 'liberty runs' were made by the squadron on two successive days in April.

His opinion is supported by an extraordinary oral testimony given to the Imperial War Museum in 2007–09 by an Austrian, Andrey Kodin, who came to Britain in 1938, joined the Pioneer Corps in 1941 and by the spring of 1945, aged 22, was working with the Intelligence Corps in Germany. On April 20 he was sent to Belsen in order to help the British troops communicate with the inmates. He, unlike Bogarde, would never confuse the date: April 20 was the birthday – the 56th – of the Führer, 'the monster' whose policies had led to the indescribable scenes that confronted him.

As Kodin stood beside his jeep, speechless with shock at the mounds of decomposing bodies nearby, another Army vehicle drove up and stopped a few yards away. Three British officers stepped out. His attention was drawn to one of them, standing with his hands on his hips and staring ahead with a look of acute sadness. The other two turned back towards their jeep, one calling: 'Come on D—-, haven't you had enough?' Their comrade stood rooted to the spot. Eventually they persuaded him to join them, but, recalled Kodin, 'he turned round and stood and looked again and I'll never forget his face.' It was the large, dark eyes in particular that haunted him.

'About 10 years later, after leaving the Army, Kodin took his wife to the cinema. As the camera closed in on the face of its star, Kodin leapt to his feet and said: 'That's him! That's him!' His wife, who was Greek, had no idea what he was so exercised about, said he was mad and made him sit down. 'Afterwards I told her about it and she wouldn't believe it. She said, "Ah, you're dreaming. You're just imagining things".'

Coldstream continued:

Fast forward another three decades and Kodin was reading *The Daily Telegraph*. Once again he leapt to his feet, saying to his wife: 'Here, Eva, you called me mad, remember? There's the proof.' For him the 'proof' was the review mentioned at the beginning of this article. The officer whose demeanour had so struck him on that fateful day in Lower Saxony was, he firmly believed, Dirk Bogarde. Yes, the fellow-officer had probably called out to Derek rather than Dirk – because 24-year-old Captain Van den Bogaerde of the Queen's Royal Regiment had yet to assume his stage name – but Andrey Kodin may be excused a slight mis-remembering.

One month and one day after their wordless encounter, the last huts at Belsen were razed to the ground. The name will never be erased, however. As Leading Aircraftman Leo Velleman, later a renowned puppeteer, wrote in the August 1945 issue of FLAP, the magazine of 39 Reconnaissance Wing RCAF: 'Belsen stands as a terrible warning to the people of the whole world … It will take unwearying vigilance and clear thinking to make sure that this does not happen again anywhere – ever.' Dirk Bogarde was passionate in endorsing that sentiment. On this gravest of anniversaries it would be gratifying to think that his own credibility as a witness at first hand is secured.

In 1982 and just after the publication of the Booker Prize winning *Schindler's Ark* by Thomas Keneally, the actor was asked if he could visit the studios of Radio Monte Carlo. This time his role was one he deemed important as he was to act as narrator to a Thames Television film about the extraordinary hero Oskar Schindler who had helped to save hundreds of Polish Jews during the Second World War by employing them in his factory. It seems Bogarde's own wartime memories of Bergen-Belsen concentration camp which he had discussed in his memoir *An Orderly Man* had attracted attention and he was deemed the ideal man to tell Schindler's story. He was passionate that the younger generation had full knowledge of the Holocaust.

What shows his vast emotional strength as an actor was his appearance as SS officer Max Theo Aldorfer in the 1974 film *The Night Porter* – a role he played 30 years after he'd witnessed the actual suffering and cruelty of Belsen. It's extraordinary to think he took on the psychology of this supremely sinister, even evocative character who had spent his war working in a concentration camp torturing and photographing Jewish victims of Hitler's monstrous regime. Bogarde, who also co-wrote the film, always insisted it was a 'love story' and nothing to do with ex-Nazis.

In *The Night Porter* we see him as Max in the black SS uniform sporting shiny boots and a riding whip. We watch him in the camp, vampire-like, take a young, skeletal Lucia Atherton (Charlotte Rampling) as a lover and subject her to a series of degrading sex acts which in her desire for survival she at first endures and then grows to accept and even yearn for.

The story then moves back to the present and it's 1957 and we see Max working as a smartly dressed night porter in a hotel in Vienna. Suddenly one day Lucia who he hasn't seen since she was liberated from the camp in 1945, drifts in wearing an elegant gown and jewellery. Lucia is accompanied by her husband who is an orchestra conductor and they are staying in Vienna as part of a musical tour. Suddenly she feels a pair of dark, glittering eyes upon her slender neck and turns around to recognise Max. She gives him a look which perversely reveals she still loves this Nazi who controlled and brutally manipulated her life in the camp. The bond between Max and 'his little girl' who he takes to restaurants and feeds by hand, had been inexplicably sealed back in the horrors of captivity. The film is based on Liliana Cavani's most famous and some say notorious work and its darkness and complicated psychology is woven into an explosive script all about power and submission. It explores too the strength of emotion and how nature can often propel its victims into a bizarre need to revisit agony.

The frightening attraction between both of the characters represented a major breakthrough in film history. Until then there had been hardly any films representing the disturbing and harrowing subject matter of the Holocaust which were about two lovers trapped within such an eerie web of perversity and passion. The affair between Lucia and Max begins when they meet again in 1957. The power of this sadomasochistic reunion appears to come from Lucia who suddenly decides to leave her husband and move in with Max and share all of his dark secrets. *The Night Porter* is unique in its ability to expose the flaws of human nature in life and death scenarios which have been co-created by ultimate lust. Also, its remarkable exploration of a post-war Nazi living in secret around the grey streets of Vienna in the 1950s confirms its identity as a film classic. Some film historians describe it as 'Gothic' in tone.

When discussing *The Night Porter* Bogarde told his friend Charlotte Rampling (with whom he had already starred in *The Damned* in 1969), how the script was 'not about Nazi guilt. It has to have the essence of a real love story, not just a sadomasochistic essay.'[60] The actor had read Liliana Cavani's extraordinary script while he was working with Visconti on *Death in Venice* (1971) and decided it would need a great deal of work to make a film from it. Also he had the prospect of playing 'another degenerate'. There was a lot to consider for an actor in his prime. Cavani got the idea for this unusual story during the making of a documentary about concentration camps. She told Bogarde she'd met a stylish and well-dressed woman standing at a graveside in a Jewish cemetery who had herself been a camp inmate. Cavani was told by the woman 'not all victims of the Nazis were innocent' and how the brutal treatment dished out by Hitler's merciless SS had exposed the depths of human nature.

Cavani wanted the story she wrote to portray the 'limits of credibility' through a sadomasochistic relationship. The perversity of the Marquis de Sade is likened to the representation of the complicated attraction Max felt towards the inmate Lucia. Love comes in many forms. Bogarde described this love story as 'rather like a tiny flower thrusting through the brutality and degradation of a battlefield.' The roles of Max and Lucia would demand the ultimate in performance technique from both actors.[61]

After 12 weeks of work on the script and with a few financial issues still to be resolved the cast assembled on the set on a rainy day in Rome. Cavani had wanted Bogarde in the role as she felt he had hidden depths as an artist. (He had worked with a female director only once before in a walk-on role for Wendy Toye in *We Joined the Navy* (1962).) He persuaded Cavani to accept Charlotte Rampling into the role of Lucia. Cavani quickly agreed that 28-year-old Rampling's quietude was as bewitching as that of the character she'd created.

Rampling described the shoot as 'unbelievably traumatic' and said how when you are young 'the impact of reality has not actually sat on you yet'. She explained: 'I felt I could stand it better because I hadn't been through anything like that of the character of Lucia. I could only imagine. For Dirk it was harder: he had been in the war.'[62]

Bogarde made a very important point when he discussed how making cinema is something people are creating together and that cameras photograph the mind so if there's 'nothing in your mind when camera X and Y are on you and there's no one at home then you can just as well play pussy because your performance won't resonate unless the camera can capture your thoughts'.

His astonishingly dominant performance as Max in *The Night Porter* no doubt reveals to audiences the actor's supreme creativity drawn from harrowing sights and sounds of that time he visited Belsen as a young army intelligence officer in 1945. To appreciate the rigorous punishment he subjects upon his very soul then the audience need only look into the deep, dark eyes of this exceptional actor to know and even attempt to understand. Rampling said *The Night Porter* had the force to shock owing to the way 'it showed how unbelievably powerful the forbidden fantasy inside us is. When we have power it is *very* exciting. And this is a subject which is as ugly as it is fascinating.'

It's important to re-iterate *The Night Porter* is a love story, a sort of warped romance, but not a treatise on Nazism alone. Critics forget that Max in the story rejects Nazism and in that rejection, he protects his love for Lucia and then they both die for it. Rampling admitted she watched him 'struggling at times to find complete fulfilment in his work' as an actor and writer but she agreed wholeheartedly with what he wrote about the making of the film in a volume of his memoirs – *An Orderly Man*.[63]

However, when it was time for the cast and crew to sit down and watch a screening of the complete film Bogarde described it as 'rather extraordinary. Marvellous. Erotic … ' and pointed out the Americans were 'shit scared' to show it. When it was released in London cinemas *The Night Porter* received glowing reviews from reviewers including Dilys Powell and Margaret Hinxman. When he was interviewed by Russell Harty in 1974 he explained how people would see *The Night Porter* as a film about burning, passionate love, explaining how it was a 'kind of warning film' and then he mentioned his own wartime experiences and went on to say the Americans gave it a bad review because the country was 'full of guilt' about the Watergate scandal and Vietnam. It seemed Bogarde's natural talents had stretched to that of historian and teacher too.

* * *

When the news came through on 4 May 1945 that Field Marshal Montgomery had accepted the German surrender, Captain van den Bogaerde and his pals of 39 Wing packed up and made their way to Lüneburg in Germany. They were all wondering what they would do or where they might be sent now the European conflict was at an end.

The 24-year-old officer returned home to Alfriston in East Sussex and spent time with his family and his then partner and Royal Naval hero Jack (Tony) Jones. He had told his father Ulric he might stay in uniform and would 'probably be shipped off to the Far East'.

His premonition was to prove correct. As the early summer of 1945 progressed there came a day when he received a telegram to report to Glasgow where he was instructed to board the SS *Carthage* bound for Bombay. Finally he knew where he was needed next so on 1 July he joined more than 1,000 troops on the ship and spent most of his 17 days on board appearing in various sketches with the onboard concert party.[64]

Once he arrived in Bally near Calcutta, No. 37 Reconnaissance Wing of the RAF were waiting for him at a grand old palace which belonged to a maharajah. Bogarde's skills were required to help pinpoint good areas for an invasion of Malaya (Operation Zipper).

Mostly, however, the planned landings to unnerve the Japanese did not take place as the war in the Pacific had come to an end. On 6 August 1945 the atom bomb devastated Hiroshima. On 15 August the Emperor of Japan and US President Harry S. Truman revealed to the world the Japanese had surrendered.

For the young British Army captain life was busy in Bally and his evenings were spent taking part in amateur theatre productions and trips to the cinema. There was time for socialising as his aerial photographic interpretation skills had been replaced by administration work.

It was here he met a senior WAAF officer and RAF Medmenham star who was to become an important friend. Edna Flavelle Holiday, known to her friends as 'Eve', was in her late thirties when she became a great friend of Captain Derek van den Bogaerde. Her war career was full of outstanding achievements. She had joined the WAAF in 1939 and is listed in *The London Gazette* as number 882898. From 1939 she learned how to work out shipping routes and identify the many different kinds of ships and submarines. Holiday's superior officer Constance Babington Smith described her as a cheerful, helpful woman during their work together at RAF Medmenham. Four years before Holiday arrived in the Far East as an Assistant Section Officer and Captain van den Bogaerde's boss, she was based in northernmost Scotland. With geographer David Linton she created a special Photographic Reconnaissance Unit. Its purpose was to monitor the movements of German Navy warships including the giant battleship *Bismarck*. The enemy ships were regularly attacking the Allies' Atlantic convoys.

John Young of the APIS, who had sailed out to Bombay the same day as Captain van den Bogaerde in July 1945, remembered Holiday well. He described her as tall with an ample figure. Her hair was in a plait bound around her head and she had an infectious sense of humour. The dashing Captain van den Bogaerde nicknamed her 'Nan' after a game of anagrams re-christened her 'Nan Baildon'. His link to Holiday would not be broken as they were to meet again and share a house in London after the war as he began to rebuild his theatrical career.

When it came to her war work Holiday was no fool. On 21 May 1941 she helped make history and had examined important aerial photographs taken by RAF Pilot Officer Michael Suckling. He had been asked to fly his reconnaissance Spitfire over the Norwegian fjords as intelligence reports revealed German shipping was moored there. Sure enough as he pointed his unheated, unarmed, unpressurised speedy little Spitfire towards the area he saw and photographed two large German ships and eleven smaller craft docked in two separate fjords. When he returned to base to the great joy of Holiday and Linton his exceptional images enabled them to pinpoint exactly where the Royal Navy and RAF should attack, and within six days the *Bismarck* was at the bottom of sea off the coast of France. It had been crippled by Allied torpedoes and then sunk by gunfire. Babington Smith recalled the day the courageous young Pilot Officer 'Babe' Suckling made history. 'His flight bought fame and glory to the PRU [Photographic Reconnaissance Unit] and his name will live on forever because of it.'[65] Sadly, two months later on 21 July as he flew over La Rochelle in France, Suckling, aged just 20 years old and a hero of nineteen missions, went missing. The news brought great sadness to the PRU staff which included of course his colleagues ASO Holiday and Babington Smith.

*   *   *

It was December 1945 when Captain van den Bogaerde received orders to board a ship bound for Batavia, Java, Indonesia. His duties in Bombay had diminished and he was bored doing administration work. In Batavia he was to join in the 23rd Indian Division which at the time had the unenviable task of attempting to sort out the struggles and violent outbursts of terrorism in the area. For while the Second World War was officially over there were still the issues of territorial rights to assess and reorganise involving the Indonesians, Dutch, and the British all of which continued to suffer various attacks from angry militant groups from all sides.

Although the Japanese had surrendered after the atom bomb was dropped on their country it didn't mean the Americans wanted to take up the challenge of restoring order in the whole of the East Indies. Boundaries were soon drawn up, however. Some of the responsibility fell on the shoulders of British naval hero Lord Louis Mountbatten who joined forces with Australian military commanders to take control of Java, Bali, Madura, Lombok and Sumatra. It was agreed the British should work closely with the Dutch and re-establish control of Indonesia. It had been ruled by the Dutch since the seventeenth century until the Japanese invasion of 1942.

Among the British military forces to arrive in troubled Indonesia in 1946 were the Gurkha Rifles who provided essential support to British troops ill-prepared to tackle the regular outbreaks of guerrilla warfare.

It would soon become clear the Dutch-Australian plan to create a harmonious 'New Indonesia' was not going to be easy. The Indonesians wanted to resist another 'takeover' in their country and Dutch residents resented British troops who marched along the streets and tried to tell them what to do. Indonesia at the time was embroiled in a tinderbox of political and military confusion. The anger of the Indonesian people had been inflamed as soon as they realised the Japanese had fooled them into believing they would 'prosper' under their rule.[66]

When Captain van den Bogaerde arrived at 'A' Mess at Batavia he was disappointed to discover he wasn't really needed at all. The area itself was chaotic and proving to be an administrative nightmare. The repatriation of prisoners of war was proving a headache as loyalties to different regimes became mixed and confusing. The British decided the Dutch government had lost touch with the people of Indonesia and just expected them to fall back into line as if the Second World War had never happened.

Then just as he thought life couldn't get any worse amidst the chaos on the streets, he suddenly found by chance the offices of a daily newspaper called *The Fighting Cock*. This publication had been founded by the General Officer Commanding Java, Major General Douglas Hawthorn, who was keen to help improve morale among the troops and population of Java. The young captain now on his editorial staff soon began contributing articles and columns and providing scenic photographs of British countryside in a bid to calm the anxious communities around him.[67]

Life in Batavia had certainly picked up as his natural gifts as a communicator had been noticed by General Hawthorn who promoted the officer and made him his ADC (Aide-de-Camp). This role along with his job at *The Fighting Cock* meant helping the General with his administration and the running of an extremely large old house in the hills. General Hawthorn, 48, had been decorated for his actions as commander of the British Army's 23rd Indian Division in Malaya, Burma and the Battle of Imphal. The newly promoted ADC van den Bogaerde must have been as impressed with his new boss just as he seemed to be taken with a new 'friend' – a half-Indonesian young woman called 'Harri' who would later inspire a character in his 1980 novel *A Gentle Occupation* which was loosely based on his experiences of the Far East. By the spring of 1946 he was to prove an exceptional ADC to General Hawthorn, a perfect organiser, brilliant communicator, journalist, morale booster and diplomat for his loud, big-hearted CO.

As the sun rose on the hot summer of 1946 the men of the 23rd Indian Division began to talk about 'demob' and often the conversations were filled with expressions of fear and dread. Many believed they would never find a job back home in Britain. It proved to be a subject of a column headed 'Cock Crow' – ADC van den Bogaerde empathised wholeheartedly with such feelings and wrote a column about how they'd 'striven for freedom and now when they had it within their grasp we baulk at it and are afraid to go forward and take our opportunities with open hands'.

On 25 July 1946 after a party without 'goodbyes' he set sail on the *Monarch* for home stopping in Singapore, a place he described as 'expensive', 'smelly' and 'British', and sent postcards to his family at Hillside Cottage in East Sussex. On 4 September, he was one of more than 2,500 men who descended the gangplank to disembark from the *Monarch* at Liverpool who had prepared themselves to don their standard 'demob' suits and look to the future.[68]

Life after military service for the former army intelligence officer proved difficult. He found it a massive gear change, the size of adjustment only the young can really grow into without regret. At the time though he was miserable in the grim rooms he had rented in Chelsea from a grumpy landlady and found himself far from the heady balm of his old life in the East Indies. Instead he was in bleak old Blighty deciding perhaps it was best to restart his stage career? It's understandable he thought it best to cling on to what he knew and had indeed begun to know very well before 1940. There is proof written on the flyleaf of a book about theatre which he had given to an army medic friend (Hugh Jolly), that he may well have talked about changing his name from 'Derek' to 'Dirk', and even considered journalism as a career. And did 'Dirk' look better than 'Derek' in a byline?

But by the end of 1946, with his army demob pay running low, he had come to the conclusion he might have to return home to live with his family until he found work. As luck would have it he bumped into a friend of the actor Tony Forwood.[69] He remembered how he'd shaken hands with Forwood in 1940 and they'd discussed his theatre career and how Forwood had suggested he would need an agent. After the war it turned out the blonde, dashing British Army officer Forwood was back in showbusiness, and now married with a son. When the two men finally met for a chat it wasn't long before Captain van den Bogaerde appeared on stage again. Within months Forwood and his wife, the well-known actress Glynis Johns, got divorced and Derek van den Bogaerde was about to become more than a client.

Various stage productions had put him back in the spotlights of the London theatres and the reviews all favourably announced him as a shining new star. Now known as Dirk Bogarde, he moved to Belgravia and his close female friend from his days in Bally, India, the WAAF Squadron Officer Eve Holiday (Nan) joined him as housekeeper and general assistant of sorts. They lived a street away from Noel Coward and those pedestrians they met in the street were often from London's artistic scene.

Soon enough he was mixing in circles which introduced him to the wonderful world of film. His good looks and enigmatic stage presence brought forward a wealth of offers. In 1947 he appeared as a policeman in *Dancing with Crime* and in *Esther Waters* he played William Latch. The following year he appeared in *Quartet* followed by *Once a Jolly Swagman*. From then on he made two or three films a year, for example *Dear Mr Prohack*, *Boys in Brown* and *The Blue Lamp* in 1949.

That year saw him on stage at his old stomping ground the Q Theatre where he played a blind former RAF pilot in a play called *Sleep on my Shoulder* written by Michael Clayton Hutton. Starring alongside the handsome dark-eyed actor in this production were Faith Brooke and Geoffrey Dunn. The drama was about a group of characters in a bombed-out public house discussing what their lives might have been if the war hadn't happened. Fresh with the memories of his own experiences knowing and working with the men and women of the RAF during the war, the play would mark the start of his opportunities to pour his experiences into a character and therefore seal in authenticity. His talent to expose the internalisation of emotion would prove an astounding magnet to the camera lens and audiences. His expressive eyes really were the windows to the soul of any character he chose to become.

Back in the late 1940s and early 1950s, with his eyes wide open to the pitfalls which came with the Hollywood manufacture of 'stars', he knew there must be other opportunities which offered more reasonable and civilised working conditions. So he turned to the British cinema and within weeks of escaping the predatory forces of America's Tinseltown he was contracted to the Rank Studios Organisation, which was under the watchful eye of the prolific independent and enigmatic film producer Betty Box. His early films were made with Wessex and Gainsborough under the Rank umbrella. He remained under contract with Rank for more than a decade until he grew weary of the way the company operated under the dictatorship and controversial behaviour of John Davis who was proving too influential and domineering in the life of elderly company chairman J. Arthur Rank.

In hindsight though we can safely argue the demands of Hollywood would definitely never have worked out well for a British poet-warrior like Captain van den Bogaerde. Having experienced gruesome horrors while serving as an Intelligence Officer during the Second World War he had a wisdom that belied his youth and pretty-boy looks. He was also quizzical, vastly intelligent, articulate and definitely not up for manipulation even though the golden goose of Hollywood had briefly fluffed her feathers at him. What he has admitted is how he made up his mind early on to look after number one and to be selfish was 'the only way to survive'. Bogarde had already written how he had to learn fast to protect himself from people who may bring him only loneliness and despair. 'During wartime you never knew if you were going to live to see the evening. Death was the ultimate cocktail,' he told a television interviewer in 1980, and 'I am the most selfish man I know. I didn't want to share my life and there's never been a change to my plan which was my own survival to do what I wanted to do.'[70] And yet friends such as the actor Michael Gough who knew Bogarde for 50 years described him as kind, generous and comical and at times most thoughtful. (Gough was a conscientious objector during the Second World War and served in the Non-Combatant Corps.)

How deeply Bogarde felt a sense of his own personal war has never been completely revealed as he lived in a shell he claimed 'nobody could crack' and never publicly discussed his sexuality. It's important to remember he grew up in an era when sexual relations between men were against the law. His privacy was all part of his art of self-protection and preservation, so much so that many of his friends describe him as someone who 'imagined his life' and even his brilliant and insightful official biographer John Coldstream found it a complexing task to unravel Bogarde's fiction from the facts of his life. Often described as mercurial, Bogarde was a sensitive man who threw himself deeply into his latest project as if it was a part of a jigsaw puzzle which added to the enigma he'd created, the camouflage if you like, which protected his personal life from unwanted intrusion.

Ironically in the 1950s and with armies of female fans the handsome actor was known as the 'British Rock Hudson'. He only mentioned his lifelong partner and agent Tony Forwood as 'Tote' – the man who organised everything and who just happened to share the house. Forwood was eight years older than Bogarde. He got divorced in 1948 and by the time Bogarde's career really took off in the 1950s he'd told his young protégé he was free to manage him full-time. In 1953 Forwood made a brief appearance in the film *Appointment in London* and Bogarde was in the starring role. Not long after making this film about Bomber Command they remained together for the rest of their lives sharing homes in England and France.

Bogarde also had women friends, some he plainly adored including artistes such as Capucine, Judy Garland, Ava Gardner and Kay Kendall. 'Judy was a monster to work with but she was magic! [*I Could Go On Singing*] What a privilege to be with this amazing artiste who I believe was killed by Hollywood,' he said.

> Ava Gardner was the sweetest woman on earth [In a letter to his friend the film critic Dilys Powell he explained how he greatly admired Ava because she appeared on set at 5am drinking a bottle of Dom Perignon!]. But I cannot commit to women emotionally as it would take too much out of me. I love them and yet those who are important to my life are those women who like me are independent and free spirits. Judy and Kay were so special to me as they felt the same about life.

'Of course during the war I lived for six years in a world of men,' he told BBC *Woman's Hour* listeners in 1980, 'I was in a world of fighting and soldiers which I loved and I wanted to be a soldier for the rest of my life. Women often fell out of love after waiting years for their husband or fiancé to come home. I believe marriage is uncivilised and unnatural.'[71]

Once he became published as the author of a bibliography totalling fifteen bestselling books, including eight volumes of memoirs and six novels, Bogarde decided to take part in the publicity whirl to help book sales. But his guard was never down when he told television presenter

Russell Harty and a few million television viewers, 'I don't see any point in somebody, a long time later, rifling through the memorabilia and the debris of my life. Those who know me will understand what I have written. What there is of me is what I have chosen to show you.'

He was resolute about keeping his personal life private. His reasons given to nosy interviewers were always delivered with a steely stare as he stacked up a protective wall aiming to quash any questions over his sexuality. And yet despite rebelling ardently against his early career label of 'matinee idol' (a term engineered by the influential Rank Organisation producer Betty Box) his army of adoring fans were mostly women who stayed loyal to him throughout his life.

Of course the leather trousers he wore as the menacing Anaclato in *The Singer Not the Song* (1961) exuded a thoroughly raunchy message and Bogarde talked about films being 'sexually charged'. His work with the great director Joe Losey proves it perfectly when we examine the brooding psychology, raw tension and desperation of the characters he played in seminal hits like Harold Pinter's *The Servant* (1963), *King and Country* (1964) and *Accident* (1967). The American Losey and the sophisticated Dirk Bogarde were to prove instrumental to the early success of each other's careers. Both men had shunned Hollywood, which had already blacklisted Losey because he was a communist. In England Losey first cast Dirk in *The Sleeping Tiger* which was released in 1954.

Bogarde once explained in a television interview: 'The cinema is a sexual thing. There's a special kind of alchemy going on. You go to the movies … you might not go there to watch porn but there is an excitement. No one wants to see tea cosies at work! I was perceived by some at Rank though like a hot water bottle and that bothered me.' His comment about tea cosies was also made about the ideas of 'method' acting and provides a rare clue into his mindful approach to his own performance style. Bogarde knew and worked with many fine 'method' actors but remarked how they often could only do one take of a scene in character and were at times unable to repeat the pinnacle of that first performance.

Of the Rank Studio executives who made him a household name as Dr Simon Sparrow in the vastly popular comedies *Doctor in the House* (1954), *Doctor at Sea* (1955) and *Doctor at Large* (1957) the actor believed they thought he was a teddy bear and that people would rather take him to bed than have him in bed! This attitude soon began to bother the Rank star and so he decided to reach out for the chance to add more artistic integrity in his roles. There was indeed so much more to him than good looks and an easy charm. To Rank he was only valuable if he filled its cinemas.

Since this time all sorts of evidence has come to light to suggest many other employees were seriously unhappy with the way in which John Davis, the managing director of Rank Studios, administrated the why, where and how the funding of 'each product' should be distributed. An accountant by trade with an ego the size of a house, Davis liked to rule supreme over Rank, take ultimate control over every production and towards the middle of his of long stay at this British film company, which began in 1942 and was to last until 1977, he began to surround himself with 'yes men' including the producer Earl St John.

Some film historians believe Davis saw productions like sausages that must be cheap and cheerful and nothing else and that he had no creative imagination. In their book *British Cinema of the 1950s: The End of Deference* Sue Harper and Vincent Porter write: 'Rank's Pinewood base was far and away the best-equipped studio in Britain, but the departmental heads always had a sceptical attitude for any request for information. No matter what a director asked for, their initial response was always a sharp intake of breath, sucked through the teeth, with the head nodding slowly from side to side.

'The studio was run like a boys' public school, where everyone was expected to behave properly. Davis was the headmaster and Earl St John the second master who was expected to iron out any difficulties.'[72] One day, St John summoned Bogarde to his office and silently handed him a note from David Lean asking him not to walk through the studio restaurant each day as though he owned it. (Bogarde writes about this incident in his memoir *Snakes and Ladders*.)

By 1977 under Davis' rule Rank had stopped making films altogether and he became known as the 'man who killed the British film industry'. By then Rank had invested in motorway services, hotels and made vast profits from Rank Xerox photocopying machines. Thirty-five years earlier in 1942 Rank had controlled two-thirds of the British film industry with its Pinewood Studios resembling a small city full of busy staff scurrying around like rabbits. Indeed Rank was behind the golden age of British cinema with pictures like *The Red Shoes* (made at Eagle-Lion Studios by Michael Powell and Emeric Pressburger) and the propaganda classic

Henry V directed by and starring Laurence Olivier, and also the famous *Brief Encounter* starring Trevor Howard and Celia Johnson. Films like these attracted audiences in their millions and are often still shown on television today.

So who was chairman J. Arthur Rank who employed stars like Bogarde? Well, he ran a flour business and was fundamentally a Victorian-style capitalist who appreciated creative people who could encapsulate on film the essence of old England. He had a Methodist approach to life. His patriotism is evident in his support for *Henry V* and he had taken up the challenge to re-build the British film industry. Author and British social commentator Dominic Sandbrook writes:

> J. Arthur put up the money for classics such as David Lean's *Brief Encounter* (1945), *Great Expectations* (1946) and *Oliver Twist* (1948), and for Powell and Pressburger's *The Life And Death of Colonel Blimp* (1943) and *The Red Shoes* (1948). He was keen to dampen the taste for Hollywood's fairyland style pictures.
>
> It was even Rank who paid for the Ealing comedies that have become synonymous with post-war Britain. Without him there would have been no *Passport To Pimlico* (1949), no *Kind Hearts And Coronets* (1949), no *The Lavender Hill Mob* (1951), no *The Ladykillers* (1955). Rank himself had nothing to do with writing or making these films. His great virtue was that he gave carte blanche to more talented people.

However, Rank ran into problems in 1947 when Harold Wilson as President of the Board of Trade slapped a tax on imported films to which Hollywood responded with a boycott on Britain. At first the company accountant Davis was delighted and used the opportunity to churn out films on tight budgets on the basis the British audiences had very little else to see. Quality didn't matter to him, raking in money did. However, when American films returned to British cinemas within six months some of Rank's recent offerings were deemed of appallingly low quality when compared with the US output of *Twelve O'Clock High*, *All the King's Men* and *Sands of Iwo Jima*.

Davis is reported to have spent five years gaining the trust of J. Arthur Rank who was described by most who knew him as a 'sweet, sentimental man of noble character'. Rank, it is claimed, was bullied by the over-ambitious Davis who was a man who fired anyone who disagreed with him or threatened his position.

In many ways the *Doctor* films starring Bogarde, the slapstick comedies with Norman Wisdom like *Trouble in Store* (1953), and the *Carry On* series helped to save the Rank Organisation from too severe a financial loss. It was their cosy and predictable nature which proved a guarantee to bring audiences back again and again. If the first one was a hit then the second one would be sure to claim a good crowd in a Rank-owned cinema.

Davis lapped up the glory of these successes owing to their low budgets but he was still regarded as a tyrant by his employees. No one, it was reported, ever had a good word to say about him. Former Granada Television director Sir Denis Forman went on to describe Davis as 'the Caligula' of British film who was the completely wrong person to be in charge of a business about human beings. One seasoned film producer of the time pointed out how Davis regarded film making as an 'industry' when in fact it was 'creation on the scale of industry', a massive difference in interpretation that Davis never understood. It seems, according to all those who took part in Phillip Kemp's 1995 documentary *The Man who Killed the British Film Industry*, Davis disliked artistes, writers and directors … anyone who cost money. Indeed anyone who disagreed with him would turn up at work on a Friday to find a note on a cleared desk which said 'cheque in the post'. Davis sacked anyone he decided to knife in the back or disagreed with him. It was always Friday the knives came out.

The late, great director Lewis Gilbert told how one of Davis' lackeys had arrived on the set of *Reach for the Sky* starring Kenneth More as the Battle of Britain pilot, Douglas Bader. Gilbert said: 'This chap arrived from Rank's headquarters in South Street, Mayfair with instructions from Davis I should cut an important scene from the film. I refused because it was an essential part of the story and suddenly the lackey started weeping and begging me to do as he asked. I was stunned that a grown man could be so intimidated by Davis.'[73]

The producer Betty Box, who was instrumental in casting Bogarde in the modestly budgeted *Doctor* films of the 1950s, recalled Davis staring at her legs every time she was called to a meeting with him in his office in Mayfair. 'He sat at a big desk like Mussolini,' she said. 'He would stare at my legs and when I sat down I pulled my skirt over my knees and we got on with the meeting.' Box, who tolerated Davis, like so many grew tired of him insisting she make more *Doctor* films. She complained he wouldn't accept there were only so many jokes about the National Health Service the British public could stomach. Bogarde agreed with her and longed to appear in more meaningful films and move on from the Davis-inspired grip of his Rank contract.

Bogarde's authorised biographer John Coldstream explained how the actor had similar thoughts about Davis to those expressed by the director Michael Powell. Indeed he might have stayed at Rank if it had not been for Davis' limited vision and restrictions imposed upon him. Coldstream writes: 'Had Dirk stayed in the confines of Rank we probably would not have had *Death in Venice, Providence, Despair, The Night Porter* and other roles that were a far cry from the safe romantic/heroic ones that sold tickets but did not stretch him as an actor.'

Another big character of the 1950s was the patriotic head of Ealing Studios Sir Michael Balcon (1896–1977), whose steady arguments with Davis over funding, contracts, and casting often left a dark cloud over many a production. From 1938 to 1955 Balcon led Ealing to the heights of success and later took control of British Lion Films and became chairman of the British Film Institute committee which helped fund new work. In 1950, five years after Bogarde had left the Army, Balcon produced a film called *The Blue Lamp* in which the actor appears as a desperate youth turned armed robber named Tom Riley who shoots PC George Dixon (Jack Warner) at the scene of one of his crimes.

Balcon meanwhile did not appreciate being bullied by Davis when Ealing was financially bailed out by Rank which had moved into Pinewood and squeezed out many of the existing talented crews and personnel. Balcon, a patriot who sought to maintain the status quo of a patriarchal society, usually cast films with a nearly all-male cast. In 1958 when he agreed to produce *Dunkirk* starring Bogarde's friend Richard Attenborough he insisted the seldom-seen female characters were in traditional roles of worried housewives, young mothers or nurses. However, we can thank Balcon for his foresight in backing the exceptionally clever *Passport to Pimlico* (1949), *The Lavender Hill Mob* (1951) and *The Ladykillers* (1953).

* * *

Now working and starring as 'Dirk Bogarde', the actor was seen on the big screen in *So Long at the Fair* and *The Woman in Question* (1950). The following year he appeared as a character called Stephen Mundy in *Blackmailed*, followed by *Hunted*. In 1952 he starred in *Penny Princess* and *The Gentle Gunman*. It was around this time he said he was weary of playing frightened, dysfunctional criminal types with soulful eyes and a way with women.

He needn't have worried as by 1953 the actor began to be cast as military figures in newly-scripted war films. No one could dispute his own genuine military experiences with the British Army and the RAF. No doubt his memories proved useful as he read the scripts which now came his way thanks to his resourceful manager Tony Forwood,

In 1953 *Appointment in London* directed by Philip Leacock proved a 'well done story of Bomber Command in the bleak days of 1943'. It was written by an RAF pilot called John De Lacy 'Dim' Wooldridge DSO DFC who had flown a whopping total of ninety-seven operational missions. Wooldridge, also an accomplished composer, joined the RAF in 1938 and was one of the few pilots to have flown the twin-engined Avro Manchester while he was with No. 207 Squadron. He was chosen to fly as a Wing Commander with the famous 'Dambuster' Guy Gibson. By 1943 Wooldridge became commanding officer of No. 105 Squadron which used Mosquito bombers to carry out low-level precision bombing raids.

In *Low Attack*, his 1944 book about these missions he wrote:

It would be impossible to forget … the sensation of looking back over enemy territory and seeing your formation behind you, wing-tip to wing-tip, their racing shadows moving only a few feet below them across the earth's surface; or that feeling of sudden exhilaration when the target was definitely located and the whole pack were following you on to it with their bomb doors open, while people below scattered in every direction and the long streams of flak came swinging up; or the sudden jerk of consternation of the German soldiers lounging on the coast, their moment of indecision, and then their mad scramble for the guns; or the memory of racing across The Hague at midday on a bright spring morning, while the Dutchmen below hurled their hats in the air and beat each other on the back. All these are unforgettable memories. Many of them will be recalled also by the peoples of

Europe long after peace has been declared, for to them the Mosquito came to be an ambassador during their darkest hours.

In his film script of *Appointment in London* RAF hero Wooldridge wanted to explain just what air crews went through during an eight-hour bombing raid on Germany. When he met Bogarde to discuss the film he was told enthusiastically 'the script is the best thing I've ever read' – praise indeed from the actor who confirmed his opinion by signing a contract with Mayflower Pictures and British Lion Productions.[74] Mayflower was owned by the financially astute lawyer Maxwell Setton who after serving in the North African desert and Italy during the Second World War had gained managerial experience with the Rank Organisation. He then set up on his own as an independent producer with Aubrey Baring, a flamboyant member of the famous banking family. Bogarde recalled it was the first time he actually made any kind of impression for good on the screen. He said: 'The director Philip Leacock made me more aware than any director up till then that it was the thought which counted more than the looks.'

Starring as Wing Commander Tim Mason made Bogarde determined to 'make every Wing Commander I played as physically attractive as I could, as mischievous or as flirty as I could. Then something happened and I started to nurse it and a little light came into my eyes and it was called "Dirk's Bar". Nobody else had it because the only thing I had was a good future and my eyes.'[75]

The film's story proved to be sound and naturalistic. Bogarde was no doubt delighted with it because he could vouch for its authenticity and he had no doubt been impressed with Woolridge's extraordinary experiences with Bomber Command. At last there was some reality for him to interpret and portray.

Appointment in London is about Wing Commander Tim Mason who is nearing the end of three tours totalling ninety missions over Germany. This in reality was an enormous feat. In fact most Bomber Command crews did thirty dangerous trips over enemy territory then if they survived the horrors of being shot down they were routinely posted to safer roles as training instructors at British airfields. In the case of the character of Wing Commander Mason he suddenly finds himself grounded and frustrated that he cannot join his squadron and complete his spectacular goal of flying ninety missions. When two crew members are injured and unable to fly he disobeys his orders to remain at base and climbs into a Lancaster ready for action. When the Pathfinder aircraft is shot down it is the cool, calm Mason at the controls of a Lanc who uses the radio to help get the mission back on track and lead the squadron to victory. The fact he had disobeyed orders proved to be a right decision as he had saved the lives of his men and ensured every target was successfully bombed. The film ends with Mason and his girlfriend Eve Canyon (played by Dinah Sheridan) arriving at Buckingham Palace where he is presented with a medal by King George VI.

Bogarde was immensely relieved to have had the chance to play a character like the noble Wing Commander Mason as 'at long last' he was in the role of hero and not the usual spiv role of a young man in a trenchcoat on the run. Those kind of films he believed were getting him nowhere. By starring in *Appointment in London* he also got to understand even more what it was like for the men of Bomber Command who had relied on his aerial photographic interpretations during the war. The essence of the film suited him perfectly. Interestingly enough Bogarde's brother-in-law George Goodings, who had married Elizabeth 'Lu' van den Bogaerde in 1947, had been a member of the 'Dambusters' during the Second World War. No doubt he proved an excellent person to have in the family when it came to Bogarde's research about life in the heroic Bomber Command.

This important film in his life also had the advantage of having Sir Arthur 'Bomber' Harris – former head of Bomber Command – as its technical advisor. It couldn't be better for authenticity. The film was shot at Shepperton Studios and at RAF Upwood where three of the Lancaster bombers which had survived the war appeared in the film alongside a few Avro Lincoln bombers which were still in service in 1953. Among the cast was a 25-year-old Bryan Forbes who enjoyed working with Bogarde and thought him 'very much the star' in all sorts of ways. 'He even had his name on his own chair!' said the admiring Forbes who noted Bogarde as 'kind, helpful and charming' and 'selfless' when working with fellow actors. (The two became lifelong friends and in 1978 Bryan Forbes and his wife the actress Nanette Newman visited Bogarde at his home in the south of France. It was also the Forbeses who informed Prime Minister John Major in 1991 that their friend was highly deserving of a knighthood for his dedicated services to cinema and culture.)[76]

Appointment in London opened in February 1953 – the year of HM The Queen's coronation. It had only moderate success at the British box office but was praised by reviewers. *The Sunday Graphic* described it as 'Mr Bogarde's finest hour – whether discreetly conveying the inward and spiritual grace of a born leader or the outward and visible signs of a young lover, he never once steps over into implausibility'. Any idea the Americans weren't overly keen on the film and allegedly wrote it off as a 'dud' can now be disputed. Film and literature academic Dr Barbara Siek, who has lectured and written on Bogarde, is one of the writing team who set up the Official Dirk Bogarde website and founded the Sir Dirk Bogarde media sites. Dr Siek considers it a matter of poor distribution of *Appointment in London* which limited access to potential filmgoers rather than the quality of the film itself which had everything going for it, for example an inspiring plot including a black airman – a big step forward then. Also there are excellent performances, stunning cinematography with actual bombing clips, and a stirring score. Bogarde loved the film and felt it had refreshed his film career. Siek said:

> The film wasn't released in the US until September 1955 – two and a half years after its British release, at which point it had missed all of the initial advertising and promotion, albeit in England.
>
> Lacking in the big budget of a US film, any wave of publicity in the US to herald its pluses was not going to happen. Even then, as a British film, it would screen in smaller art theatres and could never compete with the blockbuster that year, *Strategic Air Command*. As for American television viewers, they were on a Western kick once *Gunsmoke* starring Audie Murphy, aired that Autumn.[77]

In agreement, film critic Mark Kermode notes in his book *The Good, The Bad, and the Multiplex* (2011), that even now, for British films 'the real problem is distribution … only a scant few secure the width of distribution that allows an extensive audience'.

The actor Nigel Stock appeared in six films with Bogarde between 1947 and 1965 – three of which were Second World War films, *Appointment in London*, *High Bright Sun* and *The Password is Courage*. Like Bogarde, Stock had served in the Second World War, from 1939–41 with the London Irish Rifles, and then the Assam Regiment in the Indian Army between

1941 and 1945 in Burma, China and Kohima. With both actors having served in South-East Asia it might well have been a talking point between them especially given all the films they did together. With a role like Wing Commander Tim Mason to inspire Bogarde on to a more extensive range of characters he could offer an adoring public he went on to star in *Desperate Moment* (1953) a thriller about a Dutchman on the run.

The following year saw the release of another war film starring the former British Army intelligence officer turned film star. Indeed, Bogarde had signed up to play a character called Lieutenant Graham in *They Who Dare*. Also starring in the role of Sergeant Corcoran was real life Second World War RAF Bomber Command hero gunner/wireless operator, Denholm Elliot.

The Russian-American director Lewis Milestone, who had won an Oscar for his big screen interpretation of the First World War epic *All Quiet on the Western Front* (1930), was creating the scenes again from behind the camera. Bogarde was delighted to work with Milestone whose reputation for making anti-war films was by then firmly established in film history. According to film historian Joseph Millichap: 'Milestone avoided the "set hero and mock heroics" typical of Hollywood war movies, allowing for a measure of genuine realism reminiscent of his masterpiece, *All Quiet on the Western Front*.' The director's trademark handling of tracking shots is evident in the action scenes. How could Bogarde resist the opportunity of working with someone of Milestone's background, especially when it came to anti-war films.

They Who Dare is about six Special Boat Service commandos and two Greek officers and local guides who take part in a mission to blow up German airfields on the island of Rhodes. (Most of the action was filmed in sunny Cyprus and Malta.) As Lieutenant Graham and his men come ashore by night they must get over steep mountains in order to reach their targets. When eight of the saboteurs are captured it's only Lieutenant Graham and Sergeant Corcoran (Denholm Elliott) who make it back to the submarine which is waiting to rescue them.

The screenplay written by Robert Westerby had been inspired by a report written by wartime Commando Colonel David George Carr Sutherland CBE, MC, TD DL who had survived an incredible and courageous raid on the Germans who invaded Greece early on in 1941. More authenticity was provided by a former wartime SBS officer by the name of Walter Milner Barry who was employed by the Mayflower Film Company to work as Technical Advisor.

By then the devastation of Greece had been horrific with severe British naval losses around the island of Crete. The Germans had met fierce resistance from Australian, British, New Zealand and Greek troops including local residents. In all the Germans are believed to have suffered around 4,000 casualties. Statistics revealed by the Greek government claimed its resistance killed 21,087 Axis troops (17,536 Germans, 2,739 Italians and 1,532 Bulgarians) and captured 6,463 – of which 2,102 were Germans, 2,109 were Italians, and 2,252 were Bulgarians. The Greek government claimed these figures paid for the lives of 20,650 Greek partisans who were killed and the unknown number captured and even tortured.

As Bogarde began filming *They Who Dare* he had reached number 2 in a *Daily Mirror* poll of popular men which included Tony Curtis, Gregory Peck, Rock Hudson, Richard Todd and Alan Ladd. The handsome, talented Bogarde trailed only behind the good-looking HRH Prince Philip who was number one! 'Fair enough,' he must have said to himself. However, whilst Bogarde's name was at the top of the 'most loved' polls in 1954 the film critics weren't impressed with *They Who Dare.* Even Bogarde admitted one reviewer had called the film *'How Dare They?'*[78]

Life was as ever busy for the actor as he took on the role of Flight Sergeant MacKay in *The Sea Shall Not Have Them* co-starring Michael Redgrave who had in real life served briefly in the Royal Navy on HMS *Illustrious* during the Second World War. The film was directed by Lewis Gilbert (1920–2018) and is based on a novel by John Harris telling the story of a dangerous RAF Air-Sea Search and Rescue mission to find the endangered and stoical crew of a Hudson bomber forced to ditch into the North Sea just after the Normandy D-Day landings. Stranded in the leaking dinghy in freezing, soaked conditions with MacKay are three fellow crew members and an air commodore (Redgrave) who is carrying secret plans which could prevent the enemy air raids on London.

As war films of the time go it makes the grade with some excellent technical help from the RAF including some stunning footage shot of a now rare Sea Otter aircraft in action and of course the now extinct Hudson Bomber. It's well worth watching and waves the flag for survival against the odds. (A waspish comment from Noel Coward who worked for British Intelligence during the Second World War, is often remembered by film historians whenever the film gets mentioned. Apparently Coward happened to walk by a London cinema and saw the billboard which screamed 'Starring Dirk Bogarde and Michael Redgrave in *The Sea Shall Not Have Them*'. Coward piped up to a companion, 'I don't know why not. Everyone else has!') Bogarde's authorised biographer John Coldstream wrote how the role as the 'snivelling Cockney Flight Sgt. MacKay is almost a thankless one and doesn't allow him much dimension and neither does the script give him much wiggle-room to improve the limitations of his lines'.[79]

This film was probably one of the obligatory films the actor had to do under his contract with Rank Studios. His saving grace as MacKay is his loyalty to his injured friend, but again his lines limit him. Bogarde did his best, but he was the first to say, 'You have to have writers and the lines to work with as an actor,' which is why he revised many of his lines later on when he had the prestige to get away with it. Also it was a tough shoot for all the actors sitting in a dinghy knee-deep in water, being doused with pouring 'rain' provided by hoses for almost 95 per cent of their time on screen. And yet there is a stirring realistic energy to the film as we see the RAF rescue unit racing toward the stranded dinghy and we realise the sea battle between the Germans and the British is at an end.

Within weeks after completing his wartime adventure at sea, Bogarde was back working with producer Betty Box and director Ralph Thomas in *Doctor at Sea*. He played Dr Simon Sparrow who endures regular doses of hi-jinks and comic scenarios which take place during his chaotic career in medicine. Then in 1955 British filmgoers saw the release of *Cast a Dark Shadow*, a murder mystery directed by Lewis Gilbert, and Bogarde played the lead character of Edward 'Teddy' Bare. This was followed by a subtle if not quietly menacing performance as José – the quiet hero of *The Spanish Gardener* based on a novel by A.J. Cronin and directed by Philip Leacock.

When *Doctor in the House* hit the big screen in 1957 it helped to endorse the young actor's growing fame and increase the number of his female fans. When he received a National Film Award in 1958 he told a BBC reporter 'I don't like purely comedy roles so much but what did help put me at the top was *Ill Met By Moonlight* which was cloak and dagger with a comedy essence or background.'

This wartime-based cinematic adventure involved Bogarde working in 1956 with the genius directing and writing team of Michael Powell and Emeric Pressburger who had vast experience creating unusual, quirky and surreal wartime propaganda classics such as *The Life and Death of Colonel Blimp* (1943), *A Canterbury Tale* (1944) starring Sheila Sim (later Lady Attenborough, a friend and neighbour to Bogarde and Tony Forwood during their years in France), and the legendary, exceptionally brilliant *A Matter of Life and Death* (1946) in which Second World War hero and actor David Niven appeared in the lead role as Squadron Leader Peter David Carter.

Ill Met By Moonlight was a partly autobiographical representation of the wartime exploits of Patrick Leigh Fermor and W. Stanley Moss who were agents of the Special Operations Executive (SOE). In 1944 their mission was to kidnap Heinrich Kreipe – the commander of the 22nd Air Landing Infantry Division which was occupying Crete. Kreipe was to be smuggled to Cairo with the aid of the Cretan Resistance to be interrogated by the head of SOE. W. 'Bill' Stanley Moss had kept a lively journal of his activities as an agent and in 1945 the title of his book based on those diaries, *Ill Met By Moonlight*, came from Shakespeare's *A Midsummer Night's Dream*. However, censors instructed by SOE chief Major-General Sir Colin Gubbins took their red pens to the manuscript and it wasn't published until 1950. Despite the delay of five years it was immediately hailed as 'more thrilling than any detective story I can remember' by the great novelist Willy Somerset Maugham.

In the second volume of his memoir *Million Dollar Movie*, legendary director Powell wrote how *Ill Met by Moonlight* was 'dear to his heart not because he wanted to play at cops and robbers but because of Crete and the Cretans'. Powell made the comment long before he began actually shooting the film. He described how when he first fell in love with the story in 1952 it wasn't the right time to make it for the big screen. He wrote that:

People were still trying to forget the war and become socially conscious. Big, spectacular war pictures, like *The Guns of Navarone* and *Lawrence of Arabia*, were in the oven but not yet in production, and it was obvious that they would have to be crammed with big names and expensive special effects.

Emeric [Pressburger – Powell's co-director and scriptwriter in their production company, The Archers] already knew I wanted to start the film with Crete and the Cretans, and I proposed to open with the German paradrop on the island: hundreds of armed paratroopers turning the sky black like a crowd of locusts, while the islanders fight and die in defence of their homes and families. He had heard my stories of SOE agents Xan Fielding and Paddy Leigh Fermor, and had listened to my pleas for at least three or four subplots, love stories or murders, to criss-cross in and out of the main plot of the kidnapping of the German General. An action film like this would need to have big names and daring stunt men, and the best part would be the German General, the more formidable he was, the greater glory for his kidnappers – and then he would have to make several attempts to escape and nearly succeed.[80]

In 1956 when director Powell eventually cast Bogarde in *Ill Met By Moonlight* he said whimsically he had met 'a charmer who liked dressing up and he knew what a good actor he was'. He also hired former SOE agent in Crete, Xan Fielding DSO, to be his technical advisor throughout. Just for once Powell and Pressburger agreed to make the one film with the Rank Organisation's John Davis and his yes man Earl St John despite the fact Davis and Powell had a relationship resembling 'Clash of The Titans'.

Powell, a serious-minded and proud man who'd been born near Canterbury in Kent, stood up to Davis' autocratic behaviour and refused to cut costs and diminish quality. Powell resented the idea of joining Rank as he detested the thought of losing the autonomy he had with his own The Archers company. Sadly, *Ill Met By Moonlight* actually marked the end of the nobly independent 'Archers' as a company as Davis took it upon himself to haul in the British and European talent and go head to head with the Hollywood giants. Powell would later chide his old friend Pressburger for selling out and becoming a 'chair polisher' with the Rank brigade.

In 1956 Powell began to make *Ill Met By Moonlight* under some duress as one of the many spirit-crushing regulations imposed by Davis was his insistence it was made in VistaVision – black and white. It wasn't what he imagined at all and feared it would become too documentary-like. He had already been disappointed in his friend Pressburger's factual-style script but could hardly blame his literary colleague who had just finished making the accurately detailed *The Battle of the River Plate*. Another disappointment loomed large at the outset when the Greek government refused permission for the film to be shot on Crete because the crew and cast would arrive 'armed to the teeth'. Such behaviour would be regarded as 'provocative' and not welcome at all. The nearby Cypriot government issued the same ban and joined the Greeks in their reasoning to refuse all permits.

In his memoirs Powell wrote:

I decided to shoot *Ill Met By Moonlight* in the Alpes Maritimes, in the mountain country between Savoy and the River Var, where Italy and France share a common frontier that comes up from the sea and then mountains into the sky of Haute Savoie. It's a great country where there are no houses, only military barracks and roads, for the frontier between France and Italy has been altered three times. But the main reason why this huge, beautiful area has not been opened up and exploited with developments and roads, and even towns, is because it was the hunting grounds of the kings of Italy and of Savoy and it was alive with marmots, chamois, hawks and wild sheep, and it has been like that for eighty years. Extra shooting then took place in Corsica.

Grumpily he too wrote how during the making of the film he often had to monitor Bogarde's tendency to say the lines too subtly and this quiet acting technique was having too much influence on the rest of the cast, including Marius Goring, Cyril Cusack and David Oxley. Only the Cretan actors steadfastly played themselves as true rebellious, boisterous countrymen.

The director described what he wanted of Bogarde – 'a flamboyant young murderer, lover, bandit – a tough, Greek speaking leader of men. Bogarde would listen with attention to me while I told him what I wanted, and then he would give me about a quarter of it.' In later years Powell complained Bogarde had 'underplayed' the part.

But Sir Patrick 'Paddy' Leigh Fermor DSO OBE who was often on set during the making of the film was happy with Bogarde's performance and called him a 'brilliant actor' even though he thought the script at times was cliché-ridden. Bogarde himself insisted his favourite publicity photograph ever was him as his *Ill Met By Moonlight* character standing on a rock in the military guise of a Greek militiaman sporting jodhpurs tucked into knee-high boots, black beret and shirt.

When he saw a rough cut of the film he offered up some amendments to Powell for consideration. Powell wrote to Bogarde in 1956:

It is quite true you have always been a close-up actor... but, my dear Dirk, that was more self-preservation. I know perfectly well why you have cultivated the close-up and 'thrown away' medium shots, and put your heart and soul and excellent voice and technique into post-syncing.

You can't fool me, even if you want to: and to your surprise you are going to get quite exceptional praise for your performance in this picture – because you steal it in the most unselfish manner: by being better than the other people with you in the scene.[81]

Although Bogarde and Powell didn't work together again they always remained cordial with each other. Indeed the actor once accompanied Powell on a visit to the south of France. Powell's father had a hotel in the area near to where Dirk went on to buy his own property. Bogarde wrote: 'Mickey [Powell] knew every hamlet, track, crag and olive grove. Together we explored them.' Bogarde, Powell and his wife, the awesome Oscar-winning film editor Thelma Schoonmaker, often ran into each other at film events. Bogarde admitted he had great admiration for Powell. Dr Barbara Siek explained:

Later, in 1990 after finishing *Daddy Nostalgie*, Dirk wrote to the director Bertrand Tavernier, who had worked for Micky Powell, saying 'I was pleased I had not let you all down and that I had not forgotten the lessons I had been taught by Micky Powell, Joe [Losey], Luchino [Visconti]... ' Tavernier dedicated 'Daddy N' to Micky. In a letter to critic pal Dilys Powell, Bogarde refers to the dedication of 'Daddy N' and also the earlier award he gave to Micky 'who was 82 then... and fiercely proud of getting it. As I was giving it to him'. When Thelma and I were chatting at an event and I mentioned Dirk, she said she and Micky had fortunately seen him shortly before he suffered a stroke and his death a few years later.'

Bogarde and Powell shared a dislike for dictatorial Rank managing director John Davis. Of Powell's dislike of working with Davis, Dr Barbara Siek writes: 'John Davis was an arrogant, autocratic accountant who understood and focused almost exclusively on figures and viewed films as "products." It must have been discouraging and limiting for fine actors to work for the man, and I'm not alone in saying that.'

Davis was blamed by many for the end of the British film industry. The actor Stewart Granger said 'Michael Powell's career would have continued much longer if he hadn't fallen foul of that nasty John Davis. Rank's man – a monster. Like me [Granger] Michael said what he thought, and he thought Davis was a piece of s***! So did I!'[82]

When as an elderly man the famously uncompromising Powell watched *Ill Met By Moonlight* again in the late 1980s he was shocked he'd agreed to shoot it in black and white. He wrote in his memoir:

I was surprised how bad the film was. It wasn't entertainment. It was like a Ministry of Information documentary film: true title 'The True Story of the Kidnapping of General Kreipe, on the island of Crete, 1944.'

The Cretan atmosphere was perfect, the use of Greek dialogue resourceful, the music of Theodorakis stirring and patriotic, the acting by all and sundry B-minus, the camera work a mistake. I so should have shot the film in colour. By the time the film reached the screens in 1957 it looked like an historical document. Everyone was obviously having a good time. Nobody was cultivating what my good friend Robert de Niro describes as 'an attitude'. The script was underwritten and the gags were unoriginal, and the surprises not surprising.

The final two reels of what were supposed to be a chase film were weak. The direction concentrated so much on creating a Greek atmosphere that the director had no time or invention for anything else. The performances of the principals were atrocious. Marius Goring as General Kreipe wouldn't have scared a rabbit; David Oxley as Captain Stanley Moss *was* the rabbit; while as for Dirk Bogarde's performance as Major Patrick Leigh Fermor, Philidem to the Cretans, it's a wonder that Paddy didn't sue both Dirk and me. Dirk was determined to throw the part away and go under everything, and he succeeded. It wasn't that he couldn't have played it for blood and guts if he'd wanted to. He just didn't want to.

Despite Powell's criticism it must be pointed out the Greek villages in the film were realistic and were shot with a great degree of wit and style.

We must remember too that both Bogarde and Powell had iron wills and the director was used to people reacting quickly to his every command. Bogarde played Paddy Leigh Fermor the way he thought best after listening long and hard to Xan Fielding's comments about characterisation – Xan had been with Paddy throughout the real-life adventure. The costume worn by the actor was also 'exactly what had been worn' at the time. Powell, however, had described it as 'picture postcard'. Bogarde and his partner 'Forwood' had befriended technical adviser Xan Fielding and his wife Daphne and they enjoyed a good rapport with Leigh Fermor.[83]

During the making of the film in the Alpes Maritimes Bogarde said he enjoyed himself despite long days which went from 3.30 in the morning until well after 9 at night. Forwood described to a friend how Powell had chosen wonderful locations and there was usually somewhere to swim when the heat become too much to cope with.

Despite Powell's disappointment in the picture it proved the seventh most popular film to hit the big screen in 1957 – a year which revealed cinema was now facing fierce competition from television. When discussing British war films of the 1950s academics Sue Harper and Vincent Porter write:

> The story, which was often based on a real wartime episode, frequently consisted of an intelligently conceived and mounted attack by a small group of men on a prestigious, and often unsuspecting, enemy target. The popular war films of 1955, such as *The Dam Busters*, *Above Us the Waves*, *The Cockleshell Heroes* and *Ill Met by Moonlight*, all deployed this structure. They were all patriotic and male-dominated adventure stories, which especially appealed to men, and in some ways they were analogous to the American Western. But the significant difference was that the military hierarchy of the small band of heroes was always unproblematically mapped onto Britain's traditional class structure. Their combination of wartime history and a boy's adventure story made them ideal films to which fathers could take their sons for both nostalgic and educational purposes.[84]

And while Bogarde was busy making the *Doctor* films, he signed up in 1957 to play a grounded RAF Flight Lieutenant Michael Quinn in *The*

Wind Cannot Read which co-starred Yoko Tani in a story about forbidden love. Ralph Thomas was in the director's chair. (This film also featured Bogarde's partner and manager Tony Forwood who played a minor role as an army officer.)

Here we see how he could use his real-life wartime experiences as an intelligence officer in the tropics of Indonesia as inspiration for his characterisation of Flight Lieutenant Quinn. The film takes place in Burma and India in 1943 and is based on a novel by Richard Mason. Whilst in real life Bogarde had a close female friend (Harri) during his wartime experiences in the Far East who was a 'ravishing beauty' of half-Indonesian and half-Dutch parentage, his initial loneliness is represented well in the film some 13 years later. Once again we see the actor drawing on his own sense of reality and association. He successfully managed to emulate his own wartime experiences of a man feeling alienated and missing his home country.

In the film Flight Lieutenant Quinn falls in love with his Japanese language instructor Suzuki San 'Sabbi' – a romance and marriage they are driven to keep quiet as the Japanese are perceived as the enemy. During work in the field as an interrogator of Japanese prisoners-of-war Quinn is captured along with his Indian driver and a brigadier. A clever plan enables Quinn's escape and he returns to find Sabbi sick with a brain tumour. Sabbi dies following an operation. This was the ending which Bogarde had agreed to with Rank and as the star of the film he had some clout. He was furious when he received a call from Davis about a change to the final scene. Davis insisted the film should have a happy ending but Bogarde asked Davis to 'justify the idea'. Bogarde was able to use his massive popularity as Britain's number one star (a claim he shared at this time with Kenneth More) to indeed pull rank on the Rank managing director (Davis) who tried, unsuccessfully, to persuade the actor how market forces were dominating many of the film industry's decisions and its fight for survival. Davis lost his battle and the sad ending to the film remained as Bogarde wished, mostly he argued for quality's sake.[85] And whilst Rank was not a design-led company it is fair to say *The Wind Cannot Read* was filmed amidst appropriate backgrounds and atmospheric scenery. But whatever agitations may have loitered in the hot, sticky atmosphere of India on set that year there was still opportunity for a party to which Bogarde invited the Maharajah and Maharani of Jaipur.

When Bogarde got back home to Beel House, Amersham, Buckinghamshire, there were opportunities for publicity photographs to be taken and the private Bogarde and Forwood entertained co-star Yoko Tani. Just after *The Wind Cannot Read* opened in 1958 the reviews were enthusiastic. Director Ralph Thomas said he thought John Davis had been brave to authorise the filming in India and admired him for trusting David Lean's belief in the book as a real three-handkerchief story. Thomas described Bogarde as 'very good' as the lead character of Quinn. It wasn't the first time Bogarde had made a distinct and memorable portrayal of an RAF officer – many of who he had met during his own military service. His knowledge of air crew and pilot mentality went way back to the times the skies were threatened by the Luftwaffe. He'd known and met many heroes who'd risked all in aerial combat and bombing raids ... British, Canadians, Americans, Poles. Bogarde's performances in films such as *Appointment in London* and *The Wind Cannot Read* are a tribute to them all.

The heat of India had not failed in its fateful and mystical attempts to attract more fire into the actor's career. This time the mysterious, shimmering souls of the desert came into view as director Anthony 'Puffin' Asquith had already approached Bogarde about playing T.E. Lawrence. A picture about the enigmatic Colonel Thomas Edward Lawrence (also known as John Hume Ross and Thomas Edward Shaw) who led the Arab rebellion against the Turks during the First World War was first conceived in the early 1930s by the great director Alexander Korda. He had read Lawrence's astounding and compelling book *The Seven Pillars of Wisdom*. But in 1935 and just before his own sudden death in a motorcycle accident, Lawrence had strongly objected to a film being made about his life. In 1958 the playwright Terence Rattigan, who had served in the RAF as a tail-gunner during the Second World War and wrote the screenplay of the famous 1945 epic film *The Way to The Stars*, penned a drama called *Ross* about Lawrence. When Rank took up a proposal to make it into a film Bogarde was offered the role by director Asquith.[86]

The actor was delighted to have a chance to play such an extraordinary and enigmatic character and spent a year studying everything he could about Lawrence – the Englishman who was an archaeologist, military officer, diplomat and writer. Rank forked out a fortune on having a special blonde wig made for Bogarde in an attempt to make him physically resemble Lawrence and various locations including Iraq were suggested during discussions at Pinewood Studios.

The playwright Rattigan, a gay man and author of such theatrical hits as *The Deep Blue Sea*, *The Browning Version* and *Separate Tables*, usually wrote about outsiders and relationship issues. He made sure the play about his hero Lawrence not only examined his famous First World War exploits but delved into historic references of homosexuality. And whilst it is true Lawrence himself was a loner who had written in his own memoir *The Seven Pillars of Wisdom* about love between two men it has proved difficult for academics to provide evidence of any significance about relationships in Lawrence's personal life. Psychologists agree he was a fearless masochist full of self-loathing and then point out this was no doubt caused by the regular childhood beatings he received from his mother and his suffering at the loss of two brothers during the First World War. It is understandable why Bogarde was keen to play Lawrence who appears to be a complicated, tortured and contrary character with a noble thirst for justice.

But a few days after returning from his filming in India with *The Wind Cannot Read* Bogarde faced what he described 'his bitterest disappointment'. He was told Rank had withdrawn support from the Lawrence film when it was discovered director David Lean and producer Sam Spiegel had already raised $15 million and had begun work on *Lawrence of Arabia* – this time its writers were Robert Bolt and Michael Wilson with Peter O'Toole cast as Lawrence and Omar Sharif as Sherif Ali. This Oscar-winning blockbuster grossed $70 million at the box office after it appeared on cinema screens all over the world in December 1962.[87]

It's little wonder Bogarde was upset. When he tried to find out why his project was axed, Rank claimed there was an 'uncertainty' in the British film market at the time and the Entertainments Tax would have hammered the box office for 30 per cent of the takings. But the actor, ever wary of the prevalent homophobic atmosphere, wondered if the exposure of a supremely private man like Lawrence might send an unwanted and shocking tremor through British society which saw him as a hero. Then there was the political ramifications with Turkey at that time. Or was it more likely Rank did not wish to upset the all-powerful director David Lean who was about to be heaped with Oscars for *The Bridge on the River Kwai*? Bogarde said some years later that Lawrence was the 'greatest part

I have ever been asked to do'. Asquith, a long-time friend of Rattigan, told the actor consolingly 'No one can look like Lawrence but you [Bogarde] can probably make us feel how he felt. Much more important.'[88] The revelation he was not going to play Lawrence was a crushing blow to Bogarde who liked the fact they had both served with the RAF and British Army during their military careers. Albeit Lawrence was immersed in the Arab revolt against the Turks during the First World War.

By 1961 and though the laws against homosexuality were finally about to be challenged, homophobia wasn't going to be removed from society quickly. Bogarde, having finally left Rank in order to widen his range as an actor and escape the rigours of Davis' influences, agreed to take a risk and star as a blackmailed barrister called Melville Farr in *Victim* – a film directed by Basil Dearden which was the first British film to mention the word 'homosexual'.

It was by taking this gamble at a time when gay rights had yet to be acknowledged that the artistically ambitious Bogarde had set the course for his future identity as a ground-breaking legend of European cinema. He played the role with passion and verve and achieved an important milestone by the legitimate exposure of the hundreds of deplorable criminals who hounded wealthy and influential men who had no option but to live frustrated lives and conceal their true sexuality.

Victim, also starring Sylvia Syms, was filmed in around the Chiswick area of London. Bogarde was delighted over the years to discover it did a lot to help liberalise attitudes towards homosexuality. Although not a big hit at the box office in the early 1960s by the time the 1970s arrived it had made a profit of £51,762 indicating a growing appreciation of its cultural importance. Before the film was released in the United States a news report in *The New York Times* described it as a political work: 'the movie is a dramatized condemnation, based on the Wolfenden Report, of Britain's laws on homosexuality.' In England the well-read film critic Dilys Powell praised *Victim* because it 'made a stand' and was also a good thriller. She wrote: 'Bogarde gives the commanding performance one has long expected of him. With a fine control of gesture and tone he conveys both the suffering of the man condemned by nature and the resolve of the man bent on sacrifice.' After starring in the 'controversial' *Victim* the actor was now left to chase his own work as he was no longer earning a regular salary from Rank. Whilst he achieved great fame and acclaim he was never abundantly wealthy.

In the 1962 film *The Password is Courage* the actor was back in uniform again to play Sergeant Major Charles Coward, a senior British NCO who as a prisoner-of-war attempts to wind up and cause chaos for the German soldiers guarding him and his pals.

The film was based on a true story. Coward was the first British soldier to receive an Iron Cross during one of several daring escape attempts. The medal was presented to him when disguised as a wounded German soldier he appeared as a patient in a hospital bed! In this Metro-Goldwyn-Mayer made film, Bogarde was able to work with Coward and learn about his extraordinary wartime adventures. A publicity still released in 1962 shows Bogarde laughing with Coward in a prisoner-of-war hut. In real life Coward had also rescued Jews from Auschwitz and later gave evidence at the Nuremburg Trials of what he saw at the death camp. In the film we see Bogarde as the daring Coward finally escape with the prisoners from the camp in Poland by posing as workmen clearing rubble in a rural area. They manage to commandeer a fire engine and charge their way through to reach an area now controlled by the US Army.

A review in *Vanity Fair* of 1962 reveals:

Andrew L. Stone's screenplay, based on a biography of Sergeant-Major Charles Coward by John Castle, has pumped into its untidy 116 minutes an overdose of slapstick humour. Result is that what could have been a telling tribute to a character of guts and initiative, the kind that every war produces, lacks conviction.

Coward (Bogarde), a breezy, likeable character, is a PoW dedicated to sabotaging and humiliating his German captors. As senior soldier in Stalag 8B, he rallies the other men to escape so that they can get back to fighting the Nazis. Coward's main problem is to make contact with the Polish underground to get maps, money, etc., before escaping through a 280-foot tunnel which the prisoners have laboriously built. Bogarde gives a performance that is never less than competent, but never much more. The best male performance comes from Lynch, as Corporal Pope, a philosophical soldier devoted to Coward. He is a composite of several characters in Coward's actual story. Maria Perschy, a personable Hungarian girl making her first appearance in a British film, brings some glamour to the film as the underground worker.

The review from *Vanity Fair* was far from the actor's mind, however, as by then he was busy moving into his sixteenth-century home 'Nore' which was nestled upon a hill near Godalming, Surrey. 'Nore' with its ghosts, ten bedrooms, eight bathrooms, six reception rooms, two cottages, a separate studio, tennis court, garage block and four pools, and ten acres, was deemed by the actor as his finest home of the 1950s and 1960s.

He had sold Beel House to Basil Dearden and made a profit. Bogarde was always canny when it came to investing in property. Just before he and Forwood moved into 'Nore' he was offered the chance to appear in Daryl F. Zanuck's epic war film *The Longest Day*. He would be needed for just one day of filming and the fee on the table was £5,000. But the actor was unable to join the cast as he was in the middle of seven projects which included moving home – always a stressful business. If he'd agreed to star in *The Longest Day* he would have had to travel to France and fund his expenses and by the time he'd paid tax on the £5,000 there wouldn't be much left to show for his work. In hindsight it's arguably a pity he decided not to take up this offer as this 1962 film representing the brutalities and social history of the Normandy Landings of D-Day 6 June 1944 had as we know indeed informed much of Bogarde's real-life military experiences.

In 1962 the actor's next war-related cinematic event was *The High Bright Sun*, an intriguing story set in Cyprus during the Greek/Cypriot nationalist (EOKA) uprising against British rule which had erupted ten years previously. A novel by Ian Stuart Black had inspired this script which was co-written by Black, and by Bogarde's great friend and fellow actor who during the Second World War had served in the Intelligence Corps, Bryan Forbes CBE. The director Ralph Thomas, who had worked a lot with Bogarde on the *Doctor* films, diplomatically chose Foggia at the bottom of Italy to shoot the action as there had been recent evidence of another civil uprising in Cyprus. Bogarde starred as a British intelligence officer named Major McGuire. The film is set in 1957 and features Susan Strasberg as an archaeology student called Juno who is staying in Cyprus with family friends. When she sees an attack by two EOKA guerrillas on two British soldiers she is questioned by Major McGuire. Before long she discovers the fugitive EOKA General Skyros is hiding in the house she is staying in and her father's friend Dr Andros is a collaborator.

A dashing George Chakiris plays the EOKA guerrilla Haghios who wants to murder Juno. He is mostly motivated by her romantic involvement with McGuire. When McGuire rescues Juno and takes her to his home the furious Haghios attacks the place. Another complication in this busy film arises when another British intelligence officer, Baker (played by Denholm Elliott), reveals he's had an affair with McGuire's wife. Haghios won't give up his plan to kill Juno and even gets on the same aircraft as she flees Cyprus. As the plane lands in Athens (in real life Northolt Airport) the murderer takes aim at Juno but Baker steps in and is killed. Haghios is shot dead by McGuire. The ending sees the lovers reunited. The ordeal is over.

By 1964 and also hot on the heels of *King and Country*, Bogarde made another film in the war genre – *Little Moon of Alban*. Described as a 'cruel-twist-of-fate drama' it stars Bogarde as Lieutenant Kenneth Boyd, a character who kills a young woman's gunman boyfriend. The action takes place in Ireland just after the First World War and the grieving Brigit (Julie Harris) becomes a nursing nun who eventually finds herself caring for the 'enemy' – the injured Lieutenant Boyd. This unique television play was scripted by James Corrigan who had met Dirk and Tony during a sea voyage in the mid-1950s. They all got chatting and Corrigan included some of Bogarde's risqué stories in his script. He had wanted Bogarde to star in the original broadcast but the actor was too busy with other commitments at the time it first went into production. So the first television version of this play was produced in 1958 by Hallmark Hall of Fame starring George Peppard (Lieutenant Boyd) and Julie Harris (Brigit). (In 1960 Robert Redford appeared on Broadway in *Little Moon of Alban*.) Six years later when Dirk took up the challenge to travel to the US to star in the play he was 42 years old. His popularity at the box office had started to slide as younger stars began to arrive on the big screen – Cliff Richard, Sean Connery, Elizabeth Taylor and Marlon Brando were among those now topping the popularity polls.[89]

Whilst there was an awareness Bogarde's relationship with Hollywood was delicate, mainly because American critics believed there couldn't be much depth behind a handsome face, he agreed to join the cast. Some of his friends like Lauren Bacall believed Bogarde was 'too intelligent' for Hollywood. And according to his authorised biographer John Coldstream the actor had not wanted to make any television dramas in Britain in case his cinema audiences thought he was now 'all over the BBC'. *Little Moon of Alban* was made at the NBC Studios in New York in just three weeks and according to *The New York Times* this gritty yet romantic drama 'seems to grow in stature'. Shortly after his appearance on US television he was delighted to hear he'd won another BAFTA for 'Best Actor' after starring as Robert Gold in the 1965 film, *Darling*.

In 1969 and back on home shores Bogarde agreed to join the cast of stars in a musical about the 1914–18 conflict *Oh! What a Lovely War*. He played a character called Stephen and was among a line-up of eminent artistes – many of whom had experienced military service. His role lasted but a minute in the film and he was on set for just one day. It was directed by Richard Attenborough and this now famous commentary with its parodies and social representations was shot on Brighton's West Pier and around Bogarde's beloved East Sussex during the summer of 1968. Students from the local Falmer College also appeared as extras.

Talk to any of his lifelong followers (Bogarde always said they were the mainstay of his audiences and different from fans or fanatics) and the response is often in similar vein. 'It's safe to argue it's hard *not* love his films.' One such follower is Gillian Davis. She told the author of this book: 'Everything really was in his eyes. He was a great artiste with an enigmatic power which charmed and fascinated. I have all of his books and love them all. They are to be read and read again. Just like his films I could watch them several times and still see something new in them.'

That year, however, the actor was feeling confused after seeing a rough cut of his latest film *The Damned* (1969). He wanted more cuts and yet 'where to make them' and 'the high opera' of the acting was astounding. This award winning film is based loosely on a real-life wartime family of industrialists who ran an important steel business. When the elderly owner of the company is murdered on the night of the Reichstag fire in 1933 his relative with connections to the Nazi Party takes control. We then see Bogarde as employee Fredrich Bruckmann who works his way up through associations with the SS to gain power.

It's a sobering and powerful film which is directed by Bogarde's favourite 'genius' Luchino Visconti. In it we see big bold beautiful sets, emotive lighting and camerawork slow enough to steal the soul. Its imagery and symbolism are highly praised. The dark and sinister associations which connect money and power and the psychology of evil are interwoven into scenes which show betrayal, the company owner's family being sent to a concentration camp and the SA's (the Nazis' original paramilitary wing) battle with the SS which turned into a massacre disguised as a homosexual orgy. When the company is fully seized by the Nazis and Germany's steel output is under Hitler's control the film ends. leaving the audience believing the Nazis will triumph in their bid for world domination.

It is interesting to note the subject of the German industrialists who supported the Nazis' rise to power, is still fascinating writers today. In 2018 a wry and iconic novel *Order of the Day* by the French writer Éric Vuillard was published. In it the author argues how often by mishap or poor judgement the bosses of the great German manufacturing companies of the 1930s were manipulated and cajoled by Hitler's sly henchmen. The novel won the French Goncourt Prize for Fiction.

For Bogarde in 1969 too it was time to consider what he felt were becoming 'the crude demands of commercialism'. When talking to the director Joe Losey about a project he claimed: 'I really think that the most successful thing I have done in ten years or more is a one-minute bit in *Oh What a Lovely War* which gets applauded every time. No, why? What was wrong with three hours in *Accident*, or two in *The Servant* ... aren't people funny?' (Bogarde won the BAFTA Award in 1963 for his role as Hugo Barrett in *The Servant*).[90]

Of course the final word on his real life military service must go to Bogarde who spoke to the *Manchester Evening News* in 1986 during a promotional tour for his latest memoir, *Backcloth*, at The Connaught Hotel in London (He was also in the UK while his partner Tony Forwood was undergoing medical tests. Forwood was suffering from Parkinson's Disease and died in May 1988.)

When asked by the *MEN* reporter if he was happy being a soldier Bogarde replied he 'enjoyed it very much'. 'I was a spoiled young actor. I had had success too quickly. It was going to my head and in the army I got a good kick in the pants,' he confessed with a trace of a smile and reached out for another cigarette.

'I know it's the biggest cliché of all time but it did make a lot of difference to my life. You might cop it, get shot, killed or wounded, but somehow you don't think of that very much. There is excitement in a war and tremendous companionship and I didn't want to leave army life.'

He was also reminded of the time he tripped over a row of what he thought were dusty footballs but which were, in fact, the maggot-ridden heads of small French children who had sought shelter from the Allied bombing of an occupied village.

'I much prefer animals to people – people are awful. The things we do to each other are so appalling – animals kill for food: they don't kill each other in the random way we all do now.'

As for acting? Well Bogarde, already a legend of the screen and by now a highly successful author too, told television journalist Russell Harty he found it 'too demanding'.

'But when I do act, just as I do everything, I don't cheat – I do it to the best of my ability.'

So what made Bogarde such a great actor? Film academic Dr Barbara Siek summed it up: 'For Dirk, on screen "action" was internal, not external waving of arms, etc. He conveyed inner feeling and thought through his eyes and faces which allowed the camera to photograph that feeling. His forte was nuance. He was a master at modulating his voice to reflect shades of tenderness or evil.'

Sir Dirk Bogarde (knighted in 1992) appeared in sixty-five films, wrote fifteen books including novels and memoirs, funded theatre and film productions. He too was *The Daily Telegraph*'s 'golden' contributor and much admired for his compelling reviews of the latest books, and was a shareholder in the culturally important satirical magazine *Private Eye*. He died in 1999 aged 78 at home in Chelsea, London. His contribution to world culture was phenomenal. His military service was as astounding as it was honourable. And those evocative memories, all charged by his wartime experiences, framed the jigsaw of his enigmatic life until the end and forever after.

Today in 2022 as we celebrate Sir Dirk Bogarde's 100th anniversary he lives on via the authorised biography by John Coldstream, and online editorial content edited by Dr Barbara Siek and approved by The Dirk Bogarde Estate. His films are regularly shown today on terrestrial and satellite channels. Coldstream said: 'The war had a massive part to play in the development of Dirk's character – no question about that and the way in which he was able to somehow put some coherence to it was impressive. He made 65 movies and wrote fifteen books and somehow on his gravestone if there was such a thing it would have on it "Dirk Bogarde, Writer and Actor" because actually in the end the writing was more important than the acting. He was an enigma and of course a huge talent.'

In 2015 one of Sir Dirk Bogarde's paintings was displayed at the British Art Fair at the Royal College of Art. The piece, 'Aunay-sur-Odon, 1944' was being auctioned by Sim Fine Art. The pen, ink and watercolour painting is unusual as Bogarde decided to crop the image by using a mount, which has only recently been removed to reveal the complete work.

Notes

Audie Murphy

1. After the war … : Smith, p. 127.
2. Years later he idly … : Ibid., p. 13.
3. 'So what did you do …?': Murphy, pp. 4 and 5.
4. 'I was bored and wanted to….': (Fisher), *Memoirs of WWII* – YouTube.
5. Kesselring: Holland, p. 24.
6. Truscott III: History Net.
7. But while trooper Murphy … : Smith, p. 20.
8. '… we were given another long, monotonous … ': Murphy, p. 9.
9. '… if the landing hadn't gone snafu … ': (Murphy) Holland, p. 224.
10. Holland and Murray: YouTube, 5 February 2021.
11. 'Each of us has his own …': Murphy, p. 96.
12. Emmanuel was unable … : Holland, p. 470.
13. A Word on Westerns – Dante, YouTube.
14. '… all human life is sacred … ': Murphy, p. 11.
15. 'Audacity is a tactical weapon… ': (Murphy) Smith, p. 26.
16. '… we watched him go … ': Murphy, p. 13.
17. Corporal Murphy: Holland, p. 473.
18. '… was more than pleased': Fairbanks, p. 573.
19. Once again Murphy: Holland, p. 179.
20. '… a fiery blanket woven …': (Murphy) Smith, p. 39.
21. It was at Cisterna … : Smith, p. 39.
22. '… like ghosts prowling around … ': Murphy, p. 163.
23. Another mission: Smith, p. 54.
24. 'As if under the influence …': Murphy, p. 243.
25. On one occasion … : Murphy, p. 268.
26. Murphy's venture into politics: Smith, pp. 97 and 98.
27. For appearing in *Beyond Glory*…: Ibid., p.102
28. John Huston: Ibid., p. 116.
29. Murphy's first wife … : Ibid., p. 118.
30. '… in Kansas Raiders I remember … ': Curtis, p. 119.
31. '… it drains you. Things don't thrill … ': (Murphy) Smith, p. 130.
32. '… he'd be a good fit … ': (Murphy) ibid., p. 133.
33. Universal Studio bosses: Gossett, p. 69.
34. However, he had confessed: Smith, p. 136.

35. '... there's an awful lot of phonies... ': (Murphy) 1997 interview with Lun Chin in *Audie Murphy Research Foundation Newsletter* Vol. 7, Spring 1999.
36. '... after I finished *To Hell and Back*... ': Murphy, *Audie Murphy Research Foundation Newsletter* Vol. 7, Spring 1999.

Sir Laurence Olivier
1. '... you are here in America... .': Cottrell, p. 163.
2. '... pickle..': Ziegler, p. 76.
3. '... burst into tears... ': Laurence Olivier, p. 118.
4. '... world seemed in dread anticipation... ': Fairbanks, p. 488.
5. '... this is the end... ': Ibid., p. 489.
6. *The Four Feathers* (1939): *Alexander Korda: Churchill's Man in Hollywood*. International Churchill Society website.
7. '... a natural... ': Cottrell, p. 175.
8. '... isolationists who are... ': (Balcon) Cottrell, p. 177.
9. '... extremely well and justified... ': (Aherne) Cottrell, p. 180.
10. Merle Oberon . .: Coleman, p. 108.
11. Olivier: Michael Parkinson television interview, 1970.
12. '... there was a general directive... ': Laurence Olivier, p. 118.
13. '... shapes the role of the girl... ': (Crowther) Walker, p. 139.
14. '... saucy language... ': Ziegler, p. 12.
15. '... a masterpiece... ': Laurence Olivier, p. 75.
16. '... the Big Five ...': Thompson and Bordwell, p. 235.
17. '... a very strong pro-British feeling... ': (R C Sherriff) Kulik, p. 250.
18. *That Hamilton Woman*: International Churchill Society.
19. '... this deed I'll do before this purpose cool ...': Laurence Olivier, p. 123.
20. '... I went to the studio on Santa Monica boulevard... ': Powell, p. 376.
21. '... Vivien and I married... ': Laurence Olivier, p. 125.
22. '... there were a hundred men ... ': Powell, p. 381.
23. Elsie Fogerty: Cottrell, p. 188.
24. '... I had to take a conversion course... ': Laurence Olivier, p. 127.
25. '....it was my job... ': (Douglas) Cottrell, p. 189.
26. 'I never fired a shot in anger... ': Laurence Olivier, p. 130.
27. '... using pilots as taxi drivers... ': Ibid., p. 128
28. '... more sensible duty ... ': Olivier, p. 129.
29. 'Flying the Walrus seaplane was like flying an elephant... ': Ellis and Foreman, p. 116.
30. 'My father definitely felt out of place ...': Tarquin Olivier, p.104.
31. 'On the same day ...': Cottrell, p. 191.
32. '... *Demi-Paradise* was amusing... ': Olivier, p. 131.
33. The proposal was quickly stamped upon... : Chapman, *The Life and Death of Colonel Blimp Reconsidered*. The Powell and Pressburger Pages. www.powell-pressburger.org
34. '... *Henry V* I am to produce myself... ': (Olivier) Tarquin Olivier, p. 108.

35. '... Nothing seems to matter... ': (Leigh) Walker, p .166.
36. '... most inspiring... ': Ibid.
37. '... babbling her lines... ': Ibid., p. 168.
38. 'If I should die... ': (Betjeman) Coleman, p. 156.
39. '... this tortuous business... ': (Olivier), (Young 1943) Coleman, p. 157.
40. 'Once More Unto the Breach Dear Friends... ': Cottrell, p. 200.
41. '... encouraged to grow beards ...': Ibid., p. 201.
42. '... it was really easy... ': Coleman, p. 163.
43. '... poor old war horse...': Ibid., p. 164.
44. '... shower of arrows ... ': Cottrell, p. 203.
45. '... his balls, their three kittens ... ': Coleman, p. 161.
46. French cavalry and extras strike: (Olivier's letter to Leigh) The Susan Farrington Collection.
47. '... hail of arrows... ': Laurence Olivier, p. 139.
48. Leigh back in London: Coleman, p. 166.
49. Finances and 'Del' Giudice: Ibid., pp. 166 and 167.
50. '... crack a few heads ...': (Olivier) ibid., p. 168.
51. Selznick: Walker, p. 174.
52. Jack Merrivale: Ibid.
53. '... men in khaki... ': The Mark Amory Transcripts. (Olivier's letter to Leigh, 1944). Coleman, p. 178.
54. '... fill out a form... ': Curtis, p. 65.
55. '... people are like leaves... ': Ibid., p. 66.
56. '... the control room... ': Ibid., p. 69.
57. '... a massive junkyard...: Ibid., p. 71.
58. '... the first time we had acted together... ': Ibid., p. 224.
59. '... Air Chief Marshal Sir Keith Park... ': Mosley, p. 162.
60. '... his life's work... ': (Fisz) Mosley, p. 161.
61. *Battle of Britain*: Ibid., pp. 21–4.
62. Fisz and Saltzman: Ibid., p.18.
63. '... there was no Battle of Britain ... ': (Galland) ibid., p. 35.
64. '... the English always smile ... ': (Galland) ibid., p. 38.
65. 'I do not think ...': Galland, ibid.
66. '... he was a clot... ': (Lacey) Mosley, p. 162.
67. '... I tried to imitate Dowding's voice... ': (Olivier) Ziegler, p. 313.
68. Dowding and the Battle of Britain: Wright, p. 51.
69. '... that was it!... ': Mosley, p. 202.

Sir Dirk Bogarde
 1. '... film which made him most proud' ...: Coldstream, p. 303.
 2. '... a class conversation ...': (Losey) ibid., p. 301.
 3. Ulric van den Bogaerde: Ibid., p. 31.
 4. 'There were four kinds of shells... ': Brennan, Imperial War Museum archive.

5. 'We fired usually about... ': Walter-Symons, Imperial War Museum archive.
6. Ulric van den Bogaerde: Coldstream, p. 31.
7. 'Our job at that time was to... ': RHA Officer, Imperial War Museum archive.
8. 'Ulric van den Bogaerde': Bogarde, *Backcloth*, p. 25.
9. 'Jesus, he once told me, many years after ...': ibid.
10. '... the gentleman always responsible ...': ibid., p. 302.
11. 'How can I write a film ... ': ibid., p. 482.
12. 'I saw it happen to a bloke once before... ': ibid., p. 302.
13. '... end his own life... ': ibid..
14. 'a somewhat negating effect'...: Caute, p. 146; 'Tom, who is an extremely good actor... ': (Losey), Coldstream, p. 302.
15. A day later *The Liverpool Echo* ...: Coldstream, p. 303.
16. '... rattling around in an Oxo tin ... ': Bogarde, *Backcloth*, p. 193.
17. 'I wore two jumpers... ' Bogarde, BBC Television interview, 1961.
18. '... not all cushions and barley sugar ...': Coldstream, p. 53.
19. '... a play the rising generation must see ...': ibid., p. 72.
20. '... a modern crop of performers who... ': (Jackson) *The Daily Mirror*, 17 April 2017.
21. 'The noise of that curtain...': Bogarde, *Snakes and Ladders*, p. 193.
22. 'I hated the star thing... ': Coldstream, p. 214.
23. '... total dedication was required... ': ibid., p. 78.
24. '... it was Jack de Leon at the Q Theatre... ': ibid., p. 79.
25. '... I was unable to wear boots... ': (Scofield) O'Connor, p. 21.
26. 'Did I lose my cool... ': Bogarde, *Backcloth*, p. 73.
27. '... morale booster... ': Coldstream, p. 90.
28. '... cold dreary barns of theatres... ': Bogarde, *A Postillion Struck By Lightning*, p. 244.
29. '... train crowded – Soldiers, old women. Conscripts like self ...': (Bogarde) Coldstream, p. 91.
30. Morse Code: ibid., p. 92.
31. '... a disgrace to the regiment ... ': Bogarde, *Snakes and Ladders*, p. 12.
32. 'Although everyone was delighted ...': ibid., p. 31.
33. '... no mechanical aptitude... ': Coldstream, p. 95.
34. Lieutenant-Colonel Bowers ...: ibid.
35. '... a draft of one... ': ibid., p. 96
36. 'You bloody give me the pip! ...': ibid., p. 101.
37. 'Enemy Documents... ': ibid., p. 103.
38. Flight Officer Babington Smith ...: Downing, p. 100.
39. '... light refreshing scent... ': (Whittle) Babington Smith, p. 222.
40. '... the immeasurably vast and complex ...': Babington Smith, p. 82.
41. 'I loved the detail... ': Bogarde, *Snakes and Ladders*, p. 60.
42. '... lively – especially so as it was staffed....': Downing, p. 103.

43. '… bunch of nuts…': (Eadon), Halsall.
44. '… we were clever little fellows planning D-Day… ': Coldstream, p.104
45. Other notables of RAF Medmenham …: *Operation Crossbow*, BBC 2, 2011.
46. '… dive-bombing….': Bogarde, *Snakes and Ladders*, p. 61.
47. Marshal of the RAF The Lord Tedder: Foreword, Babington Smith.
48. '… the silver ring… ': Coldstream, p. 106.
49. Many of these men were waiting to be sent to Normandy: Coldstream, p.107.
50. '… an overwhelming sense of doom… ': Bogarde, *Cleared for Take Off*, pp. 28–9.
51. '… On August 1, 1944, I was flying back to Sommervieu… ': (Rohmer) Coldstream, p. 111.
52. 'My motivation was to defeat the enemy… ': Rohmer, Veterans' Voices, Juno Beach Centre, Normandy.
53. '… soggy airfield… ': Coldstream, p. 115.
54. '… noise all over the place..': Gregg, *Rifleman* (YouTube).
55. '… effete and mincing… ': Foster, p. 393.
56. '… Bogarde felt his friend, recently knighted… ': Attenborough, p. 153.
57. '… a cross between Terry Thomas and Ralph Reeder… ': Coldstream, p. 398.
58. '… laughed it off as 'tripe'…': ibid., p. 400.
59. Author interview – *Kent Evening Post/Kent Today*, September 1991.
60. '… not about Nazi guilt…': (Bogarde) Coldstream, p. 376.
61. '… limits of credibility… ': (Cavani) ibid.
62. '… unbelievably traumatic… ': (Rampling) ibid., p.377.
63. '… struggling at times… ': (Rampling) ibid.
64. The SS *Carthage*: Coldstream, p. 126.
65. 'His flight bought fame and glory to the PRU … ': Babington Smith, p. 114.
66. Although the Japanese…: McMillan, p. 10.
67. '… The Fighting Cock… ': Coldstream, p. 135.
68. '… a party without goodbyes… ': ibid., p. 146.
69. By the end of 1946 …: ibid., p. 156.
70. '… during wartime you never knew… ': Bogarde, TV interview, 1980.
71. '… Judy was a monster to work with but she was magic! . . ': Bogarde, BBC *Woman's Hour* 1980.
72. 'Rank's Pinewood base…': Harper and Porter, p. 41.
73. 'This chap arrived from Rank's headquarters… ' (Gilbert) Kemp, *The Man Who Killed the British Film Industry*, TV documentary 1995.
74. '… the script is the best thing I've ever read… ': (Bogarde to Wooldridge) Coldstream, p. 195.
75. '… the director Philip Leacock made me more aware …': (Bogarde) ibid.
76. '… he even had his name on his own chair! … ': (Forbes) ibid.
77. 'Appointment in London… ': Dr Barbara Siek (comments supplied to author).

78. '... *How Dare They?...* ': (Bogarde) Coldstream, p. 199.
79. '... doesn't allow him much dimension ...': ibid., p. 208.
80. '... people were still trying to forget the war... ': Powell, *Million Dollar Movie*, p. 218.
81. '... it is quite true you have always been a close up actor... ': (Powell) Coldstream, p. 221.
82. '... Davis was an arrogant, autocratic accountant... ': Dr Barbara Siek (comments supplied to Author).
83. '... exactly what had been worn at the time ...': Coldstream, p. 221.
84. '... the story which was often based on a real wartime episode... ': Harper and Porter, p. 255.
85. Davis insisted the film should have a happy ending ...: Coldstream, p. 233
86. Anthony 'Puffin' Asquith: ibid., p.236.
87. '... his bitterest disappointment... ': ibid., p. 238.
88. '... no one can look like Lawrence... ': (Asquith) ibid.
89. Six years later ...: ibid., p. 300.
90. 'I really think the most successful thing I've done ...': (Bogarde) ibid., p. 349.

Bibliography

Hoopes, Roy, *When the Stars Went to War* (US Random House, 1994).

Kelly, Andrew, *Filming All Quiet on the Western Front* (I B Tauris Books 1998).

LaRocca, David (ed.), *The Philosophy of War Films* (The University of Kentucky Press 2018).

Audie Murphy

Curtis, Tony, *American Prince: My Autobiography* (Virgin Books/Random House, 2008).

Fairbanks Jr, Douglas, *The Salad Days* (William Collins, 1988).

Gossett, Sue, *The Films and Career of Audie Murphy: America's Real Hero* (Empire Publishing, 1996).

Harris, Mark, *Five Came Back: A Story of Hollywood and the Second World War* (Canongate Books, 2014).

Holland, James, *Sicily '43: The First Assault on Fortress Europe* (Penguin Random House UK, 2020)

Murphy, Audie, *To Hell and Back* (Henry Holt US, 1949/ Picador, 1977).

Smith, David A., *The Price of Valor* (Regnery Publishing US, 2015)

Sir Laurence Olivier

Aherne, Brian, *A Proper Job* (Boston Houghton Mifflin, 1969).

Coleman, Terry, *Olivier: The Authorised Biography* (Bloomsbury, 2005).

Cottrell, John, *Laurence Olivier: The Definitive Biography of the Greatest Actor of all Time* (Coronet, Hodder and Stoughton, 1977).

Curtis, Tony, *American Prince: My Autobiography* (Virgin Books/Random House, 2008).

Fairbanks Jr, Douglas, *The Salad Days* (William Collins, 1988).

Foreman, Melody and Ellis, Mary, *A Spitfire Girl* (Frontline/Pen & Sword, 2016).

Galland, Adolf, *The First and Last* (Methuen, 1955).

Kulik, Karol, *Alexander Korda: The Man Who Could Work Miracles* (W. H. Allen, 1975).

Mosley, Leonard, *Battle of Britain Film Biography* (Weidenfeld and Nicholson, 1969).

Olivier, Laurence, *Confessions of an Actor* (Coronet edition, Weidenfeld and Nicholson, 1983).

Olivier, Tarquin, *My Father Laurence Olivier* (Headline Books, 1992).

Powell, Michael, *A Life in Movies: An Autobiography* (1992 edition, first published by William Heinemann Ltd, 1986).

Thompson, Kristin and Bordwell, David, *Film History: An Introduction* (McGraw Hill Higher Education, 1994).

Walker, Alexander, *Vivien: The Life of Vivien Leigh* (Weidenfeld and Nicholson, 1987).

Wright, Robert, *Dowding and the Battle of Britain* (Corgi, 1970).

Ziegler, Philip, *Olivier* (MacLeHose Press, an imprint of Quercus New York & London, 2014),

Sir Dirk Bogarde

Attenborough, Richard, *Entirely Up to You Darling* (Arrow Books, 2009).

Babington Smith, Constance, *Evidence in Camera* (Chatto and Windus, 1957).

Beevor, Antony, *Arnhem: The Battle for the Bridges 1944* (Viking, 2018).

Bogarde, Dirk, *A Postillion Struck By Lightning* (Chatto & Windus, 1977).

Bogarde, Dirk, *Snakes & Ladders* (First published by Chatto & Windus, 1978).

Bogarde, Dirk, *An Orderly Man* (Chatto and Windus, 1983),

Bogarde, Dirk, *Backcloth* (Viking, 1986).

Bogarde, Dirk, *Cleared for Take Off: A Memoir* (Viking/Bloomsbury, 1989).

Caute, David, *Joseph Losey: A Revenge on Life* (Faber & Faber, 1994).

Coldstream, John, *Dirk Bogarde: The Authorised Biography* (Weidenfeld and Nicholson, 2004).

Downing, Taylor, *Spies in the Sky* (Abacus, 2012).

Forster, Margaret, *Daphne du Maurier* (Chatto & Windus, 1993).

Gregg, Victor and Stroud, Gregg, *Rifleman: A Frontline Life* (Bloomsbury, 2018).

Halsall, Christine, *Women of Intelligence: Winning the Second World War with Air Photos* (Spellmount, 2021),

Harper, Sue and Porter, Vincent, *British Cinema of the 1950s: The End of Deference* (Oxford University Press, 2003).

McMillan, Richard, *The British Occupation of Indonesia 1945 – 1946* (Routledge, 2006).

O'Connor, Gary, *Paul Scofield: An Actor for All Seasons* (Applause Books, 2016).

Powell, Michael, *Million Dollar Movie: The Second Volume of A Life in Movies* (William Heinemann Ltd, 1992).

Salwolke, Scott, *The Films of Michael Powell and the Archers* (Scarecrow Press, 1997).

Index

Audie Murphy

Agrigento, 14
Aix-en-Provence, 26
Anzio, 2, 21, 22
Archer, Pamela, 33, 35
Arzew, 11
Audie Murphy/American Cotton Museum, 2
Autobiography, *see To Hell and Back*

Battipaglia, 20
Battle fatigue, *see* PTSD
Beach Jumpers, 19
Besançon, 26
Bogart, Humphrey, 6, 7
Brandon, *see* Tipton, Lattie
Brouvelieures, 26

Cagney Productions, 30, 31
Camp Kilmer, 6
Camp Wolters, 5
Canicatti, 16
Casablanca, 9
Casablanca (Movie), 6
Chin Lun, 38
Cisterna, 21, 22
Colmar Pocket, 26, 27
Curtis, Tony, 34–5, 36

Dante, Michael, 16
Death, 39
Drake, Charles, 36
Duck boat, *see* DUKW
DUKW, 12, 13

Early life, 3–4
Enlistment, 3, 4–5

Fairbanks Jnr, Douglas, 18–19
Farmersville, 3, 28
Fiala, Andrew, 6
Fisher, Ancil, 8–9
Fort Meade, 6
France, invasion, 23
Furiano River, 17

Greenville, 2
Guinness, Alec, 12

Harman, Estelle, 31
Hendrix, Wanda, 33, 35
Hibbs, Jesse, 36, 37
Holtzwihr, 27, 33
Huston, John, 32, 33

Incident (TV Drama), 38
Influenza, 22

Kasserine Pass, 9
Kelly, Jack, 37

Ladd, Alan, 31
Le Tholy, 25
Licata, 12
L'Omet, 26

Malaria, 17, 21
Marriages, 33
McClure, David, 31, 33, 38
Medals and Awards, 2, 3, 22, 25, 26, 27, 28, 33
Messina, 17, 18
Mignano, 22
Mike Novak, *see* Sieja, Joe
Montélimar, 24, 25
Movies, 16, 30, 31, 32, 33, 34, 36
Murphy, Corinne, 3, 5, 28
Murphy, Emmett, 3
Murphy, Josie, 3, 4
Murphy-Lokey, Nadine, 3

North Africa Campaign, 6, 7, 8, 9–10, 11

Operation Avalanche, 19
Operation Husky, 12, 19
Operation Shingle, 21
Operation Torch, 6

Paramount Pictures, 30, 31
Paulick, Michael, 37

Port Lyautey, 10
Price, Carolyn, 26
Promotions, 9, 12, 17, 21, 26
PTSD, 4, 29, 34–5

Rabat, 9
Ramatuelle, 2
Rome, 23
Rosenberg, Aaron, 36

Salerno, 20
Salzburg, 28
Shell shock, *see* PTSD
Sieja, Joe, 2, 13, 20, 21
St Tropez, 23

Thompson, Marshall, 37
The Waltons (TV Drama), 11
Tipton, Lattie, 2, 13, 20, 24, 34, 36
To Hell and Back (Book), 2, 13, 33, 34
To Hell and Back (Movie), 4, 26, 31, 36, 37, 38
Training, 5, 6, 12
Truscott II, Lucian, 10–11

Volturno River, 20
Vosges, 25, 37

West Point, 27
Wounds, 26

Laurence Olivier

Bader, Douglas, 53–4, 107
Birmingham Repertory Company, 55

Casson, John, 70–1
Channel Dash, 78–80
Churchill, Winston, 45, 61
Curtis, Tony, 99–104

Del Giudice, Filippo, 82, 84, 92–3
Deserters, *see* Shirkers
Divorces, 65, 98
Douglas, Kirk, 98–9
Dowding, Hugh, 104 *et seq*, 117–18, 119

Early life, 53–4
Enniskerry, *see* Ireland
Esmond, Jill, 50, 62, 77

Fairbanks Jnr, Douglas, 42–3, 64
Films, *see* Movies
Finch, Peter, 97–8
Fisz, Ben, 110, 111, 112, 113, 115, 118
Fleet Air Arm, 62, 65, 70 *et seq*
Flying lessons, 46–7

Galland, Adolf, 113–15, 116

Hamilton, Guy, 112, 113, 115, 118
Hays Code, 57–8, 93
Howard, Leslie, 67, 69

Injury, 90–1
Ireland, 88, 89

Korda, Alexander, 45, 52, 53, 58, 59, 60, 61, 62

Laurie, John, 89
Leigh, Vivien, 42, 49, 51–2, 58, 59, 75–6, 84–7, 91, 94–5

Movies:
    49th Parallel, 62, 63, 64, 66–9
    Adventure for Two, *see The Demi-Paradise*
    Battle of Britain, 54, 104 *et seq*
    Clouds Over Europe, *see Q Planes*
    Fire Over England, 58
    Hamlet, 97
    Henry V, 50, 81, 83, 84, 87 *et seq*
    Marathon Man, 121
    Oh! What a Lovely War, 104
    Q Planes, 41, 45–6
    Rebecca, 50
    Spartacus, 98
    That Hamilton Woman, 53, 59–61, 78
    The Boys from Brazil, 121–2
    The Demi-Paradise, 74, 81–2
    The Entertainer, 112
    The Invaders, *see 49th Parallel*
    Wuthering Heights, 41, 44, 49, 50

Newton, Robert, 89
Niven, David, 44, 64, 82, 98

Operation Cerberus, *see* Channel Dash
Order of Merit, 122

Plays, *see* Theatre
Plowright, Joan, 98
Portman, Eric, 67, 68, 69
Powell, Dilys, 46
Powell, Michael, 62, 63, 66, 68
Pressburger, Emeric, 63, 68, 69

Richardson, Ralph, 45, 46, 55, 65, 66, 72, 77, 95, 116

Saltzman, Harry, 111–12, 115, 118
Selznick, David, 42, 50, 91, 94
Shirkers, 41–2, 47–9, 76
Special Lifetime Achievement Award, 122

Theatre:
  Beau Geste, 56
  Hamlet, 58
  Journey's End, 55, 56
  Othello, 45

Richard III, 97
Romeo and Juliet, 58, 61
The Skin of Our Teeth, 94–5, 97
The School for Scandal, 97

The World At War (TV series), 120–1
Toland, Greg, 50

Vansittart, Robert, 45

Walton, William, 92
Wyler, William, 50, 84, 89

Dirk Bogarde

ACIU, 158
Aerial Photographic Interpretation Service, *see* APIS
Aerial Photographic Interpreters, *see* RAF Medmenham
Allied Central Interpretation Unit, *see* ACIU
Amersham Playhouse, 144, 145
APIS, 161
Arnhem, *see* Operation Market Garden
Attenborough, Richard, 168, 169, 170

Babington Smith, Constance, 153–5
Balcon, Michael, 195
Bally, 184
Batavia, 185–7
Belsen, 174, 175–8
Bergen-Belsen, *see* Belsen
Bogaerde, van den Ulric, 127, 128, 129
Box, Betty, 188, 194
Browning, Frederick, 167–8, 172

Caen, 162
Catterick Camp, 146–9
Cavani, Liliana, 180, 181
Central Interpretation Unit, *see* CIU
Chelsea Polytechnic School of Art, 138
CIU, 153
Courtney, Tom, 126, 132–3

Danesfield House, *see* RAF Medmenham
Davis, John, 188, 191–2, 193–4, 206, 207
Deans, Annie, 144–5
Demobilisation, 187
du Maurier, Daphne, 168

Early life, 137–8
ENSA, 145, 146, 173

Entertainments National Service Association, *see* ENSA
Essame, Hubert, 150, 152, 173
Évreux, 164

Films, *see* Movies
Forwood, Tony, 187, 189–90

Greaves, Christopher, 160, 161

Holiday, Eve, 156, 184–5, 188

India, *see* Bally
Indonesia, *see* Batavia
Interview with Author, 174–7
Interview with *Manchester Evening News*, 217

Java, *see* Batavia

Lawrence, T.E., 210–12
Liverpool lecture, 133
Losey, Joe, 130, 191, 206

Medals, 136
Medmenham, *see* RAF Medmenham
Military training, 146–52
Movies:
  A Bridge Too Far, 167–72
  Appointment in London, 196–9
  Death in Venice, 141–2
  Ill Met By Moonlight, 202–06, 207–08
  King and Country, 126–7, 129, 130–2
  Little Moon of Alban, 215
  Oh! What a Lovely War, 216
  The Damned, 216
  The High Bright Sun, 214–15
  The Night Porter, 180–3

The Password is Courage, 213
The Sea Shall Not Have Them, 201–02
The Wind Cannot Read, 208–10
They Who Dare, 200–01
Victim, 143–4, 212

Newick Amateur Dramatic Society, 139

Odiham, *see* RAF Odiham
Operation Crossbow, 154
Operation Market Garden, 165–7, *see*
   Movies: *A Bridge Too Far*

Photographic Interpretation Unit, *see* PIU
PIU, 153
Plays, *see* Theatre
Powell, Michael, 203–08
Pressburger, Emeric, 203

Q Theatre, 144, 188

RAF Medmenham, 152–9
RAF Odiham, 159, 160–1
Rampling, Charlotte, 180, 181, 182
Rohmer, Richard, 162–4

Sandhurst Military Training College, 150
Schindler's Ark, 180
Sommervieu, 161

Theatre:
   Journey's End, 139
   Sleep on my Shoulder, 188
   The Ghost Train, 146

Ustinov, Peter, 143, 145

Visconti, Luchino, 141, 206, 216
Volpi Cup, 132

Wyndham's Theatre, 145